Section 5 — Home and Environment

Names of Buildings 58
Asking Directions 59
Where You're From 60
Talking About Where You Live 61
Inside Your Home 63
Celebrations 64
The Environment 65
Revision Summary 67

Section 6 — Education and Work

School Subjects 68
The School Routine 69
Talking About School 70
Classroom Language 71
More School Stuff 72
Problems at School 73
Work Experience 74
Plans for the Future 75
Types of Job 76
Jobs: Advantages and Disadvantages 77
Working Abroad 78
Getting a Job 79
Telephones 81
The Business World 82
Revision Summary 83

Section 7 — Grammar

The Wonderful Truth About Cases (Cases: Nominative and Accusative) 84
More Cases and Noun Endings (Genitive, Dative and Noun Endings) 85
Words for People and Objects (Nouns) 86
Word Order 88
Words to Join Up Phrases (Conjunctions) 89
'The' and 'A' (Articles) 90
Words to Describe Things (Adjectives) 91
Making Sentences More Interesting (Adverbs) 93
Comparing Things (Comparatives and Superlatives) 94
Sneaky Wee Words (Prepositions) 95
I, You, Him, Them... (Pronouns) 97
Someone, No One, Who? & What? (Pronouns) 98
'That', 'Which', 'Whom' & 'Whose' (Pronouns) 99
The Lowdown on Verbs (Verbs, Tenses and the Infinitive) 100
Verbs in the Present Tense (Present Tense) 101
Talking About the Future (Future Tense) 103
Talking About the Past (Perfect Tense) 104
Talking About the Past (Imperfect Tense) 105
More Verb Forms (Pluperfect Tense and Imperatives) 106
Myself, Yourself, etc. (Reflexive Verbs) 107
Separable Verbs 108
How to Say 'No', 'Not' and 'Nobody' (Negatives) 109
Modal Verbs 110
Odds and Ends (Impersonal Verbs and 'Um ... zu...') 112
Revision Summary 113

Do Well in Your Exam 114
German–English Dictionary 121
Index 128

Published by Coordination Group Publications Ltd.

Contributors:

Angela Billington
Charley Darbishire
Chris Dennett
Paul Jordin
Andy Park
Katherine Stewart
Claire Thompson
Hayley Thompson
Jennifer Underwood
Tim Wakeling
James Paul Wallis
Karen Wells

With thanks to Polly Cotterill and Janet Sheldon for the proofreading.

One corny cliché about German people was harmed in the making of this book.

ISBN: 978 1 84762 363 8

Groovy website: www.cgpbooks.co.uk
Jolly bits of clipart from CorelDRAW®
Printed by Elanders Hindson Ltd, Newcastle upon Tyne.

Based on the classic CGP style created by Richard Parsons.

Text, design, layout and original illustrations © Coordination Group Publications Ltd. 2009
All rights reserved.

C900596699

FOR REFERENCE

Do Not Take From This Room

PORTADOWN

2 6 AUG 2014

BRANCH LIBRARY

PWN

You can renew your book at any library or online at
www.librariesni.org.uk

If you require help please email - enquiries@librariesni.org.uk

...ty Book from CGP

...g GCSE Foundation German.

...'re doing it's the same
...of facts and you've just got
...German is no different.

...es you all that important
...nd concisely as possible.

...n to try and make the whole
...ely entertaining for you.

...is all about

*Our sole aim here at CGP is to produce the highest quality
books — carefully written, immaculately presented and
dangerously close to being funny.*

*Then we work our socks off to get them out to you
— at the cheapest possible prices.*

Contents

Section 1 — General Stuff

Numbers and Amounts 1
Times and Dates 2
Asking Questions 4
Being Polite 5
Opinions 7
Writing Informal Letters 10
Writing Formal Letters 11
Revision Summary 12

Section 2 — Lifestyle

Food 13
Mealtimes 14
Daily Routine 16
About Yourself 17
Family and Pets 18
Personality 19
Relationships and Future Plans 20
Social Issues and Equality 21
Feeling Ill 22
Health and Health Issues 24
Revision Summary 26

Section 3 — Leisure

Sports and Hobbies 27
Television 29
Talking About the Plot 30
Music 31
Famous People 32
New Technology 33
E-mail and Texting 34
Shopping 35
Inviting People Out 39
Going Out 40
Revision Summary 42

Section 4 — Holidays

Holiday Destinations 43
Catching the Train 44
All Kinds of Transport 45
Planning Your Holiday 46
Holiday Accommodation 47
Booking a Room / Pitch 48
Where / When is...? 49
Problems with Accommodation 50
At a Restaurant 51
Talking About Your Holiday 53
The Weather 56
Revision Summary 57

Numbers and Amounts

No two ways about it, you've got to know the numbers — so get cracking.

Eins, zwei, drei — One, two, three...

1 It all starts off easy enough. Learn zero to twelve — no probs.

0	null
1	eins
2	zwei
3	drei
4	vier
5	fünf
6	sechs
7	sieben
8	acht
9	neun
10	zehn
11	elf
12	zwölf

13	dreizehn
14	vierzehn
15	fünfzehn
16	sechzehn
17	siebzehn
18	achtzehn
19	neunzehn

2 You can work out the teens using numbers one to ten — for example thirteen is just 'three' and 'ten' stuck together (drei+zehn).
BUT 16 and 17 are different — they lose the '-s' and '-en' from the ends of 'sechs' and 'sieben'.

20	zwanzig	60	sechzig
30	dreißig	70	siebzig
40	vierzig	80	achtzig
50	fünfzig	90	neunzig

3 After dreißig all the ten-type numbers are easy.

21	einundzwanzig	24	vierundzwanzig	27	siebenundzwanzig
22	zweiundzwanzig	25	fünfundzwanzig	28	achtundzwanzig
23	dreiundzwanzig	26	sechsundzwanzig	29	neunundzwanzig

100	hundert
1000	tausend
1,000,000	eine Million

4 The in-between numbers are the tricky ones. For these you say the numbers backwards. Say 'two and thirty' instead of 'thirty-two'.

zweiunddreißig = Thirty-two

5 When you get to hundreds and thousands it's simple again — thousands come before hundreds, and hundreds before the rest of the numbers.

tausendfünfhundertzweiunddreißig

1000   500   32   = 1532

Erste, zweite, dritte — First, second, third...

1st	das erste		
2nd	das zweite	8th	das achte
3rd	das dritte	9th	das neunte
4th	das vierte	10th	das zehnte
5th	das fünfte	20th	das zwanzigste
6th	das sechste	21st	das einundzwanzigste
7th	das siebte	100th	das hundertste

In German, '1st' is written '1.'.

Sometimes the endings change, see pages 84-85 for help.

1) For most numbers between 1 and 19, just add '-te' to the number in German. The three exceptions are in purple.
2) From 20 onwards, just add '-ste' to the German number.

Nehmen Sie die erste Straße links.

= Take the first street on the left.

Wie viel? — How much?

Little words for 'how many' or 'how much' are really vital. There are a lot of them to learn down there, but don't skimp — write each one out in different sentences and make sure you don't miss any.

Ich habe beide Äpfel.

= I have both apples.

all:	alle	*some:*	einige
other:	andere	*many:*	viele
no:	keine	*few:*	wenige

Jeden Tag fahre ich Rad.

= I go cycling every day.

See page 92 for more on 'jeder'.

Ich weiß nichts. = I know nothing.

lots: viel   *little:* wenig

It's as easy as 1, 2, 3...

You might already know great chunks of this — that's great. Then you can spend more time checking that you know the rest of the page. Make sure you know all of those words about amounts. The best way to check is to cover up the page, and then try to write them down.

Times and Dates

Knowing how to say the time is <u>vital</u> — examiners love it.

Wie viel Uhr ist es? — What time is it?

There are loads of ways of saying the time in German — just like English.
You need to learn 'em all of course.

| Wie viel Uhr ist es? | ← | = What time is it? | → | Wie spät ist es? |

1) **Something o'clock:**

It's 1 o'clock:	(Es ist) ein Uhr	← ein Uhr, not eine Uhr.
It's two o'clock:	(Es ist) zwei Uhr	
It's 8pm:	(Es ist) zwanzig Uhr	

Be <u>careful</u> with 'halb':
'<u>halb drei</u>' means 'half <u>to</u>
three' (i.e. <u>half past two</u>)
not half past three.

2) **Quarter to and past, half past:**

quarter past two:	<u>Viertel nach</u> zwei
half past two:	<u>halb</u> drei
quarter to three:	<u>Viertel vor</u> drei

Wie viel Uhr
ist es?

3) **'... past' and '... to':**

twenty past seven:	<u>zwanzig nach</u> sieben
twelve minutes past eight:	<u>zwölf nach</u> acht
ten to two:	<u>zehn vor</u> zwei

4) The <u>24-hour clock</u>:
They use it a lot in Germany
— and it's easier too.

03.14:	drei Uhr vierzehn
20.32:	zwanzig Uhr zweiunddreißig
19.55:	neunzehn Uhr fünfundfünfzig

Die Woche — The week

This is '<u>must-learn</u>' stuff — it'll gain you simple marks in your assessments.

Hmm... did I put
my 'Montag'
underpants on?

DAYS OF THE WEEK

Monday:	Montag
Tuesday:	Dienstag
Wednesday:	Mittwoch
Thursday:	Donnerstag
Friday:	Freitag
Saturday:	Samstag/Sonnabend
Sunday:	Sonntag

Days of the week are all
<u>masculine</u>. If you want to
say '<u>on Monday</u>', it's either
'<u>Montag</u>' or '<u>am Montag</u>'.

SOME USEFUL WORDS ABOUT THE WEEK

today:	heute
tomorrow:	morgen
yesterday:	gestern
week:	die Woche (-e)
weekend:	das Wochenende (-n)
on Mondays:	montags

Dienstags gehe ich einkaufen.

= I go shopping on <u>Tuesdays</u> (every Tuesday).

Dienstag fahre ich weg.

= I'm going away
on <u>Tuesday</u>.

Remember, plurals are always 'die'.

Wie viel Uhr ist es, Herr Wolf?

Time is <u>ultra-important</u>. In the mark schemes they specifically mention being able to say
<u>when</u> you do things — and you can't do that if you don't know how to say the <u>days of the
week</u> and things like '<u>tomorrow</u>' or '<u>weekend</u>'. So what are you waiting for... <u>Learn it</u>.

Times and Dates

You're <u>bound</u> to get asked about something to do with dates. When you're going on holiday, when Billy went to the concert... that sort of thing. It's practically <u>guaranteed</u>.

Januar, Februar, März, April...

Yippee, holiday...

German month names are blummin' similar to the English — make sure you learn what's different.

January:	Januar	*July:*	Juli
February:	Februar	*August:*	August
March:	März	*September:*	September
April:	April	*October:*	Oktober
May:	Mai	*November:*	November
June:	Juni	*December:*	Dezember

Er fährt Juli / im Juli **weg.** = He's going away <u>in July</u>.

① Like the days, the months are masculine. Say '<u>Januar</u>' or '<u>im Januar</u>', <u>not</u> 'in Januar'.

season:	die Jahreszeit (-en)
spring:	Frühling
summer:	Sommer
autumn:	Herbst
winter:	Winter

② The seasons are masculine too.

Im Jahre zweitausendelf — In the year 2011

See <u>pages 10-11</u> for letters.

Write the date out like this for an informal letter...

den 5. März = 5th March

...and like this for a formal letter.

den 12.11.2011 = 12th November, 2011

Here's how to <u>say</u> the date — it's a bit different because you have to pronounce all the numbers.

In German you **NEVER** say 'In 2011...' like we do in English, you say:

Im Jahre *zweitausendelf* ... = In the year <u>2011</u>.

The special endings are because this is the <u>dative</u> case, <u>see page 85</u>.

Ich komme <u>am</u> zweitausend<u>en</u> Oktober. = I am coming on the 20th of October.

Like in English, the year is 'neunzehnhundert...' rather than 'tausendneunhundert...'.

Ich bin <u>am</u> dritt<u>en</u> März neunzehnhundertfünfundneunzig geboren. = I was born on the 3rd of March 1995.

Morgen — Tomorrow... Gestern — Yesterday

Use these with the <u>stuff</u> on the <u>page 2</u> — together they're <u>great</u> for sorting out your social life.

tomorrow:	morgen
yesterday:	gestern
this morning:	heute Morgen
this afternoon:	heute Nachmittag
tonight:	heute Nacht
tomorrow morning:	morgen früh
this week:	diese Woche
next week:	nächste Woche
last week:	letzte Woche
every day:	jeden Tag
at the weekend:	am Wochenende
recently:	neulich

Was machst du heute Abend **?**

= What are you doing <u>this evening</u>?

i.e. <u>not</u> 'morgen Morgen' even though the word for tomorrow is 'morgen' as well.

always:	immer
never:	nie
often:	oft
seldom:	nicht oft
sometimes:	manchmal

Ich fahre selten **Ski.** = I <u>seldom</u> go skiing.

Dates — better at the cinema than in German...

This stuff is absolutely <u>crucial</u>. It's got to be worth making the effort to learn it — it'll get you loads more marks. And as an added bonus, it's not that hard. Hurrah. Make sure you learn all that <u>heute Abend / morgen früh</u> business too, cos it might well come in handy somewhere.

Asking Questions

You've got to be able to understand questions. You might have to ask them too.

Wann — when... warum — why... wo — where

It's really important that you learn these question words:

when?:	wann?
why?:	warum?
why?:	wieso?
where?:	wo?
where (to)?:	wohin?
where (from)?:	woher?
how?:	wie?
how much?:	wie viel?
how many?:	wie viele?
who/whom?:	wer/wen/wem?
what?:	was?
which (one)?:	welche/r/s?

Wann kommst du wieder nach Hause?

= When are you coming back home?

Wie viele Karotten möchten Sie?

= How many carrots would you like?

Reverse word order to ask a question

In English you change 'I can go' to 'Can I go?' to make it into a question — you can in German too.

Ich kann mitkommen. = I can come along.

subject   verb

Put the verb (the doing word/action) first and then the verb's subject (the person or thing doing the verb) to show it's a question:

Kann ich mitkommen? = Can I come along?

verb   subject

Don't forget to stick a question mark on the end.

Kommt dein Bruder auch? = Is your brother coming too?

verb   subject

Learn how to say 'isn't it?'

The most common words used for this are 'nicht (wahr)?', 'ja?' and 'oder?'. Just stick them on the end of a statement with a comma first and bung a question mark on the end — lovely.

Gut, nicht ?

= Good, isn't it?

Du warst auch da, oder ?

= You were there too, weren't you?

Sie ist freundlich, ja ?

= She is friendly, isn't she?

Word order — I'll have 2 six-letter words please...

The secret to most of GCSE German is to learn a phrase, and learn the words you can change in it, and what you can change them to. Once you know how to ask 'How many carrots would you like?', it doesn't take much more to be able to ask 'How many apples would you like?'...

Being Polite

This stuff is <u>dead important</u> — without it you'll lose marks and sound rude — 'nuff said.

Wie geht's? — How are you?

You've <u>absolutely</u> got to know these phrases. You need to be able to <u>say</u> them, and to <u>understand</u> them. It's utterly crucial — so make sure you know these <u>inside out</u>.

'Wie geht es (dir)?' is often shortened to 'Wie geht's?'.

Wie geht es dir? = How are you?

How are you? *(formal):* Wie geht es Ihnen?
How are you? *(informal plural):* Wie geht es euch?

Bitte — Please... Danke — Thank you

Easy stuff — probably the first German words you ever learnt.
When someone says '<u>danke</u>' it is polite to say '<u>bitte</u>' or '<u>bitte schön</u>'.

please: bitte   *you're welcome:* bitte schön/bitte sehr
thank you: danke/danke schön

Erm, could you take a step forward please, thank you very much. Errm, bitte...danke schön...

Ich hätte gern — I would like

It's more polite to say '<u>ich hätte gern</u>' (I would like) than '<u>ich will</u>' (I want).

1 Here's how to say you would like <u>a thing</u>:

I would like: Ich möchte ⮕ **Ich hätte gern** *das Salz.*   = <u>I would like</u> the salt.

2 Here's how to say you would like <u>to do</u> something:

Ich würde gern *singen.*   = <u>I would like</u> to sing.

I would like: Ich möchte

See <u>pages 110-111</u> for more info on the grammar behind these phrases and <u>pages 14–15</u> for help on asking for things.

Darf ich — May I

Here's how to ask for something. Use '<u>May I?</u>' to be more polite.

Can I?: Kann ich? ⮕ **Darf ich** *bitte das Salz haben?*   = <u>May I</u> have the salt, please?

Darf ich *mich hinsetzen* **?**   = May I <u>sit down</u>?

use the toilet: die Toilette benutzen
please have something to drink: bitte etwas zu trinken haben

Mind your P's and Q's please...

Little niceties will help you to excel as a social butterfly in Germany... oh yes, and they'll help shed-loads when it comes to those <u>speaking assessments</u>. These little jokers are absolutely <u>vital</u> — they make you sound like you <u>really</u> know how to speak great German. And examiners like that.

Being Polite

Polite conversation just means being able to talk to people in everyday social situations, and doing it properly and politely in a way your mother would be proud of. And it gets you marks too.

Guten Morgen! Wie geht's?

— Good Morning! How are you?

Good day / hello: Guten Tag
Good evening: Guten Abend
How are you?: Wie geht es dir/Ihnen?

To reply to 'Guten Tag', simply say 'Guten Tag' back.
Do the same with 'Guten Abend'.

Mir geht's gut *, danke.*   = I'm fine thanks.

not too well: nicht so gut
badly/I'm ill: schlecht
great: klasse/super
OK: OK

You could just say 'Gut, danke' (you'll get more marks for the whole thing, though).

Darf ich Petra vorstellen? — May I introduce Petra?

All useful stuff for your speaking assessments.

Dies ist Petra.   = This is Petra.

Freut mich.   = Pleased to meet you.

you (plural, informal): Kommt herein. Setzt euch.

Komm herein. Setz dich.   = Come in. Sit down. (Informal)

Kommen Sie herein. Setzen Sie sich.   = Come in. Sit down. (Formal)

you (singular & plural formal): Ihnen
you (plural, informal): euch

Vielen Dank. Das ist sehr nett von dir *.*   = Thank you. That is very nice of you. (Informal)

Es tut mir Leid — I'm sorry

Learn both these ways of apologising — and how they're used.

I'm sorry (when you've done something wrong): Es tut mir Leid
Sorry! (to a friend): Entschuldige!

Don't just barge in and demand things — it'll lose you marks, and friends.

Excuse me! (e.g. wanting to ask someone the way): Entschuldigung / Entschuldigen Sie!

Entschuldigung! Erm... do you come here often?

Es tut mir Leid — you'll need to learn this stuff...

It's a bit boring, I know. But grin, bear it, and most of all learn it, and you'll be fine. Not only that, if you ever go to Germany, everybody will think you're lovely and want to be your friend. Aww.

Opinions

To get a decent mark, you need to be able to say what you think about things. So get <u>learning</u> this little lot...

Magst du...? — *Do you like...?*

| Magst du | diese Band | ? | = Do you like <u>this band</u>? |

This needs to be in the <u>accusative</u> case, see the grammar section <u>page 84</u>.

this film: diesen Film
this newspaper: diese Zeitung
this book: dieses Buch

| Ich mag | diese Band | nicht. Ich finde | sie | schlecht | . | = I don't like <u>this band</u>. I think <u>it's bad</u>.

There are more opinion words on <u>pages 8 and 9</u>.

These are <u>linked</u>. If the <u>first bit</u> is <u>feminine</u>, then the <u>second bit</u> must be feminine too.

it: ihn/sie/es

These are good, <u>all-purpose</u> ways of asking whether somebody <u>agrees</u> with what you've just said:

Ich denke, diese Zeitung ist langweilig. Und du?

= I think this newspaper is boring. What about you?

Denkst du das auch?

= Do you agree?
(Literally: 'Do you think that too?')

Ich mag... — *I like...*

You'll often be asked what you think of stuff. So get learning these handy phrases.

LIKING THINGS

I like ... :	Ich mag ...
I like ... :	... gefällt mir
I love ... :	Ich liebe ...
I'm interested in ... :	Ich interessiere mich für ...
I find ... great:	Ich finde ... toll
I like ... :	Ich habe ... gern

DISLIKING THINGS

I don't like...:	Ich mag ... nicht
I don't like...:	... gefällt mir nicht
... doesn't interest me:	... interessiert mich nicht
I find ... awful:	Ich finde ... furchtbar

| Tischtennis | gefällt mir | , aber | Fußball | interessiert mich | nicht | .

= <u>I like</u> table tennis, but football <u>doesn't</u> <u>interest me</u>.

<u>Watch out</u> — say '<u>ich mag Hermann</u>' if you want to say you <u>like him</u>. If you say '<u>Hermann gefällt mir</u>', it means you <u>fancy him</u>.

OTHER USEFUL PHRASES

It's all right:	es geht
I don't mind/care:	es ist mir egal
I prefer to do ...:	ich mache lieber

Die Band — the opposite of a live band...

This is another must-know topic. It's one of those that they specifically mention in the <u>mark schemes</u>. If you're asked your <u>opinion</u> about something, and you <u>can't remember</u> how to say what you really think, then <u>make something up</u>. Get these phrases <u>learnt</u> for loads of marks.

Opinions

Yep, still on opinions I'm afraid — that's cos you really need to know this stuff. You'll get given other people's opinions in your exams and you'll need to come up with some of your own in the speaking and writing tasks. This page gives you loads more ways to tell the world what you think...

Wie findest du...? — What do you think of...?

Look out for these words, they all mean the same thing — 'what do you think of ...?'.
If you can use loads of these then your German will be dead interesting — that means more marks of course. But be really careful about 'ich meine' — it means 'I think', not 'I mean'.

FINDING OUT SOMEONE'S OPINION

What do you think of... ?:	Was hältst du von...?
What do you think of...?:	Wie findest du...?
What do you think of...?:	Was denkst du über...?
What's your opinion of that?:	Was ist deine Meinung dazu?
What do you think?:	Was meinst du?

I THINK...

I think that ... :	Ich meine, dass ...
I think that ... :	Ich denke, dass ...
I think ... is ... :	Ich halte ... für ...

Wie findest du | meinen Freund?   = What do you think of my boyfriend?

Ich halte ihn für verrückt.   = I think he's mad.

This is in the accusative case — see page 84.

See page 7 for how to ask if somebody agrees.

Ich finde es... — I think it's...

You might have to say whether you like something or not.

Ich finde | diese Band | gut .   = I think this band is good.

See page 9 for more opinion words.

this team:	diese Mannschaft
this music:	diese Musik

bad:	schlecht
excellent:	ausgezeichnet
terrible:	schrecklich
boring:	langweilig
quite good:	ziemlich gut

Opinion words

Rob could never understand why his air guitar band wasn't more popular...

Ich finde | diese Musik | schrecklich .

= I think this music is terrible.

If I hear one more word about this band...

Giving your opinion about things gets you big marks in speaking and writing. It's quite easy to say whether you like something or not, so you've got no excuses — just learn these phrases.

Opinions

After you've <u>impressed</u> the examiners by saying you like or hate something, really <u>knock their socks off</u> by explaining <u>why</u>.

Toll — Great... Furchtbar — Terrible

Here are some words you can use to <u>describe</u> things you <u>like</u> or <u>don't like</u>. They're <u>really easy</u> to use, so it's worth <u>learning</u> them.

great:	toll / prima super / klasse	*friendly:*	freundlich	*not nice (person):*	unsympathisch
good:	gut	*excellent:*	ausgezeichnet	*bad:*	schlecht / schlimm
lovely:	schön	*fantastic:*	fantastisch	*terrible:*	furchtbar / schlimm
beautiful:	wunderschön	*interesting:*	interessant	*ugly / nasty:*	hässlich
		nice (person):	nett / sympathisch		

Bob ist toll . = <u>Bob</u> is <u>great.</u>

Tennis ist furchtbar . = <u>Tennis</u> is <u>awful.</u>

Weil — Because

'Weil' is <u>ultra-important</u> — it's the main German word for <u>because</u>.
When you use '<u>weil</u>' the <u>verb</u> in that part of the sentence gets shoved to the <u>end</u>.

Remember: a <u>verb</u> is a <u>doing</u> word.

This means that...

Der Film gefällt mir. Er ist interessant. = I like the film. It is interesting.

verb

See <u>page 89</u> for other words like 'weil'.

... becomes:

Der Film gefällt mir, weil er interessant ist. = I like the film, because it is interesting.

Ich finde sie sehr nett , weil sie freundlich ist. = I think she's very <u>nice</u> because she is <u>friendly.</u>

There's always a comma before 'weil'.

Ich mag ihn nicht, weil er langweilig ist. = I don't like him because he is <u>boring.</u>

Denn — Because

It's handy to know that '<u>denn</u>', like 'weil', means '<u>because</u>'.
'Denn' is <u>dead useful</u>, cos it <u>doesn't</u> change the word order.

<u>Don't</u> confuse '<u>denn</u>' with '<u>dann</u>', which means '<u>then</u>'.

Ich mag ihn nicht, <u>denn er ist</u> langweilig. = I don't like him because he is boring.

Deutsch ist toll/prima/furchtbar...*

It's no good only knowing how to ask someone else's opinion, or how to say 'I think', without being able to say <u>what</u> you think. All these phrases are great, because you can just <u>stick them together</u> to get a sentence. Just make sure you don't say something <u>daft</u> like 'I like it because it's boring'.

Writing Informal Letters

You might have to <u>write a letter</u> in German at some point.
So <u>learn</u> how to lay out a letter and how to say Dear Jim, and all the stuff like that.

Lieber Hermann — Dear Hermann

You've got to be able to <u>start</u> and <u>end</u> a letter properly.
OK, this one's a bit short, but it shows you how to start and end it, and where to put the <u>date</u>.

Put where you live and the date up here. Check out <u>page 3</u> on dates.

This means Dear Hermann. If you're writing to a woman, you'd put <u>Liebe</u> instead of <u>Lieber</u>.

This means: 'Many thanks for your letter.'

These two are really great phrases to use in letters.

You <u>don't</u> need a capital letter here.

This means: 'I was so pleased to hear from you again.'

Many greetings.

If you're female, you put <u>deine</u> instead of <u>dein</u>.

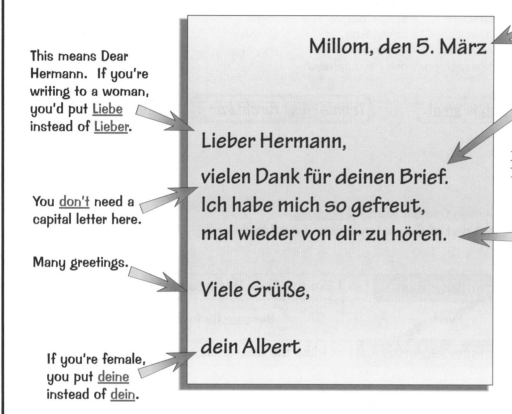

Millom, den 5. März

Lieber Hermann,

vielen Dank für deinen Brief.
Ich habe mich so gefreut,
mal wieder von dir zu hören.

Viele Grüße,

dein Albert

"Lieber Hermann,
willkommen in Dumpsville..."

Use these phrases in your letters

One thing that you can use for just about <u>every</u> informal letter is asking how the person is:

Wie geht's? = How are you?

You can use this one to start a letter, just after Dear whoever.

Just before you <u>sign off</u>, you can put: *Bis bald!* = See you soon.

German letters — keep them Brief...

This is pretty <u>easy</u> stuff, but it could well help with your writing assessment. Make sure you can use the German <u>stock phrases</u> — then your letter will sound <u>authentic</u>. There <u>aren't</u> any secrets to the <u>main part</u> of the letter — just stick to what you know and it'll all be tickety-boo.

Writing Formal Letters

It might not be fair, but they expect you to be able to write a _formal_ letter as well.
Most often they want you to write to _book_ a _hotel room_. For more hotel vocab see _page 47_.

Put your name _and_ address _at the top_

Put _your_ name and address up here.

The _name and address_ of who you're writing to goes here.

You _don't_ need a capital letter here.

This lot means:
I would like to reserve three rooms with you for the 4th - 18th June, inclusive. We need a double room and two single rooms. Please can you tell me how much they will cost?

> Aleesha Thompson
> 16 Rusland Drive
> Manchester
> M14 7QE
> Großbritannien
>
> Manchester, den 23.6.2009
>
> Brandenburger Hotel
> Unter den Linden 115
> 10159 Berlin
>
> Sehr geehrte Damen und Herren,
>
> ich möchte drei Zimmer für den 4. - 18. Juni inklusive bei Ihnen reservieren. Wir brauchen ein Doppelzimmer und zwei Einzelzimmer. Können Sie mich bitte informieren wie viel sie kosten werden?
>
> Mit freundlichen Grüßen
>
> _A. Thompson_
>
> Aleesha Thompson

Put the date over here.

You write this when you _don't know_ the name of the person you're writing to.

If you do know, put 'Sehr geehrte' for a woman, or 'Sehr geehrter' for a man, then the person's name.

Yours sincerely

Remember that 'Sie' and 'Ihnen' _always_ start with a _capital letter_.

Schön.

Monks love formal letters.

Learn _these ways to_ end _a letter_

The examiner _won't_ be impressed if you can't _end_ a letter properly. So _learn_ this:

Hochachtungsvoll = Yours faithfully/sincerely

You can use the ending from the letter above, as well.

Use '_entschuldigen_' _to apologise_

You might find you have to _apologise_ for something. This is the phrase you'll need:

Ich möchte mich bei Ihnen entschuldigen. = I wish to apologise.

You might also have to _complain_ about something:

Ich möchte mich über Ihrem Hotel beschweren. = I wish to complain about _your hotel_.

Formal 'your'.

Put whatever you need in here.

H in a dinner jacket — a formal letter...

OK, there's a lot to _learn_ for these, but they might come in _pretty handy_. There are _set polite phrases_ for formal letters in German just like there are in English — this page might look pretty scary, but once you've _learnt them_, the whole thing doesn't look so bad. So get _practising_.

Revision Summary

This section is the absolute basics that you need to have <u>totally sorted</u> come exam time.
The stuff on your <u>opinions</u>, and on <u>times</u> (including today, tomorrow, every week, on Mondays etc.),
can make a really <u>big difference</u> to your marks. The only way to make sure that you've got it sorted
is to do <u>all</u> of these questions. Go over the section again and again (and again) until you know it.

1) Count out loud from 1 to 20 in German.

2) How do you say these numbers in German? a) 22 b) 35 c) 58 d) 71 e) 112 f) 2101

3) What are these in German? a) 1st b) 4th c) 7th d) 19th e) 25th f) 52nd

4) What do these words mean? a) alle b) manche c) viel d) wenig

5) Give two ways to ask 'What time is it?' in German.
   Look at your watch, and say what time it is, out loud and in German.

6) How would you say these times in German? a) 5.00 b) 10.30 c) 13.22 d) 16.45

7) Say all the days of the week in German.

8) How do you say these in German? a) yesterday b) today c) tomorrow

9) Say all of the months of the year in German.

10) How do you say the <u>date</u> of your birthday (including the <u>year</u>) in German?

11) 'Was machst du heute Abend?' means 'What are you doing this evening?'
    How would you say 'What are you doing a) this afternoon?' b) tonight?' c) next week?'

12) 'Ich fahre nicht oft Ski' means 'I seldom ski.'
    How would you say: a) 'I never ski.' b) 'I often ski.' c) 'I sometimes ski.'

13) 'Du singst' means 'You sing' or 'You are singing'. What do these questions mean?
    a) Wann singst du? b) Wo singst du? c) Was singst du?
    d) Wie singst du? e) Warum singst du? f) Wie viel singst du?

14) How do you say these in German? a) Please b) Thank you c) How are you?

15) Here are some phrases: 'ich hätte gern', 'ich möchte', 'ich würde gern'.
    Which two could you use to say you'd like a) some coffee? b) to dance?

16) How would you ask someone what they think of Elvis Presley? (In German.)
    Give as many ways of asking it as you can.

17) How would you say these things in German? Give at least one way to say each of them.
    a) I like Elvis Presley. b) I don't like Elvis Presley. c) I find Elvis Presley interesting.
    d) I love Elvis Presley. e) I find Elvis Presley terrible. f) I think that Elvis Presley is fantastic.

18) To win this week's star prize, complete the following sentence in
    10 words or less (in German): 'I like Elvis Presley because...'

19) To win last week's potato peelings, complete the following sentence
    in 10 words or less (in German): 'I don't like Elvis Presley because...'

20) Which of the following phrases would you use to start a <u>formal</u> letter in German?
    a) Sehr geehrter Herr Presley, b) Lieber Elvis, c) Yo Elvis.

You need 'General Stuff' to do well in the exam.

Leave me alone.

Food

The <u>more</u> of this lot you learn, the <u>better</u>. Luckily, a lot of these are <u>similar</u> to the English words.

Gemüsehändler und Metzger — Greengrocer and butcher

This is basic, <u>meat and two veg</u> vocab. You really do need to know it.

VEGETABLES: DAS GEMÜSE

potato:	die Kartoffel (-n)
carrot:	die Karotte (-n)
tomato:	die Tomate (-n)
cucumber:	die Gurke (-n)
onion:	die Zwiebel (-n)
cauliflower:	der Blumenkohl (-e)
cabbage:	der Kohl (-e)
lettuce:	der Kopfsalat (-e)
pea:	die Erbse (-n)

Remember, plurals are always 'die'.

FRUIT: DAS OBST

apple:	der Apfel (die Äpfel)
banana:	die Banane (-n)
strawberry:	die Erdbeere (-n)
lemon:	die Zitrone (-n)
orange:	die Orange (-n)
	die Apfelsine (-n)
raspberry:	die Himbeere (-n)
peach:	der Pfirsich (-e)
pear:	die Birne (-n)

MEAT: DAS FLEISCH

beef:	das Rindfleisch
pork:	das Schweinefleisch
chicken:	das Hähnchen
sausage:	die Wurst (die Würste)
lamb:	das Lamm(fleisch)

Getränke und Süßigkeiten — Drinks and sweets

You'll need to know these — you can't describe a meal without mentioning <u>dessert</u> and a <u>drink</u>.

SWEET THINGS: DIE SÜßIGKEITEN

cake:	der Kuchen (-)
biscuit:	der Keks (-e)
ice cream:	das Eis (-)
chocolate:	die Schokolade
sugar:	der Zucker
jam / marmalade:	die Marmelade
cream:	die Sahne
gateau:	die Torte (-n)

DRINKS: DIE GETRÄNKE

beer:	das Bier
red wine:	der Rotwein
white wine:	der Weißwein
tea:	der Tee
coffee:	der Kaffee
orange juice:	der Orangensaft
	/ der Apfelsinensaft
apple juice:	der Apfelsaft
mineral water:	das Mineralwasser

I'm on a seafood diet. I see food and I eat it.

Sergeant Stern, dodgy old joke squad. You're nicked, sunshine.

Andere Lebensmittel — Other foods

You'll need to know <u>lots</u> of other foods too. Learn <u>as many</u> of these as you can.

OTHER FOODS: ANDERE LEBENSMITTEL

bread:	das Brot (-e)
bread roll:	das Brötchen (-)
milk:	die Milch
butter:	die Butter
cheese:	der Käse (-)
egg:	das Ei (-er)
salt:	das Salz
pepper:	der Pfeffer
rice:	der Reis
pasta (plural):	die Nudeln
yogurt:	der Joghurt (-s)

GERMAN SPECIALITIES: DEUTSCHE SPEZIALITÄTEN

pickled cabbage:	das Sauerkraut
boiled sausage:	die Bockwurst (die Bockwürste)
fried sausage:	die Bratwurst (die Bratwürste)
sausage with curry sauce:	die Currywurst (die Currywürste)
veal slice fried in breadcrumbs:	das Schnitzel (-)

What's Kuchen...

Phew — that's made me hungry. Now, you might need to talk or write about <u>healthy and unhealthy foods</u> or say what your <u>favourite meal</u> is — so make sure you're properly prepared. <u>Learn</u> these.

Mealtimes

This page is full of stuff that you can use all the time — not just at mealtimes. Use it to say <u>what you like</u>, and to ask people <u>politely</u> for things. You've just <u>got</u> to know it.

Ich mag... — I like...

These expressions <u>aren't</u> just for food — use them to talk about <u>anything</u> you <u>like</u> or <u>dislike</u>.

Ich mag Äpfel . = I like <u>apples</u>.

bananas: Bananen   *cream:* Sahne

Ich mag kein Gemüse . = I <u>don't</u> like <u>vegetables</u>.

apples: keine Äpfel   *coffee:* keinen Kaffee

Ja bitte — Yes please

It doesn't come any <u>easier</u> than this.

Ja bitte. = Yes please.

Nein danke. = No thanks.

Important:
Always say 'Ja bitte',
not 'Ja danke'.

Könnten Sie...? — Could you...?

Two <u>mega-important</u> phrases that you've got to <u>learn</u> and be able to use <u>properly</u>.

Könnten Sie mir bitte den Pfeffer **reichen?**

a napkin: eine Serviette
the sugar: den Zucker
the cream: die Sahne
the milk: die Milch

= Could you pass me <u>the pepper</u>, please?

Darf ich bitte das Salz **haben?** = May I have <u>the salt</u>, please?

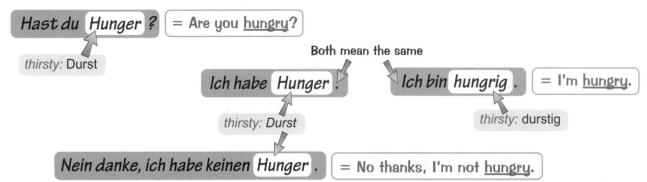

Hast du Hunger oder Durst? — Are you hungry or thirsty?

Common enough questions. Make <u>sure</u> you can answer them.

Hast du Hunger **?** = Are you <u>hungry</u>?

thirsty: Durst

Both mean the same

Ich habe Hunger . = I'm <u>hungry</u>.

thirsty: Durst

Ich bin hungrig . = I'm <u>hungry</u>.

thirsty: durstig

Nein danke, ich habe keinen Hunger . = No thanks, I'm not <u>hungry</u>.

OK, forget the pepper — just pass your exams...

This is pretty <u>easy</u>. They're bound to ask what you <u>like and don't like</u> — so you need to know what to say. And make sure you can ask questions <u>politely</u>... so you don't go offending anyone.

Mealtimes

This is stuff you <u>should know</u> — especially if you want <u>good marks</u>. Again, a lot of it could be used in <u>different</u> sorts of situations — <u>not just</u> in conversations at the dinner table.

Hat das geschmeckt? — Did that taste good?

A fairly <u>common</u> question. Learn these answers and it won't cause you any <u>trouble</u>.

Das Essen hat **gut** geschmeckt.   = The food tasted <u>good</u>.

very good:	sehr gut
not especially good:	nicht besonders gut
bad:	nicht
very bad:	gar nicht

Das Frühstück war **lecker**, danke.   = Breakfast was <u>delicious</u>, thanks.

Hat das geschmeckt?

Möchten Sie...? — Would you like...?

It's that word '<u>möchten</u>' again. These sentences are <u>dead important</u> — you can use them to make <u>different</u> sorts of offers, not just ones about <u>food</u>.

Möchten Sie **das Salz** haben?   = Would you like <u>the salt</u>?

This is <u>similar</u> to what's on the previous page — see <u>page 13</u> for more possible <u>vocab</u>.

the pepper:	den Pfeffer
the red wine:	den Rotwein
the butter:	die Butter
a napkin:	eine Serviette

Ein wenig... — A little...

These quantity words are dead <u>useful</u>. There'll be loads of times in your speaking and writing tasks that you can use them and bag yourself <u>more marks</u>.

Ich möchte **viel** Zucker, bitte.   = I would like <u>lots</u> of sugar, please.

a bit: ein bisschen/ein wenig

See <u>page 1</u> for more on quantities.

Ich möchte **ein großes Stück** Torte.   = I would like <u>a big piece</u> of cake.

Ich habe **genug** gegessen, danke.   = I've eaten <u>enough</u>, thanks.

Ich bin satt.   = I'm full.

Ooh, I'd like a nice cuppa tea please...

These quantity words are really <u>handy</u> — learn them and you're cooking on gas. There are loads of ways you can use this stuff, so get cracking and make sure you know it <u>inside out</u>.

Daily Routine

More useful stuff for if you're <u>staying</u> with someone.

<u>Wann isst du...?</u> — <u>When do you eat...?</u>

Meals are <u>important</u> — so get <u>learning</u> these phrases.

| Wann | isst du | zu Abend | ? | = When <u>do you eat</u> <u>dinner</u>? |

See <u>page 2</u> for more times.

do you eat (plural, informal):   esst ihr
do you eat (formal):   essen Sie

breakfast: das Frühstück
lunch: zu Mittag

| Wir essen | um sieben Uhr | zu Abend | . | = We eat <u>dinner</u> <u>at seven o'clock</u> <u>in the evening</u>. |

<u>Musst du zu Hause helfen?</u>
— <u>Do you have to help at home?</u>

Even if you <u>never</u> help at home — <u>learn</u> these words.

| Ich wasche zu Hause ab. | = I wash up at home. |

| Ich muss | abwaschen | . | = I have to <u>wash up</u>. |

I tidy my room: Ich räume mein Zimmer auf.
I make my bed: Ich mache mein Bett.
I vacuum: Ich sauge Staub.
I clean: Ich putze.

clean: putzen
tidy up: aufräumen
make my bed: mein Bett machen
empty the dishwasher: die Spülmaschine leeren

'Abwaschen' and 'aufräumen' are separable verbs.
If you don't know much about these, have a look at <u>page 108</u>.

<u>Brauchst du etwas?</u> — <u>Do you need anything?</u>

These are <u>easy</u> phrases — so there's <u>no excuse</u> for not <u>knowing</u> them.
Remember to use the formal '<u>Sie</u>' if you're asking someone older.

| Darf ich mich | duschen | ? | = May I have <u>a shower</u>? |

bath: baden

a towel: ein Handtuch   some soap: etwas Seife

| Haben Sie | Zahnpasta | ? | = <u>Have you</u> <u>any toothpaste</u>? |

Have you (informal): Hast du

<u>Essen — the ESSENtials of life...</u>

You should have <u>no problem</u> learning the <u>meals</u> — but those <u>separable verbs</u> take a bit of getting used to. <u>Learn one</u>, and all the others follow the same <u>pattern</u>. It's almost as <u>fun</u> as washing up...

About Yourself

You'll probably have to give all sorts of <u>personal details</u> about yourself in your speaking and writing tasks. You should <u>know</u> all this already, just make <u>sure</u> you <u>really</u> know it backwards.

Erzähl mir etwas von dir... — Tell me about yourself...

You might need to answer these questions in your <u>speaking assessment</u>:

What are you called?: **Wie heißt du?**

Ich heiße George . = I'm called <u>George</u>.

How old are you?: **Wie alt bist du?**

Ich bin fünfzehn Jahre alt. = I'm <u>15</u> years old.

When is your birthday?: **Wann hast du Geburtstag?**

Ich habe am 12. Dezember Geburtstag. = My birthday is on the <u>12th of December</u>.

Where do you live?: **Wo wohnst du?**

Ich wohne in Lancaster .

= I live in <u>Lancaster</u>.

What do you like?: **Was magst du?**

Ich mag Fußball .

= I like <u>football</u>.

Use this to say you like or dislike any person or thing, e.g. I like you: ich mag dich.

See <u>pages 61-62</u> for where you live, <u>page 1</u> for more numbers and <u>page 3</u> for more dates.

Wie siehst du aus? — What do you look like?

You might have to <u>describe</u> how gorgeous you are as well — shouldn't be too hard should it?

Ich bin groß . = I am <u>tall</u>.

medium height:	mittelgroß
small:	klein
fat:	dick
thin:	dünn
slim:	schlank

Ich habe braune Augen. = I have <u>brown</u> eyes.

blue: blaue
green: grüne

Ich trage eine Brille. = I wear glasses.

Ich habe lange Haare. = I have <u>long</u> hair.

short:	kurze	dark:	dunkle	red:	rote
straight:	glatte	light:	helle	brown:	braune
curly:	lockige	blond:	blonde	black:	schwarze

moustache: Schnurrbart

Ich habe einen Bart . = I have a <u>beard</u>. OK — so <u>you</u> might not have a beard, but you might have to describe someone <u>who does</u>.

Wie schreibt man das? — How do you spell that?

You may have to <u>spell</u> your name and home town letter by letter in your <u>speaking assessment</u> or <u>listen</u> to someone spell something in the listening exam.

Kannst du das buchstabieren? = Can you spell that?

Nooool!!!
...er... I mean...
Nein!!!

That means you have to be able to <u>pronounce</u> the German alphabet.
Helpfully, the alphabet's all written out on the <u>inside front cover</u> for you.

Appearances matter — to the exam board...

<u>Learn</u> how to <u>describe</u> how scrumptious you look — so you can do it without a second thought.
You have to be able to <u>pronounce</u> the German <u>alphabet</u> as well — so get <u>practising</u>.

Family and Pets

You might have to talk about <u>family</u> and <u>pets</u> in your speaking assessments or writing tasks.

Ich habe eine Schwester — I have one sister

If you're talking about <u>more than one person</u>, use 'heißen', not 'heißt'.

| Meine Mutter | heißt | Janet | . | = <u>My mother</u> <u>is called</u> <u>Janet</u>.

my father:	mein Vater
my brother:	mein Bruder (meine Brüder)
my sister:	meine Schwester (-n)
my stepmother:	meine Stiefmutter
my stepfather:	mein Stiefvater
my aunt:	meine Tante (-n)
my uncle:	mein Onkel (-)
my female cousin:	meine Cousine (-n)
my male cousin:	mein Cousin (-s)
my grandmother:	meine Großmutter (meine Großmütter)
my grandfather:	mein Großvater (meine Großväter)
my male friend:	mein Freund (-e)
my female friend:	meine Freundin (-nen)
my parents:	meine Eltern
my siblings:	meine Geschwister

Remember, it's 'meine' for plurals.

Ich habe einen Bruder . = I have <u>one brother</u>.

Ich bin Einzelkind. = I am <u>an only child</u>.

To <u>describe</u> your relatives, use these sentences:

Er ist zwölf Jahre alt. = He's <u>12</u> years old.

Er hat blaue Augen. = He has <u>blue</u> eyes.

Sie hat glatte Haare. = She has <u>straight</u> hair.

Sie ist groß . = She is <u>tall</u>.

You can stick the other words from <u>page 17</u> in the white boxes.

Hast du Haustiere? — Have you any pets?

Ich habe einen Hund . = I have <u>a dog</u>.

a dog:	einen Hund (-e)
a cat:	eine Katze (-n)
a budgie:	einen Wellensittich (-e)
a guinea pig:	ein Meerschweinchen (-)
a rabbit:	ein Kaninchen (-)
a horse:	ein Pferd (-e)
a goldfish:	einen Goldfisch (-e)

Mein Hund heißt Rudi .

= My dog is called <u>Rudi</u>.

See <u>page 38</u> for colours and <u>page 17</u> for sizes and things like fat and thin.

Er ist gelb . = He is <u>yellow</u>.

Swap in <u>any</u> descriptive word here.

Who are you calling yellow?

Ist er verheiratet? — Is he married?

Here's some more <u>fancy stuff</u> to learn...

Ich liebe Gerald. = <u>I love</u> Gerald.

He loves: Er liebt
She loves: Sie liebt

She is: Sie ist
They are: Sie sind

Er ist verheiratet . = <u>He is</u> <u>married</u>.

| single: | ledig | separated: | getrennt |
| divorced: | geschieden | engaged: | verlobt |

Meine Familie — they're familiar to me...

Most of this page is <u>basic stuff</u> you have to <u>know</u> — like how to say what <u>relations</u> you have (or don't have). If you don't <u>already</u> know it like the back of your hand — get <u>learning</u>.

Personality

Personality, character, whatever you want to call it, I'm sure you've got bags of it.
It'd probably be useful if you could talk about it in German though...

Meine Persönlichkeit — My personality

You might have to describe your personality in one of your speaking assessments — here's how...

Ich bin **fantastisch** .

= I am fantastic.

nice:	sympathisch/nett	*helpful:*	hilfsbereit
intelligent:	intelligent	*patient:*	geduldig
funny:	lustig	*busy:*	beschäftigt
friendly:	freundlich	*hard-working:*	fleißig
happy:	glücklich		

quite/fairly:	ziemlich
very:	sehr

Ich bin **ein bisschen** **schüchtern** .

= I am a bit shy.

stupid:	blöd / dumm	*serious:*	ernst
noisy:	laut	*impolite:*	unhöflich
lazy:	faul	*impatient:*	ungeduldig
boring:	langweilig	*unfriendly:*	unfreundlich

Die Persönlichkeiten anderer Leute
— Other people's personalities

So you know how to talk about yourself, here's how to talk about other people...

Mein kleiner Bruder ist sehr **laut** . = My little brother is very loud.

Meine Schwester ist wirklich **sympathisch** . = My sister is really nice.

Mein Vater ist oft **beschäftigt**, aber er ist immer **glücklich** .

You can put any of the personality traits above in these white boxes.

= My father is often busy, but he is always happy.

'DAD! It's stuck up my nose!'

'Dad, can you lend me a tenner?'

'Dad, I crashed the car...'

No matter what his kids threw at him, Colin was always happy. His secret was cotton wool...

I'm nice, funny, intelligent — and a born liar...

There's quite a bit of vocab on this page, but learn it and you're sure to impress those pesky examiners. Make sure you know how to write this stuff as well as say it — that's important.

Relationships and Future Plans

OK, we're about to get all <u>deep and meaningful</u> here.
Tissues at the ready? Let's plough on...

Rob didn't have much in common
with his brother and sister.

Wir verstehen uns gut — We get on well

Now's your chance to pour out all your <u>relationships woes</u> in German.

not so well: nicht so gut

This is the <u>dative case</u> — see <u>pages 85 and 92</u> for more info.

Ich verstehe mich gut *mit* meiner Schwester.   = I get on <u>well</u> with <u>my sister</u>.

This is a reflexive verb. If you don't know much about these, take a look at <u>page 107</u>.

my brother: meinem Bruder
my friend: meinem Freund / meiner Freundin
my parents: meinen Eltern

'<u>Ein Freund</u>' is a male friend and '<u>eine Freundin</u>' is a female friend.

You can also say: *Ich komme gut mit* meiner Schwester *aus.*   = I get on well with <u>my sister</u>.

Ich streite mich oft mit meinem Bruder.

= I often argue with <u>my brother</u>.

'Auskommen' is a separable verb. Take a look at <u>page 108</u> to find out more.

Wir streiten uns oft.   = We often argue.

Get more marks, say why...

Really knock the examiner's socks off by saying <u>why</u> you do or don't get on with your <u>loved ones</u>...

Ich streite mich oft mit meinem Bruder, weil er so faul *ist.*

= I often argue with my brother because he's so <u>lazy</u>.

You can put any of the personality words from <u>page 19</u> in the white box.

In der Zukunft — In the future

You need to be able to say what your <u>relationship plans</u> for the <u>future</u> are in German.
If you don't have any yet, learn how to <u>say so</u>.

There's more about future plans on <u>page 75</u>.

Ich möchte heiraten.   = I would like to <u>get married</u>.

to get engaged: mich verloben
to have a family: eine Familie haben
to be in a relationship: in einem Verhältnis sein

Im Moment, weiss ich nicht.

= At the moment, I don't know.

We're just one big happy family...

OK, so this page might involve you <u>thinking</u> a bit, but once you've learnt a few <u>key phrases</u> you should be just fine. You know what I'm going to say: <u>look</u>, <u>cover</u>, <u>scribble</u>... Lovely jubbly.

Social Issues and Equality

Argh, social issues... Talking about them can seem <u>daunting</u> enough in your own language, let alone another one, but keep a <u>cool head</u> and don't start anything you can't <u>finish</u>.

Die Arbeitslosigkeit und die Obdachlosigkeit
— Unemployment and Homelessness

There's not really very much that needs saying here. These things suck whichever way you look at it.

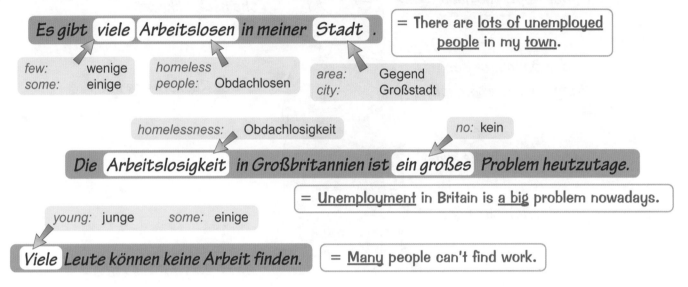

Es gibt viele Arbeitslosen in meiner Stadt. = There are <u>lots of unemployed people</u> in my <u>town</u>.

few: wenige
some: einige

homeless people: Obdachlosen

area: Gegend
city: Großstadt

homelessness: Obdachlosigkeit   no: kein

Die Arbeitslosigkeit in Großbritannien ist ein großes Problem heutzutage.

= <u>Unemployment</u> in Britain is <u>a big</u> problem nowadays.

young: junge   some: einige

Viele Leute können keine Arbeit finden.   = <u>Many</u> people can't find work.

Die Diskriminierung — Discrimination

This is your chance for a good <u>rant</u>, in German of course.

Einige Leute sind gemein zu mir, weil ich aus Indien komme.

= Some people are <u>mean</u> to me because I <u>come from India</u>.

nasty: böse
unfriendly: unfreundlich

am a girl: ein Mädchen bin
wear glasses: eine Brille trage
am foreign: ausländisch bin

For more countries see <u>page 43</u>.

poverty: Armut   discrimination: Diskriminierung   violence: Gewalt
vandalism: Vandalismus   AIDS: AIDS

Ich denke, dass Rassismus ein großes Problem in unserer Gesellschaft ist.

= I think that <u>racism</u> is a big problem in our society.

Das ist rassistisch.   = That's <u>racist</u>.

unfair: unfair

Es geht mir auf die Nerven.

= It gets on my nerves.

Phew — serious stuff this...

There are some really <u>important</u> topics on this page and examiners just love testing you on 'em. They could come up anywhere from <u>speaking</u> to <u>reading</u> too, so make sure you <u>learn</u> this vocab.

Feeling Ill

You've got to be able to <u>tell</u> the doctor <u>what's wrong</u> with you. To do that, you've got to know the names of all the <u>parts of your body</u> in German. It's not hard, so get <u>learning</u>.

Der Körper — The body

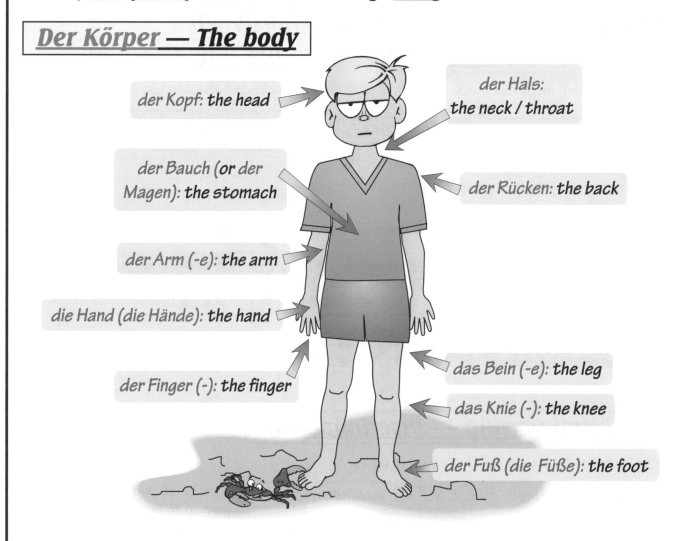

der Kopf: the head

der Hals: the neck / throat

der Bauch (or der Magen): the stomach

der Rücken: the back

der Arm (-e): the arm

die Hand (die Hände): the hand

der Finger (-): the finger

das Bein (-e): the leg

das Knie (-): the knee

der Fuß (die Füße): the foot

Der Kopf — The head

Remember, plurals are always 'die'.

die Haare (plural): hair

das Auge (-n): the eye

das Ohr (-en): the ear

der Zahn (die Zähne): the tooth

die Nase: the nose

der Mund: the mouth

All together now — heads, shoulders, knees and toes...

When you think you know <u>all</u> those body parts, <u>cover</u> the page and scribble down a rough body picture with <u>all</u> the German words — <u>with</u> the <u>der</u>, <u>die</u> or <u>das</u>. Keep learning till you can get them <u>all</u> — <u>without</u> looking back. Der <u>Arm</u>, die <u>Hand</u> and der <u>Finger</u> should be pretty <u>easy</u>...

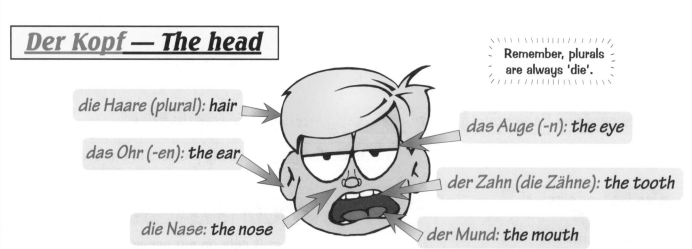

Feeling Ill

Pain, illness and suffering... ah, it's all good fun. OK, roll your sleeves up and get stuck in.

Wie fühlen Sie sich? — How do you feel?

An important question, this. You want to be able to answer it.

Mir ist **schlecht** .   = I am ill.

hot: heiß
cold: kalt

These sentences mean the same here — but the alternative words you can use in each sentence are different.

Ich bin **krank** .   = I am ill.

hungry: hungrig
thirsty: durstig
tired: müde

Ich muss **zum Arzt** gehen.   = I need to go to the doctor's.

| to the hospital: | ins Krankenhaus | to the chemists: | zur Drogerie |
| to the pharmacy: | zur Apotheke | to the dentist: | zum Zahnarzt |

Cuthbert thought he had Foot and Mouth disease.

Was tut weh? — What hurts?

Here's how you say what bit hurts. The parts of the body are all on the previous page.

Use 'mein' for 'der' and 'das' words — and 'meine' for 'die' words.

Mein Bein **tut weh** .   = My leg hurts.

hurt (plural): tun weh

My head: Mein Kopf
My hand: Meine Hand

Was ist los? — What's wrong?

If you want to say your stomach aches, you stick '-schmerzen' ('pains') on the end of the word for stomach and make one long word. Magen+schmerzen = Magenschmerzen.

Ich habe **Magenschmerzen** .   = I have stomach ache.

a headache:	Kopfschmerzen	a sore throat:	Halsschmerzen
flu:	die Grippe	a temperature:	Fieber
a cold:	eine Erkältung		

Ich habe mich **am Bein** geschnitten.   = I've cut my leg.

finger: am Finger   hand: an der Hand

Going to the doctor's — it's a pain in the neck...

It's not the most pleasant page in the world, but you've got to learn it.
You know the score — cover the page, scribble it down, and check you've got it right.

Health and Health Issues

First up, how to live a <u>healthy lifestyle</u>. Ah the joys of GCSE German.
There's a fair bit to say on this topic, mind...

Diät — Diet

No, I'm not talking about any ridiculous <u>lettuce-only</u>, weight-loss diet.
This is about your normal everyday diet and how <u>healthy</u> it is, or isn't.

unhealthily: ungesund

Isst du **gesund** ? = Do you eat <u>healthily</u>?

For more food see
<u>page 13</u>.

NEIN!

Nein, ich esse Pommes fast jeden Tag und ich trinke nur Cola.

= No, I eat chips almost every day and I only drink cola.

Nein, ich esse zu viel Fett und Zucker.

= No, I eat too much fat and sugar.

JA!

Ja, ich esse viel Salat und frisches Obst.

= Yes, I eat a lot of salad and fresh fruit.

Ja, ich trinke nur Mineralwasser.

= Yes, I only drink mineral water.

Bewegung — Exercise

It doesn't matter if you don't do any, just be able to say so.

Was machst du, um fit zu bleiben? = What do you do to stay fit?

Sport isn't always good for you...

Ich mache oft Aerobic, weil es sehr gut für das Herz ist.

= I often do aerobics because it's very good for the heart.

For more sports
see <u>page 27</u>.

Ich treibe viel **Sport** . = I do a lot of <u>sport</u>.

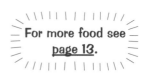

tennis: Tennis
football: Fußball

Ich treibe keinen Sport. Es ist langweilig. = I don't do sport. It's boring.

I eat healthily — a chip is a vegetable, right...

There's loads you might want to say about these <u>exciting</u> things, but learning the stuff on this page is a <u>good start</u>. <u>Think</u> about what else you might want to say, write it down, and <u>practise</u> it.

Health and Health Issues

This bit's all about <u>smoking</u>, <u>drugs</u>, <u>alcohol</u> and <u>rock 'n' roll</u>. Alright. I'm lying about the rock 'n' roll part. It's still pretty interesting though, and you should have an <u>opinion</u> on this stuff without having to try too hard.

Rauchen — Smoking

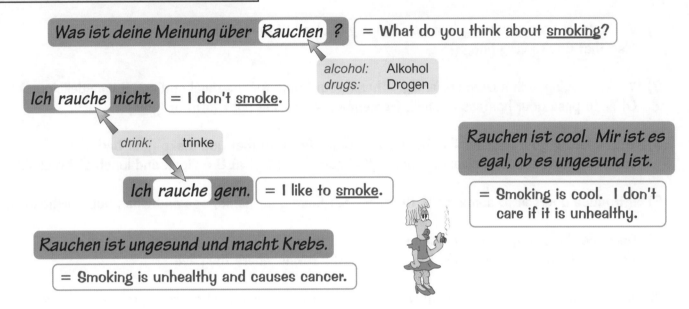

Was ist deine Meinung über Rauchen ? = What do you think about <u>smoking</u>?

alcohol: Alkohol
drugs: Drogen

Ich rauche nicht. = I don't <u>smoke</u>.

drink: trinke

Ich rauche gern. = I like to <u>smoke</u>.

Rauchen ist cool. Mir ist es egal, ob es ungesund ist.

= Smoking is cool. I don't care if it is unhealthy.

Rauchen ist ungesund und macht Krebs.

= Smoking is unhealthy and causes cancer.

Trinken und Drogen — Drink and drugs

You could get asked about your views on <u>drugs</u>, so here's some <u>vocab</u> you might need to know:

alcoholism is: Alkoholismus... ist

Ich glaube, dass Drogen ein großes Problem in unserer Gesellschaft sind .

= I think that <u>drugs</u> <u>are</u> a big problem in our society.

Ich nehme keine Drogen, weil es zu gefährlich ist.

= I don't take drugs because it's too dangerous.

Man kann abhängig werden. = You can become dependent.

Man kann Alkoholiker werden. = You can become an alcoholic.

Just say 'nein'...

I admit, this page is pretty <u>heavy going</u>, but at least it's <u>interesting</u>. Again, there's plenty more to say about this lot — so get your <u>thinking cap</u> on. And learn as much of the <u>tricky vocab</u> as you can.

Revision Summary

The idea isn't that you just do these questions and <u>stop</u>. To <u>really</u> make sure you've learnt this stuff, you need to <u>go back</u> through the section and look up the ones you couldn't do. Then try them all again. Your aim is to eventually be able to <u>glide</u> through them all with the greatest of ease.

1) You're making a fruit salad for a party. Think of the German words for as many fruits as you can to put in it — at least 5. Make a list of 5 drinks you could offer people at the party.

2) Write down how you'd say that you like vegetables but don't like sausage.
Also that you're very hungry.

3) You're staying with a German family. Thank your hosts for the meal and say it was delicious.
Offer to pass your hostess the milk (remember to use the right form of 'you').

4) You're telling your host family about your home life. Say that you make your bed and sometimes vacuum and clean at home. You have breakfast at 8 o'clock and lunch at 1 o'clock.

5) Introduce yourself to someone in German. Tell them your name, age and when your birthday is.

6) Describe three of your friends and say how old they are.
Spell out loud their names and the names of the towns where they live.

7) Tell your German pen friend what relations you have — including how many aunts, cousins etc.

8) Your animal-loving friend has six rabbits, a budgie, a guinea pig and two cats.
How will she say what these are in her German speaking assessment?

9) Describe the personalities of two of your family members. Say how well you get on with them.

10) A German news reporter asks your opinion on unemployment in the UK.
What would you say to them?

11) Say in German that you feel ill. You have a headache and a temperature.

12) Do you play a lot of sport? Why? Why not?
Write down how you'd explain this to your German friend.

13) What's your opinion on smoking? Give your answer in German.

Hallo. Mein Name ist Heidi und ich bin zwanzig Jahre alt.

Sports and Hobbies

Loads of <u>dead useful vocab</u>. Look back to this page if you need to know the name of a <u>hobby</u>.

Treibst du Sport? — *Do you do any sport?*

Quite a lot of the stuff you'll be expected to say about yourself will be to do with <u>sport</u>.
Even if you're no demon on the pitch, you <u>need</u> to be good at talking about it.

Usually when you talk about sports you just say their name, e.g. 'Fußball', not 'der Fußball'.

VERBS FOR OUTDOOR SPORTS

to fish:	angeln	*to ski:*	Ski fahren
to go out:	ausgehen	*to go for a walk:*	spazieren gehen
to run:	laufen	*to play:*	spielen
to cycle:	Rad fahren	*to walk, hike:*	wandern
to swim:	schwimmen	*to jog:*	joggen

Remember, plurals are always 'die'.

NAMES OF SPORTS

badminton:	das Badminton
football:	der Fußball
tennis:	das Tennis
table tennis:	das Tischtennis
squash:	das Squash
hockey:	das Hockey

PLACES YOU CAN DO SPORTS

fitness centre:	das Fitnesszentrum (-zentren)
open-air pool:	das Freibad (die Freibäder)
swimming pool:	das Schwimmbad (die Schwimmbäder)
indoor swimming pool:	das Hallenbad (die Hallenbäder)
sports field:	der Sportplatz (die Sportplätze)
sports centre:	das Sportzentrum (die Sportzentren)
park:	der Park (-s)

Hast du ein Hobby? — *Do you have a hobby?*

There are <u>other things</u> to do apart from sports — that's where these <u>tasty selections</u> come into play.

GENERAL BUT VITAL

hobby:	das Hobby (-s)
interest:	das Interesse (-n)
club:	der Club / Klub (-s)
member:	das Mitglied (-er)
game:	das Spiel (-e)

VERBS FOR INDOOR ACTIVITIES

to meet:	(sich) treffen
to dance:	tanzen
to sing:	singen
to collect:	sammeln
to bowl:	kegeln
to read:	lesen

To see how to use verbs with different people, see <u>pages 100 to 105</u>.

OTHER IMPORTANT NOUNS

chess:	das Schach
film:	der Film (-e)
performance:	die Vorstellung (-en)

MUSICAL INSTRUMENTS

violin:	die Geige
drums (plural):	die Schlagzeuge
guitar:	die Gitarre
trumpet:	die Trompete
piano:	das Klavier
flute:	die Flöte
clarinet:	die Klarinette

MUSICAL WORDS

band, group:	die Band (-s)
CD:	die CD (-s)
cassette:	die Kassette (-n)
concert:	das Konzert (-e)
stereo:	die Stereoanlage (-n)

I've got hobbies — what's 'eating cheese' auf Deutsch?

This is dead <u>important</u>. You can <u>look back</u> at this page while you're learning the rest of the section — but you'll <u>still have to learn it</u> in the end. <u>Cover</u> up the <u>German</u> bits and <u>scribble</u> down the ones you know. <u>Look back</u>, find out the ones you don't know and <u>try again</u>... and again... and again...

Sports and Hobbies

You might be asked about what you do in your <u>free time</u> in either your speaking assessment or writing task. Chances are you'll get asked for your <u>opinions</u> on other <u>hobbies</u> too, so you've got to learn this page.

Was machst du in deiner Freizeit?
— What do you do in your free time?

You'll get asked this question <u>a lot</u> — so <u>learn it</u>.

Ich spiele am Wochenende **Fußball** . = I play <u>football</u> <u>at the weekend</u>.

every day:	jeden Tag
every week:	jede Woche
twice a month:	zweimal im Monat

badminton: Badminton
tennis: Tennis

For more about times,
see <u>pages 2–3</u>.

Ich spiele Klavier . = I play the <u>piano</u>.

Put in any of the instruments
on <u>page 27</u> here.

Ich bin Mitglied eines Tennisklubs .

youth club: Jugendklubs

= I'm a member of
a <u>tennis club</u>.

IMPORTANT
In German, you just say,
'<u>I play piano</u>' — you don't
need to use '<u>the</u>'.

Handy Hint:
If you need to talk about any
sport club, just add '<u>-klub</u>' to
the end of the sport.

The '<u>-s</u>' on '<u>-klubs</u>' isn't to make a plural — it's
the <u>genitive case</u> (see <u>page 85</u>). This is a little
bit tricky because the plural of 'der Klub' is also
'Klubs' — be careful.

Wie findest du Fußball? — What do you think of football?

Here's how to say what you <u>think</u> of different hobbies — <u>learn</u> these phrases even if you don't really <u>care</u>.

Ich finde Fußball okay . = I think <u>football</u>'s <u>okay</u>.

the cinema:	das Kino
hiking:	Wandern

good:	gut
bad:	schlecht
excellent:	ausgezeichnet
terrible:	furchtbar

Put 'gern' here if you like doing
something, or 'ungern' if you don't.

Ich spiele gern **Fußball** .

= I <u>like</u> playing <u>football</u>.

I think that too:	Das denke ich auch.
I don't think that:	Das denke ich nicht.
That's true:	Das ist wahr.
That's not true:	Das ist nicht wahr.

For <u>agreeing</u> and
<u>disagreeing</u> you can
use these phrases.

But
jogging's
so boring...

Warum denkst du das? = Why do you think that?

For more about giving
opinions, see <u>pages 7–9</u>.

Ich jogge ungern **, weil es** langweilig **ist.** = I <u>don't like</u> jogging because it's <u>boring</u>.

interesting:	interessant	*difficult:*	schwierig
exciting:	aufregend		

I guess 'because I do' isn't a good enough answer...

Right-o, more things to learn. Get your head round how to say <u>what you do</u> in your free time
and what <u>hobbies</u> you have. <u>Don't forget</u> to learn how to say <u>when</u> you do them. Oh, and one
more thing — make sure you can say <u>what you think</u> of loads of <u>other hobbies</u> and activities.

Television

This page is about <u>TV</u> — dead easy. It also covers <u>explaining</u> the kind of things you've done recently. This is dead important. <u>Learn it well</u>.

Meine Lieblingssendung ist...

— My favourite programme is...

You've probably got quite a bit to say about <u>TV</u> — here's how to do it <u>auf Deutsch</u>:

Welche **Fernsehsendungen** **siehst** du gern? = Which <u>TV programmes</u> do you like to <u>watch</u>?

books: Bücher   *read:* liest

Ich **sehe** gern **Westenders** . = I like to <u>watch</u> <u>Westenders</u>.

listen to: höre   *read:* lese

Put what you like to watch, listen to or read here.

For more about giving opinions, see <u>pages 7–9</u>.

When I said, "Ich mag fernsehen", this wasn't quite what I meant...

TELEVISION VOCAB

programme:	die Sendung (-en)	*documentary:*	der Dokumentarfilm (-e)
series:	die Serie (-n)	*quiz show:*	die Quizsendung (-en)
weather report:	der Wetterbericht (-e)	*comedy:*	die Komödie (-n)
news:	die Nachrichten (plural)	*cartoon:*	der Zeichentrickfilm (-e)
soap opera:	die Seifenoper (-n)		

Remember, plurals are always 'die'.

Die Sendung fängt um **acht Uhr** an und endet um **halb zehn** . = The programme starts at <u>8 o'clock</u> and finishes at <u>half past nine</u>.

For more on telling the time, see <u>page 2</u>.

Was hast du neulich gemacht?

— What have you done recently?

This <u>past tense</u> stuff is <u>really</u> important — to get <u>good marks</u>, you have to be able to <u>use it</u>. See <u>pages 104-105</u> for more info.

Ich habe **neulich** **Godzilla** **gesehen** . = I <u>saw</u> <u>Godzilla</u> <u>recently</u>.

heard: gehört
read: gelesen

last week: letzte Woche
two weeks ago: vor zwei Wochen
a month ago: vor einem Monat

the new song by Antarctic Apes:
das neue Lied von Antarctic Apes
a great book:
ein tolles Buch

For more about times and dates, see <u>pages 2–3</u>.

Godzilla — ein Dokumentarfilm about a giant lizard...

OK, so it turns out that talking about TV in German isn't <u>quite</u> as much fun as actually watching TV in real life. But (you guessed it) you've got to learn it anyway. Saying what you've been doing and <u>when you did it</u> is another <u>handy</u> thing that'll get you loads of gorgeous <u>marks</u>.

Talking About the Plot

It could be last night's Westenders episode or the twists and turns of the last book you read, but you might well get asked to talk about the plot.

Welche Filme hast du neulich gesehen? — Which films have you watched recently?

Another great opportunity to practise using the past tense. If you need some help, see pages 104-105.

Letzte Woche habe ich 'Pirates of the Mediterranean' gesehen.

= I saw 'Pirates of the Mediterranean' last week.

Was für ein Film ist das? = What sort of film is that?

Don't try to translate the titles of films or books into German — it's OK to just use the English name.

Er ist ein Abenteuerfilm. = It is an adventure film.

| a horror film: | ein Horrorfilm | a romance: | ein Liebesfilm |
| a comedy: | eine Komödie | a crime drama/thriller: | ein Krimi |

Kannst du den Film beschreiben? Was ist passiert?

= Can you describe the film? What happened?

When it comes to talking about this sort of thing, don't panic. Just pick a film (or a book, or a play...) that's got a relatively simple plot and remember to use the past tense.

War der Film gut? — Was the film good?

You're bound to get asked for your opinion at some point — so get learning these little gems...

Wie fandst du den Film? = What did you think of the film?

| the book: das Buch | the performance: die Vorstellung |

If you're talking about a book, use 'Es' here.
If you're talking about a performance use 'Sie'.

Er hat mir gefallen. = I liked it.

Er hat mir nicht gefallen. = I didn't like it.

Er war interessant. = It was interesting.

For more on giving opinions, see pages 7-9.

amusing:	amüsant	quite good:	ziemlich gut
fascinating:	faszinierend	very good:	sehr gut
sad:	traurig	bad:	schlecht

Der Film war gut — that's my gut reaction...

There's some pretty useful vocab on this page, so make sure you know it. Also, even if you couldn't really care less, make sure you have an opinion to give. That's what grabs you marks.

Music

Whether it's Kylie or Bach, everybody likes a bit of <u>music</u>. You need to be able to talk about your <u>musical preferences</u>, as well as saying <u>where</u> and <u>when</u> you listen to it.

Was für Musik magst du?
— What sort of music do you like?

This bit's about <u>giving your opinion</u> again. Try and find something a bit <u>interesting</u> to say and <u>jazz</u> up those sentences.

Ich höre gern Popmusik. = I like listening to <u>pop music</u>.

rock music:	Rockmusik
rap music:	Rapmusik
modern music:	moderne Musik
classical music:	klassische Musik

Volksmusik gefällt mir nicht. Ich höre lieber moderne Musik.

= I don't like folk music. I prefer listening to modern music.

Meine Lieblingssängerin ist Beyoncé. = <u>My favourite (female) singer</u> is <u>Beyoncé</u>.

my favourite (male) singer:	Mein Lieblingssänger
my favourite group:	Meine Lieblingsgruppe

For more on giving opinions, see <u>pages 7–9</u>.

Wo magst du Musik hören?
— Where do you like listening to music?

This is all about <u>how</u> and <u>where</u> you listen to music. Easy peasy.

in the shower:	in der Dusche
in the car:	im Auto

Ich höre gern Musik im Radio *, wenn ich* in meinem Zimmer *bin.*

on my iPod®:	auf meinem iPod®
on my MP3 player:	auf meinem Mp3-Player/Mp3-Spieler
on CD:	auf CD

= I like listening to music <u>on the radio</u> when I'm <u>in my room</u>.

Examiners will <u>love it</u> if you talk about the <u>latest technologies</u>.

German — it's music to my ears...

Now this is fairly <u>straightfoward</u> stuff, but you still have to <u>learn it</u>. It could really come in handy. Also, if you happen to have heard any German pop music then <u>say so</u>. Not only does it make life <u>more interesting</u>, the examiners will be over the moon that you've taken an interest in German culture.

Famous People

Now this choice of topic seems a tad weird to me, but apparently you are supposed to be <u>fascinated</u> by celebs. So much so that you wanna <u>talk</u> about them in German with your pen friends and <u>exchange partners</u>.

Welche berühmten Persönlichkeiten findest du gut?

Which celebrities do you like?

Talking about celebrities and famous people you admire mostly involves all the same old <u>straightforward</u> stuff that you need to talk about yourself and your family. Start with their <u>name</u>, then <u>what</u> they do, and follow that up with <u>why</u> you like them.

WHO → *Ich finde Beyoncé fantastisch.* = I think Beyoncé is fantastic.

WHAT → *Sie ist eine berühmte amerikanische Popsängerin.* = She is a famous American pop singer.

WHY → *Beyoncé sieht so hübsch aus und trägt immer schicke modische Klamotten.* = Beyoncé looks so pretty and always wears smart trendy clothes.

Berühmte Persönlichkeiten — Celebrities

Möchtest du berühmt sein? = Would you like to be famous?

JA!

Ich möchte berühmt sein, weil **...** = I would like to be famous because**...**

...celebrities have lots of friends.:	berühmte Personlichkeiten viele Freunde haben.
... celebrities have lots of money.:	berühmte Personlichkeiten viel Geld haben.
... you go to lots of parties.:	man zu vielen Partys geht.

NEIN!

Ich möchte nicht berühmt sein, weil **...** = I wouldn't like to be famous because**...**

... it's stressful.:	es stressig ist.
... you have no privacy.:	man kein Privatleben hat.
... it's lonely.:	es einsam ist.

PRETTY DARNED USEFUL VOCAB: RELATIV NÜTZLICHE VOKABELN

famous:	berühmt	*anorexic:*	magersüchtig
pop singer:	Popsänger/Popsängerin	*responsibility:*	die Verantwortung
actor/actress:	Schauspieler/Schauspielerin	*responsible:*	verantwortlich
celebrity:	die berühmte Persönlichkeit	*example:*	das Beispiel (-e)

Don't you know who I am?

One day I very much hope to be a <u>world-famous</u> revision guide writer — at which point this book'll be worth millions, so I'd hang on to it if I were you. In the meantime, get <u>learning</u> this page.

New Technology

Computers are taking over the world, or so they say.
They'll almost definitely be cropping up somewhere in <u>GCSE German</u>.

Computer und das Internet
— Computers and the internet

It's a good idea to be able to talk about what you <u>use</u> computers for...

webpage: Webseite/Internetseite

Ich habe eine Website für meinen Schachclub gemacht.

= I have made a website for my <u>chess club</u>.

football team: meine Fußballmannschaft
band: meine Band

Our computer really is like a member of the team...

Foolish humans! Soon I shall render you all obsolete! Mwa-ha-ha-haa!

COMPUTER HARDWARE

computer:	der Computer
printer:	der Drucker
screen/monitor:	der Bildschirm
keyboard:	die Tastatur

Ich will meine Fotos downloaden .

= I want to <u>download</u> my photos.

download: herunterladen
upload: hochladen

Wir chatten über MSN®.

= We chat over MSN®.

Ich surfe im Internet.

= I surf the internet.

Technologie: Vorteile und Nachteile
— Technology: Advantages and Disadvantages

There are lots of things you can say about the <u>pros and cons</u> of computers.
Here are a few to <u>get you started</u>:

Computer sind wirklich nützlich. Ohne Computer könnte ich nicht meine Schularbeit machen.

= Computers are really useful. Without a computer I couldn't do my schoolwork.

Computer können viel Zeit sparen.

= Computers can save a lot of time.

Man kann zu viel Zeit vor dem Computer verbringen. Es ist nicht gut für die Gesundheit.

= You can spend too much time in front of the computer.
It's not good for your health.

It were all done wit' horses back in my day...

You're probably familiar with the arguments <u>for and against</u> technology, so think about what you'd say to someone asking you in English. Make sure you can talk about how you <u>use</u> computers too.

E-mail and Texting

Ah, the joys of <u>digital communication</u>. Exam boards like to move with the times, so here's a bit about text messages and electronic-post. Great stuff.

Ich möchte eine E-mail senden
— I would like to send an e-mail

Ich werde eine E-mail schicken. = I'm going to send an e-mail.

my inbox: meinen Posteingang

Ich muss *meine E-mails* lesen. Darf ich deinen Computer benutzen, bitte?

= I need to read <u>my e-mails</u>. Please may I use your computer?

You can write an <u>e-mail</u> in pretty much the same way as an <u>informal letter</u> — see <u>page 10</u>.

Eine SMS — A text message

<u>Text messages</u> could crop up anywhere. You might get asked to <u>write</u> a text message in one of your writing tasks, or <u>read</u> one in the reading exam.

If you do get asked to write a text, <u>don't panic</u>.

You probably send them all the time in English — just think about the sort of things you'd <u>normally say</u> to your friends and remember to use the informal '<u>du</u>'. Same goes for <u>e-mails</u>.

text message: die SMS, die (SMS-)Mitteilung
mobile phone: das Handy

16:04

Hallo Berta. Wie geht's? Möchtest du heute Abend mit mir ins Kino gehen? Der neue Film von Danny Kraig beginnt um 20h00. Bis später. Alex.

= Hello Berta. How's it going? Do you want to go to the cinema with me tonight? The new Danny Kraig film starts at 8 o'clock. See you later. Alex.

Ich blogg, du bloggst... — I blog, you blog...

A blog is basically just 'a day in the life of...'. Here's an <u>example</u> to get you started:

Cumbria	11/05/2009	22h15

Heute habe ich einen tollen Tag gehabt. Ich bin mit meinen Freunden ins Kino gegangen und wir haben den neuen Film von Danny Kraig gesehen. Normalerweise mag ich keine Abenteuerfilme aber er war eigentlich sehr lustig. Ich würde diesen Film bestimmt empfehlen!

Cumbria	11/05/2009	22h15

Today I've had a great day. I went to the cinema with my friends and we saw the new Danny Kraig film. Normally I don't like adventure films, but it was actually very funny. I would definitely recommend this film!

This blog is written (mainly) in the <u>perfect tense</u>. See <u>page 104</u> for help.

It's pretty 'Handy', this mobile phone thing...

This is the sort of stuff that might appear in one of your <u>writing tasks</u>, so it's <u>important</u> you're familiar with it. Be warned though: your e-mail, text or blog could be about a whole host of <u>different topics</u>. And <u>don't</u> try and <u>use txt spk</u>* in your writing assessment or the exams. * That's 'text speak' by the way.

Shopping

This is bread-and-butter stuff and you really have to <u>know it</u>. Basically, if you learn this stuff, you'll be able to use it when it comes up. You'd be <u>nuts</u> not to.

Wo ist...? — Where is...?

A <u>dead useful</u> question — and luckily the word order is the <u>same</u> in English and German.

Wo ist der Supermarkt **, bitte?** = Where is <u>the supermarket</u>, please?

butcher's: die Metzgerei (-en)
bakery: die Bäckerei (-en)
grocer's: das Lebensmittelgeschäft (-e)

Wo ist der Supermarkt, bitte?

Dort drüben!

Wann...? — When...?

To say when a shop is <u>open</u> or <u>closed</u>, you need these handy little phrases. Chances are they'll come up at some point — so make sure you know them like the back of your hand.

Wann hat **der Supermarkt** auf **?** = When <u>is the supermarket open</u>?

shut: zu

Or any other shop.

These verbs are separable — see <u>page 108</u> for more info.

Wann macht **der Supermarkt** zu **?** = When <u>does</u> the supermarket <u>close</u>?

For times, see <u>page 2</u>.

open: auf

Der Supermarkt macht **um** neunzehn Uhr **zu .** = The supermarket <u>closes</u> at <u>7:00pm</u>.

Andere Läden — Other shops

The words '<u>der Laden</u>' and '<u>das Geschäft</u>' both mean '<u>shop</u>'.
You'll often find them stuck to other words telling you what <u>type</u> of shop it is.

pharmacy: die Apotheke (-n)
chemist's: die Drogerie (-n)
bookshop: die Buchhandlung (-en)
department store: das Kaufhaus (die Kaufhäuser)
shopping centre: das Einkaufszentrum (-zentren)
cake shop: die Konditorei (-en)

fishmonger's: das Fischgeschäft (-e)
market: der Markt (die Märkte)
electrical shop: das Elektrogeschäft (-e)
stationer's: das Schriebwarengeschäft (-e)

Remember, plurals are always 'die'.

<u>Note:</u> you pick up <u>prescriptions</u> from the <u>Apotheke</u>, but buy your <u>toothpaste</u> from the <u>Drogerie</u>.

Oh, wo ist me...

Asking <u>where things are</u> and <u>when they open</u> isn't too difficult, so get those questions <u>learnt</u>.
Try and remember <u>as many</u> of those shops as possible too — they could well come up in an exam.

Shopping

These are the kind of phrases that can be used in lots of <u>different situations</u>, so it's <u>definitely</u> going to be <u>worth learning</u> them. Well, get to it — and enjoy.

Ich möchte... — I would like...

You'll be using this <u>all the time</u>. You should be pretty comfortable with '<u>Ich möchte</u>' by now.

Ich möchte **ein großes Stück Brot**, bitte. = I'd like <u>a big piece of bread</u>, please.

Ich möchte **eine Hose**. Meine Größe ist **sechsundvierzig**. = I'd like <u>a pair of trousers</u>. I'm <u>size 46</u>.

For clothing, see <u>page 38</u>.

Important Bit:
Another good way to say '<u>I would like</u>' is '<u>Ich hätte gern</u>'.

CONTINENTAL SIZES
size: die Größe / die Nummer
dress size 10 / 12 / 14 / 16: 38 / 40 / 42 / 44
shoe size 5 / 6 / 7 / 8 / 9 / 10: 38 / 39 / 41 / 42 / 43 / 44

Do you think my bum looks big in this? / I do.

Deutsches Geld — German money

German money's easy. There are <u>100 cents</u> in a <u>euro</u>, like there are 100 pence in a pound.

This is what you'd <u>see</u> on a German <u>price tag</u>:  € 5,50

This is how you'd <u>say</u> the price: 'Fünf Euro fünfzig Cent' = 5 euros 50 cents

For numbers, see <u>page 1</u>.

Ich gehe gern einkaufen — I like going shopping

Lots of <u>useful</u> shopping-related vocab for you to <u>get your teeth into</u> here. First up, how to talk about your <u>shopping habits</u>...

Ich gehe einmal pro Woche einkaufen. = I go shopping once a week.

Ich kaufe oft in der Bäckerei ein. = I often shop in the bakery.

'<u>Einkaufen</u>' is a separable verb. For more on these, see <u>page 108</u>.

SALES VOCAB
special offer: das Sonderangebot (-e)
per cent: Prozent
reduction: die Ermäßigung
sale: der Ausverkauf (die Ausverkäufe)

Ich kaufe gern Bücher ein. = I like shopping for books.

You'll be shopping mad if you forget this...

Lots of bits and pieces here, I know. The thing is they're all <u>really useful</u> — so make sure you're prepared for anything and <u>learn them properly</u>. You'll thank me for it in the long run. Honest.

Shopping

Another <u>important</u> topic that you might well need to <u>know</u>. It's not a difficult one — and there are some <u>standard</u> questions and answers that save you having to <u>think</u>.

Kann ich Ihnen helfen? — Can I help you?

Use '<u>Ich möchte...</u>' or '<u>Ich hätte gern...</u>' for saying what you'd like:

Ich hätte gern fünfhundert Gramm **Zucker, bitte.** = I'd like <u>500 g</u> of sugar, please.

1 kg: ein Kilo
2 kg: zwei Kilo

1 You don't need to make words like '<u>Gramm</u>' and '<u>Kilo</u>' plural. Just say, '<u>Ein Kilo...</u>', '<u>Zwei Kilo...</u>' and so on.

2 In German, you can also just say '<u>500 g sugar</u>' — you don't need to use '<u>of</u>'.

USEFUL VOCAB

several:	mehrere
a tin/box of:	eine Dose
a bottle of:	eine Flasche
a jar of:	ein Glas
a piece of:	ein Stück
a bag of:	eine Tüte
a bar of:	eine Tafel

The <u>shop assistant</u> may say:

Sonst noch etwas? ...or... **Sonst noch einen Wunsch?**

= Will there be anything else?

<u>You</u> could reply:

Nein danke. = No thank you.

two apples: zwei Äpfel
three pears: drei Birnen

See <u>page 1</u> for numbers.

...or...

Ja, ich möchte auch eine Kartoffel **, bitte.** = Yes, I'd like <u>a potato</u> as well, please.

Haben Sie...? — Do you have...?

Maybe you're not sure this shop will have what you want — in which case, you'll have to <u>ask</u>.

Entschuldigung, haben Sie Brot **, bitte?** = Excuse me, do you have any <u>bread</u>, please?

milk: Milch *cheese:* Käse

Ja, hier ist es **.** = Yes, here <u>it</u> is.

it: er / sie / es

Nein, haben wir nicht. = No, we don't.

Can I help you?

Nehmen Sie das? — Will you be taking that?

<u>Decision time</u>. It happens every time you go into a shop. <u>Make sure</u> you know these.

Ich nehme es **.** = I'll take <u>it</u>.

it: ihn / sie / es

Which word you use for 'it' depends on the gender and case of the noun — see <u>page 97</u>.

I'll leave it. I'm not sure this shade of blue suits me.

Ich lasse es. Die Farbe gefällt mir nicht **.** = I'll leave it. <u>I don't like the colour.</u>

It's the wrong size: Es ist die falsche Größe   *It's too expensive:* Es ist zu teuer

Will you be taking that? — No, I was going to pay...

There's lots of <u>important stuff</u> here. You don't have to make those '<u>quantity words</u>' like '<u>Gramm</u>' and '<u>Kilo</u>' plural — just use them as they are. Also, you <u>don't</u> need to use '<u>of</u>' like in English. <u>Remember</u> — there are <u>no tricks or catches</u> in the tasks — you just need to know your stuff.

Shopping

This is the sort of vocab you'll need if you ever have to give a <u>description</u> of somebody.
Useful if your best mate ever goes missing in Germany...

Die Kleidung — Clothing

Most of this stuff is <u>pretty common</u> — so you <u>need</u> to know it.

| Dieser Mantel | gefällt mir (nicht). | = I (don't) like <u>this coat</u>. |

> Watch out: 'die Hose' is feminine singular, <u>not plural</u> as in the English 'trousers'. Same with '<u>die Strumpfhose</u>'.

| *fashionable:* modisch | *old-fashioned:* altmodisch |

| Dieser Mantel | ist wirklich | bequem | . | = <u>This coat</u> is really <u>comfortable</u>. |

> Remember, plurals are always 'die'.

shirt: das Hemd (-en)	*coat:* der Mantel (die Mäntel)	*scarf:* der Schal (-e)	
blouse: die Bluse (-n)	*hat:* der Hut (die Hüte)	*glove:* der Handschuh (-e)	
trousers: die Hose (-n)	*cap:* die Mütze (-n)	*miniskirt:* der Minirock (die Miniröcke)	
skirt: der Rock (die Röcke)	*T-shirt:* das T-Shirt (-s)	*tie:* die Krawatte (-n), der Schlips (-e)	
sock: die Socke (-n)	*suit:* der Anzug (die Anzüge)	*tights:* die Strumpfhose (-n)	
shoe: der Schuh (-e)	*jacket:* die Jacke (-n)	*shorts:* die Shorts (plural), die kurze Hose (-n)	
dress: das Kleid (-er)	*jumper:* der Pullover (-)	*a pair of socks:* ein Paar Socken	

Welche Farbe...? — What colour...?

Another <u>vital</u> little topic. You <u>won't</u> get away with not learning this one.

| Ich möchte eine | blaue | Jacke. | = I'd like a <u>blue</u> jacket. |

For adjective endings, see <u>page 91</u>.

Add '<u>hell-</u>' or '<u>dunkel-</u>' to the start of a colour to say it's <u>light</u> or <u>dark</u>.

| Ich möchte ein | hellgrünes | Kleid. | = I'd like a <u>light green</u> dress. |

The colours '<u>rosa</u>', '<u>lila</u>' and '<u>orange</u>' don't take endings.

| Ich möchte einen | rosa | Rock. | = I'd like a <u>pink</u> skirt. |

COLOURS: DIE FARBEN

black:	schwarz
white:	weiß
red:	rot
yellow:	gelb
green:	grün
blue:	blau
brown:	braun
orange:	orange
pink:	rosa
purple:	lila
light blue:	hellblau
dark green:	dunkelgrün

Es besteht aus... — It's made out of...

| Ich hätte gern eine neue Jacke aus | Leder | . |

cotton: Baumwolle
silk: Seide
wool: Wolle

= I'd like a new <u>leather</u> jacket.

Eisen
Plastik
Metall
Holz

OTHER MATERIALS: ANDERE STOFFE

iron:	das Eisen	*metal:*	das Metall	*plastic:*	das Plastik
wood:	das Holz	*paper:*	das Papier	*silver:*	das Silbe

He's got a Hut on his head — in German, that's normal...

Lots of these clothes are pretty easy to remember — <u>S</u>chuh, <u>S</u>ocke, <u>H</u>ut, <u>B</u>luse and so on.
Others need a bit more effort. It's <u>important stuff</u> though, so it's worth it. Honestly.

Inviting People Out

As well as finding out <u>how much</u> things cost, <u>when</u> they're open and <u>where</u> they are, you've <u>got to learn</u> how to <u>ask someone</u> to come <u>with you</u>.

<u>Gehen wir aus — Let's go out</u>

These are all really <u>useful</u> phrases, so get them <u>learnt</u>.

Gehen wir | ins Schwimmbad | . = Let's go <u>to the swimming pool</u>.

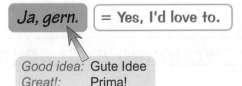
to the theatre: ins Theater
to the park: zum Park

For other places you might want to invite someone to, and more activities or sports, see <u>page 27</u>.

Ja, gern. = Yes, I'd love to.

Good idea: Gute Idee
Great!: Prima!

Nein, danke. = No, thank you.

I'm sorry: Es tut mir Leid.
I don't have enough money: Ich habe nicht genug Geld.

<u>Wo treffen wir uns? — Where shall we meet?</u>

Now to sort out the details of <u>where</u> and <u>when</u> to meet.

Wir treffen uns | vor dem Rathaus | . = We'll meet <u>in front of the town hall</u>.

But I was sure she said, 'In front of the Rat-house'...

at your house: bei dir
next to the church: neben der Kirche

For other places, see <u>pages 27 & 58</u>. For more on 'in front of'/ 'at'/ 'next to' etc. see <u>pages 95-96</u>.

Um wie viel Uhr treffen wir uns? = What time shall we meet?

Wir treffen uns um | 10 Uhr | . = We'll meet at <u>10 o'clock</u>.

For more about times, see <u>page 2</u>.

two thirty: vierzehn Uhr dreißig
half past three: halb vier

The verb 'sich treffen' is reflexive. For more on this, see <u>page 107</u>.

<u>Es tut mir Leid, I'm washing my hair...</u>

Now you've got that <u>sorted</u> you should be able to ask Boris Becker out to the theatre or arrange to meet Claudia Schiffer in front of the park. If you <u>can't</u> then <u>go back</u> over it until you darn well can.

Going Out

You're going to <u>need</u> this stuff — you may need to <u>talk</u> about it and you'll definitely have to be able to <u>understand it all</u>. Don't just sit there, <u>get into gear</u> and get down to it.

Was gibt es hier in der Nähe? — What is there near here?

Gibt's hier in der Nähe **ein Theater** ? = Is there <u>a theatre</u> near here?

a sports field: einen Sportplatz
a bowling alley: eine Kegelbahn

For hobbies & more places, see <u>pages 27 & 58</u>.

play tennis: Tennis spielen
go for walks: spazieren gehen

Kann man hier in der Nähe **schwimmen** ? = Can people <u>swim</u> near here?

Wann macht das Schwimmbad auf?

— When does the swimming pool open?

For more on verbs like this one, see <u>page 108</u>.

the sports centre: das Sportzentrum

Wann **macht** **das Schwimmbad** **auf** ? = When does <u>the swimming pool</u> <u>open</u>?

close: macht ... zu

This is in the <u>present tense</u>, but it's talking about something that's going to happen in the <u>future</u>. <u>For more info see page 103</u>.

Es macht um **halb zehn** auf . = It opens at <u>half past nine</u>.

Es macht um **fünf Uhr** zu. = It closes at <u>five o'clock</u>.

For more times, see <u>page 2</u>.

Ich möchte bitte **eine Karte** . = I'd like <u>one ticket</u>, please.

two tickets: zwei Karten

Wie teuer ist es...? — How expensive is it...?

Wie viel kostet es, **schwimmen zu gehen** ? = How much does it cost <u>to go swimming</u>?

For other sports and activities, see <u>pages 27 and 58</u>.

to go cycling: Rad zu fahren
to play tennis: Tennis zu spielen

Es kostet **2 Euro** . = It costs <u>2 euros</u>.

For more about prices see <u>page 36</u>.

Es kostet **5 Euro** pro Stunde. = It costs <u>5 euros</u> per hour.

A noisy horse near here — a 'Nähe'...

This is the sort of thing that might well turn up in a <u>listening exam</u>, so make sure you're familiar with it all. The best way to <u>learn it</u> is the good old <u>look</u>, <u>cover</u>, <u>scribble</u>, <u>check</u>... <u>biscuit</u>.

Going Out

Almost everyone likes the cinema, and whatever kind of films tickle your fancy you're
gonna need to know <u>how to arrange</u> going there with someone else. Away you go.

Was läuft im Kino? — What's on at the cinema?

Some useful <u>cinema-related</u> phrases for you:

Wie viel kostet eine Eintrittskarte **?** = How much does <u>one entry ticket</u> cost?

How much do two entry tickets cost?:
Wie viel kosten zwei Eintrittskarten?

Eine Karte kostet 10 Euro. = One ticket costs 10 euros.

<u>Plural ending</u> — see <u>page 101</u>.

'<u>Eintrittskarte</u>' means 'entry
ticket' and '<u>Karte</u>' means
'ticket', so they're basically the
<u>same thing</u>. You need to be
able to <u>understand</u> the longer
word and you'll get <u>more</u>
<u>marks</u> if you can <u>use it</u> too.

Ich möchte zwei Karten **, bitte.** = I'd like <u>two</u>
<u>tickets</u>, please.

one ticket: eine Karte
three tickets: drei Karten

If you want to know how to describe a film you've seen, see <u>page 30</u>.

Um wie viel Uhr...? — At what time...?

It's no good if you don't know what <u>time</u> the film starts.
You'll miss all the nice adverts at the beginning for one thing...

Um wie viel Uhr beginnt die Vorstellung? = What time does the performance begin?

'<u>fängt ... an</u>' comes from '<u>anfangen</u>', which is a separable strong verb. See <u>page 108</u> for more info.

Wann fängt die Vorstellung **an?** = When does <u>the performance</u> start?

the film: der Film   *the concert:* das Konzert

Wann endet die Vorstellung **?** = When does <u>the performance</u> end?

Sie fängt um acht Uhr **an.** = It starts at <u>8 o'clock</u>.

Sie endet um halb elf **.** = It finishes at <u>half past ten</u>.

You use '<u>sie</u>' here because '<u>die Vorstellung</u>' is <u>feminine</u>.
For '<u>der</u> Film' use '<u>er</u>' and for '<u>das</u> Konzert' use '<u>es</u>'.

I'm not going out till I've learnt this German...

So you should now be able to ask for <u>tickets</u>, ask <u>when</u> the film or performance <u>starts</u>, and be
able to <u>understand</u> the answer. And when you've watched the film or play you have to give
your own expert <u>opinion</u> of it. If you can <u>do</u> all that then you've got this bit <u>sorted</u>.

Revision Summary

These questions really do check what you <u>know</u> and don't know — which means you can spend your time learning the bits you're shaky on. But it's not a good idea to do this one day, then forget about it. <u>Come back</u> to these a day later and try them again. And then a week later...

1) Franz asks Christine if she has a hobby. She says that she plays the guitar, plays football and reads books. Write down their conversation in German.

2) Hermann and Bob are having an argument. Hermann says that he likes tennis because it's exciting. Bob finds tennis boring. Write down their conversation in German.

3) You're talking to your German pen friend.
How do you tell her what TV programmes you like to watch?

4) Tell your German friend you went to see 'Night of the Zombie-Mummies 26' last week.
Tell her it was a horror film and that you thought it was very sad.

5) You and your pen friend are having an unlikely conversation about where and how you listen to music. Your friend says she listens to her iPod when she's in the car.
How did she say that in German?

6) Nadja thinks she's fallen in love with Justin Timberlake. Write a paragraph to her saying what you think of him, and telling her which celebrities you admire. Don't forget to give reasons.

7) Give one advantage of using a computer and one disadvantage.
Don't cheat — give them in German.

8) Write out a text message in German asking your friend Joe if he wants to go swimming with you on Saturday. Don't forget to be a good friend and ask how he is.

9) What are the German names for the shops where you'd buy: paper, a cake, some sausages, some soap? (And don't just say 'Supermarkt' for all four.)

10) You're in Munich and you need to buy a brown jumper, size 48, and three pairs of socks.
How do you say this to the shop assistant?

11) Dave invites Gabriela to see 'Romeo und Julia' at the cinema.
They arrange to meet in front of the cinema at 8pm.
Write down their conversation in German. *(Watch out for word order here.)*

12) You're in Germany and you want to play squash. Ask when the sports centre is open and how much it costs to play squash. Ask for two tickets.

Holiday Destinations

I know there's a lot to <u>learn</u> on this page, but it's really pretty <u>important</u>. It could come up <u>anywhere</u>.

Learn these foreign places

You need to <u>understand</u> where <u>other people</u> are from when they tell you. And you'll probably have to talk about <u>holidays</u> and <u>trips abroad</u> at some point. So get <u>learning</u> this little lot:

An adjective is a describing word. See <u>pages 91-92</u>.

	Place	*People (male/female)*	*Adjective*
Germany:	Deutschland	Deutscher/Deutsche	deutsch
France:	Frankreich	Franzose/Französin	französisch
Italy:	Italien	Italiener/Italienerin	italienisch
Spain:	Spanien	Spanier/Spanierin	spanisch
Austria:	Österreich	Österreicher/Österreicherin	österreichisch
Ireland:	Irland	Ire/Irin	irisch
America:	Amerika	Amerikaner/Amerikanerin	amerikanisch

So your (male) German friend might say:

Ich bin Deutscher . Ich komme aus Deutschland . = I am <u>German</u>. I come from <u>Germany</u>.

And you'd describe him as: Mein deutscher Freund. = My <u>German</u> friend.

For even more lovely marks, learn these too:

Greece:	Griechenland	*India:*	Indien	*Russia:*	Russland
Belgium:	Belgien	*Poland:*	Polen	*Africa:*	Afrika
Denmark:	Dänemark	*China:*	China	*Australia:*	Australien

For more on talking about where <u>you're</u> from, including countries in the <u>UK</u>, see <u>page 60</u>.
Women and girls need the <u>feminine versions</u> — usually that just means adding '<u>-in</u>' to the end.

Some countries are a bit more tricky...

1) <u>Watch out:</u> you always have to put '<u>die</u>' before these countries:

The Netherlands:	die Niederlande	*Turkey:*	die Türkei
The USA:	die USA, die Vereinigten Staaten	*Switzerland:*	die Schweiz

2) <u>BUT</u> after '<u>aus</u>', the '<u>die</u>' changes to '<u>der</u>' for Turkey and Switzerland (because they're singular and feminine) and '<u>den</u>' for the others (cos they're plural). See <u>pages 90, 95 and 96</u> for stuff about 'die' and 'aus'.

Ich komme aus den USA . = I come from the USA.

You need to know these holiday destinations

Um... not that I'm really suggesting you go on holiday in the Channel Tunnel, but I'm sure you catch my drift — learn this little lot, they just might come in <u>handy</u>:

the English Channel:	der Ärmelkanal	*the Black Forest:*	der Schwarzwald	*the Rhine:*	der Rhein
the Channel Tunnel:	der Tunnel	*Lake Constance:*	der Bodensee	*the Danube:*	die Donau
the Alps (plural):	die Alpen	*Bavaria:*	Bayern		

We're all going on a summer holiday...

You've got to <u>learn</u> all those <u>countries</u> and <u>nationalities</u>. With ones that are <u>similar</u> in German and English, make sure you get the <u>spelling</u> right. There's a pretty ridiculous amount of vocab here, but keep <u>testing yourself</u> until you know it back to front. It's really the <u>only way</u>.

Catching the Train

Trains, planes and automobiles... Well, just trains for now. You'll need loads of vocab if you want the best marks. And you must know a few bog-standard sentences — things you'll always need.

Ich möchte mit dem Zug fahren

— I'd like to travel by train

Fährt ein Zug nach Berlin ? = Is there a train to Berlin?

Cologne: Köln	Geneva: Genf		Some German-speaking cities have
Munich: München	Vienna: Wien		different names in German and English.

This is in the genitive case — see page 85.

Einmal einfach nach Berlin, erster Klasse . = One single to Berlin, first class.

Two: Zweimal	return(s): hin und zurück	second class: zweiter Klasse
Three: Dreimal		

There's another word for 'return ticket' — 'die Rückfahrkarte':

Eine Rückfahrkarte nach Berlin, bitte. = One return ticket to Berlin, please.

Wann fahren Sie? — When are you travelling?

This stuff is more complicated, but it's still dead important.

Ich möchte am Samstag nach Köln fahren. = I would like to travel to Cologne on Saturday.

today: heute   next Monday: nächsten Montag   on the tenth of June: am zehnten Juni

'Abfahren' and 'ankommen' are separable verbs. See page 108 for more info.

Wann fährt der Zug nach Köln ab? = When does the train for Cologne leave?

Wann kommt der Zug in Köln an? = When does the train arrive in Cologne?

More vocab... Yes, it's as dull as a big dull thing, but it's also vital to know as much as you can.

to depart:	abfahren	arrival:	die Ankunft	to get on:	einsteigen
to arrive:	ankommen	ticket:	die Fahrkarte (-n)	to get out:	aussteigen
to change (trains):	umsteigen	ticket window:	der Fahrkartenschalter	through train:	der D-Zug
platform:	das Gleis (-e)	ticket machine:	der Fahrkartenautomat	suburban train:	die S-Bahn
departure:	die Abfahrt	timetable:	der Fahrplan	intercity express train:	der ICE-Zug

Remember, plurals are always 'die'.

Whoops, I've dropped the train...

Be careful with verbs like 'abfahren' and 'einsteigen'. They're 'separable' — you say 'der Zug fährt ab', not 'der Zug abfährt'. Apart from that, this is all fairly straightforward — so learn it. Then getting around in Germany will be a whole lot easier — more importantly, so will your GCSE.

All Kinds of Transport

Here's what you need to <u>know</u> about other forms of <u>transport</u>. This is another of those topics that you'll need to know <u>really well</u> — and you need to know loads of <u>vocab</u> for it, too.

Wie kommst du dahin? — **How do you get there?**

You'll need to say how you get about. Use the verb '<u>fahren</u>' with vehicles, but '<u>gehen</u>' if you're on foot. Also, you have to use '<u>mit</u>...' with vehicles — but if you're on foot, say '<u>zu</u> Fuß'.

Ich gehe zu Fuß.   = I'm going on foot.

Ich fahre | *mit dem Zug* | .   = I'm travelling <u>by train</u>.

by bus:	mit dem Bus
by tram:	mit der Straßenbahn
on the underground:	mit der U-Bahn
by bike:	mit dem Fahrrad
by car:	mit dem Auto
by motorbike:	mit dem Motorrad
by coach:	mit dem Reisebus
by boat:	mit dem Boot
by plane:	mit dem Flugzeug

Abfahrt und Ankunft — **Departure and arrival**

These are the kinds of questions you'd <u>have</u> to ask at a station.

Fährt | *ein Bus* | *nach Mannheim?*   = Is there <u>a bus</u> that goes to Mannheim?

This doesn't look like Stuttgart - I must've taken the wrong bus...

a tram:	eine Straßenbahn	*a coach:*	ein Reisebus
a plane:	ein Flugzeug	*a boat:*	ein Boot

Wann fährt | *der nächste Bus* | *nach Stuttgart ab?*   = When does <u>the next bus</u> to Stuttgart leave?

the (next) coach:	der (nächste) Reisebus
the (next) boat:	das (nächste) Boot

Wann kommt | *das Flugzeug* | *in Frankfurt an?*   = When does <u>the plane</u> arrive in Frankfurt?

Welcher Bus...? — **Which bus...?**

No doubt about it — you need to be able to ask <u>which bus</u> or <u>train</u> goes <u>where</u>. Just learn <u>this</u>.

Welcher Bus | *fährt* | *zum Stadtzentrum* | *, bitte?*   = <u>Which bus</u> goes <u>to the town centre</u>, please?

Which tram: Welche Straßenbahn

to the bus stop:	*zur Bushaltestelle*
to the airport:	*zum Flughafen*
to the harbour/port:	*zum Hafen*

Take the bus — no, leave it there...

Think about how you usually <u>get around</u>, and how you get around when you're on <u>holiday</u>. Then tell someone <u>in German</u>. They'll be dead impressed by your language skills, and really interested to hear about all the different modes of transport you use for different occasions. Promise.

Planning Your Holiday

So you've finally made it to your destination. Now you need to know what there is <u>to do</u>. Unfortunately there are quite <u>a lot</u> of things to learn about this. Better get started then...

Das Verkehrsamt — The Tourist Information Office

Here's where you <u>find out</u> what a town's got to offer. Get these phrases <u>between your ears</u>:

Wo ist der Zoo **?** = Where is <u>the zoo</u>?

See <u>page 59</u> for info on asking for directions.

the swimming pool: das Schwimmbad

For more places in town see <u>page 58</u>.

Wann macht **das Museum** auf **?** = When does the museum <u>open</u>?

close: zu

Ausflüge — Excursions

Learning this lot'll get you <u>big bonus marks</u>.

the museums in Cologne: die Museen in Köln

Haben Sie Broschüren über Ausflüge in der Nähe von München **?**

= Do you have any leaflets about <u>excursions near Munich</u>?

Was für einen Ausflug möchten Sie machen?

= What kind of excursion would you like to go on?

Ich möchte ein Schloss sehen **.** = I'd like to <u>see a castle</u>.

go to a museum: in ein Museum gehen

Was kostet es? = What does it cost?

Oooooooohhhhhh! A Magical Mystery Tour!

Es kostet fünf Euro pro Person. = It costs 5 euros for one person.

Dieser Bus fährt nach Neuschwanstein.
Der Bus **fährt um** halb drei vom Rathaus **ab.**

= This bus goes to Neuschwanstein. <u>The bus</u> leaves <u>from the town hall</u> at <u>half past two</u>.

The train: Der Zug

2 pm: vierzehn Uhr
3.15 pm: fünfzehn Uhr fünfzehn

from the church: von der Kirche
from the marketplace: vom Marktplatz

Forget museums — tell me when the shops open...

You might have to <u>answer questions</u> about a tourist brochure in the <u>reading</u> exam, or you could end up <u>writing a letter</u> to a tourist office in the <u>writing</u> assessment. Either way, this stuff's dead <u>useful</u>.

Holiday Accommodation

Okay, this page has all the words you need to know about <u>hotels</u>, <u>hostels</u> and <u>camping</u>.
You may not find it exactly riveting, but it <u>is</u> dead useful. Better get <u>learning</u> then...

Der Urlaub — Holiday

They like to <u>test</u> you on booking the right kind of <u>room</u> in the right kind of hotel — <u>learn it</u>...

GENERAL VOCABULARY

holiday:	der Urlaub (-e)
abroad:	im Ausland
person:	die Person (-en)
night:	die Nacht (die Nächte)
overnight stay:	die Übernachtung (-en)

VERBS USED IN HOTELS

to reserve:	reservieren
to stay the night:	übernachten
to stay:	bleiben
to cost:	kosten
to leave:	abfahren

THINGS YOU MIGHT ASK FOR

room:	das Zimmer (-)
double room:	das Doppelzimmer (-)
single room:	das Einzelzimmer (-)
place/space:	der Platz (die Plätze)

TYPES OF ACCOMMODATION

full board:	die Vollpension
half board:	die Halbpension
bed and breakfast:	Übernachtung mit Frühstück

For more on meals see <u>pages 51-52</u>.

Remember: plurals are always 'die'.

hotel: das Hotel (-s)

guest house: das Gasthaus
(die Gasthäuser)

campsite: der Campingplatz
(die Campingplätze)

youth hostel: die Jugendherberge (-n)

Die Rechnung — The bill

After all that, you need to be able to ask about
your <u>room</u>, where <u>things are</u>... and <u>paying the bill</u>.

PARTS OF A HOTEL

reception:	der Empfang (die Empfänge)
restaurant:	das Restaurant (-s)
dining room:	der Speisesaal (die Speisesäle)
lift:	der Aufzug (die Aufzüge)
stairs:	die Treppe (-n)
car park:	der Parkplatz (die Parkplätze)

Donnie had finally located the drinking water.

OTHER HOTEL VOCAB

key:	der Schlüssel (-)
balcony:	der Balkon (-e)
bath:	das Bad (die Bäder)
shower:	die Dusche (-n)
washbasin:	das Waschbecken (-)

PAYING FOR YOUR STAY

bill:	die Rechnung (-en)
price:	der Preis (-e)

EXTRA WORDS FOR CAMPING

tent:	das Zelt (-e)
sleeping bag:	der Schlafsack (die Schlafsäcke)
to camp:	zelten
pitch:	der Platz (die Plätze)
drinking water:	das Trinkwasser

You'll need a holiday after this...

A page bristling with vocab — <u>learn</u> all the stuff on this page and you're <u>well away</u> if anything on hotels
comes up... and it often does. Check you know the words by <u>covering</u> the page and <u>scribbling</u> them down.

Booking a Room / Pitch

Looking for a relaxing post-exam break this summer? Here's how to book yourself a room in Deutschland.

Haben Sie Zimmer frei? — Do you have any rooms free?

You'll have to say what sort of room you want and how long you'll be staying.

Ich möchte ein Einzelzimmer . = I'd like a single room.

double room: Doppelzimmer

You could be a bit more specific and use these:

room with a bath: Zimmer mit Bad
room with a balcony: Zimmer mit Balkon

Ich möchte zwei Nächte hier bleiben. = I'd like to stay here for two nights.

On the plus side this is only costing us 5.95 a night.

See page 1 for more numbers.

If you're staying for one night, use 'eine Nacht' (not ein Nacht).

Was kostet es pro Nacht für eine Person ? = How much is it per night for one person?

If there's more than one person, use 'zwei Personen', 'drei Personen' etc.

Ich nehme es. = I'll take it.   **Ich nehme es nicht.** = I won't take it.

Kann man hier zelten? — Can you camp here?

Whether you like the outdoor life or not — you'll need these phrases.

Ich möchte einen Platz für drei Nächte , bitte.

= I'd like a pitch for three nights, please.

Put how long you want to stay here.

You might need these phrases too:

Is there drinking water here?: Gibt es hier Trinkwasser?
Where can I get...?: Wo bekomme ich...?

pitch (place for a tent): **der Platz** (die Plätze)

tent: **das Zelt (-e)**

caravan: der Wohnwagen (-)

sleeping bag: **der Schlafsack** (die Schlafsäcke)

Remember, plurals are always 'die'.

You may have to book ahead. See page 11 for information on how to write a formal letter.

Do you have any rooms free? — No, you have to pay...

Going to a hotel or campsite could well come up somewhere like your listening exam.
So even if you're never going to go on holiday to Germany, get this page learnt.

Where / When is... ?

Being able to ask questions is pretty darn useful — as is understanding the answers.
This lot'll also help when you go on holiday...

Wo ist... ? — Where is... ?

Knowing how to ask where things are is essential — get these learnt:

Wo ist der Speisesaal , bitte?   = Where is the dining room, please?

See **page 47** for more things you might need to ask about.

the car park:	der Parkplatz (die Parkplätze)
the games room:	das Spielzimmer (-)
the play area:	der Spielplatz (die Spielplätze)
the toilet:	die Toilette (-n)
the loo:	das Klo (-s)

Remember, plurals are always 'die'.

The floor number takes a dative ending here. See page 91.

Er ist im dritten Stock .   = It's on the third floor.

Only 13 more floors to go...

fourth floor:	vierten Stock
second floor:	zweiten Stock
first floor:	ersten Stock
ground floor:	Erdgeschoss

For higher floor numbers, see **page 1**.

These are other words you might need when you describe where something is.

outside:	draußen
on the left/right:	links/rechts
upstairs:	oben
downstairs:	unten
at the end of the corridor:	am Ende des Ganges

Wann ist... ? — When is... ?

And then when you've found out where everything is, you'll need to know when things happen...

Wann wird das Frühstück serviert, bitte?

lunch:	das Mittagessen (-)
evening meal:	das Abendessen (-)

= When is breakfast served, please?

For more times, see **page 2**.

Wann wird das Abendessen serviert?

Gulp!

Es wird um acht Uhr serviert.   = It's served at eight o'clock.

What d'you mean 'das Klo' is on the 49th floor...

That stuff on 1st floor, 2nd floor etc. comes up for other things, like shops... — so it's well worth learning. You need to know all of this vocab to get good marks. The best way to make sure you know it is to cover up the page and try to scribble the words down. If you can't, you haven't learnt it.

Problems with Accommodation

Whatever your problem, sometimes it's good to get it all off your chest. Nobody wants their holiday ruined by dodgy plumbing and itchy sheets, so here's how to make yourself heard auf Deutsch...

Es gibt ein Problem mit... — There's a problem with...

Here are a few common complaints to be getting on with:

The room: Das Zimmer → **Das Wasser ist kalt .** = The water is cold.

too hot: zu heiß

Es gibt keine Handtücher in meinem Zimmer. = There are no towels in my room.

soap: Seife

Once you get started it's hard to stop...

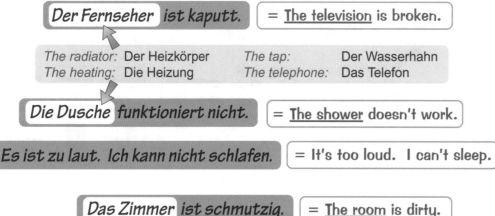

Der Fernseher ist kaputt. = The television is broken.

The radiator: Der Heizkörper   *The tap:* Der Wasserhahn
The heating: Die Heizung   *The telephone:* Das Telefon

Die Dusche funktioniert nicht. = The shower doesn't work.

Es ist zu laut. Ich kann nicht schlafen. = It's too loud. I can't sleep.

> It's too loud, I can't sleep.

Das Zimmer ist schmutzig. = The room is dirty.

The bath: Das Bad   *The bed linen:* Die Bettwäsche

Können Sie mir helfen, bitte? — Can you help me, please?

So you've told them what the problem is, now you need to get it fixed.

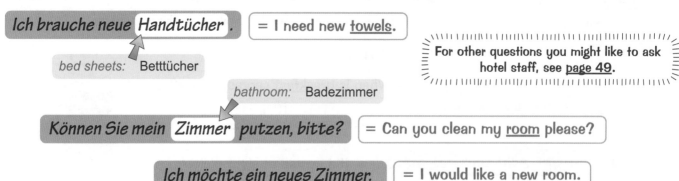

Ich brauche neue Handtücher . = I need new towels.

bed sheets: Betttücher

bathroom: Badezimmer

For other questions you might like to ask hotel staff, see page 49.

Können Sie mein Zimmer putzen, bitte? = Can you clean my room please?

Ich möchte ein neues Zimmer. = I would like a new room.

'There's water everywhere' — 'This is a cruise, Sir...'

This sort of thing could come in really useful if you ever find yourself in a dodgy German hotel. Even if you don't, I'd still suggest learning this page. You never know when it'll come in handy.

At a Restaurant

You might've seen some of these sentences before in different situations and with different vocabulary. That's because they're important, so get them learnt.

Im Restaurant — At the restaurant

Herr Ober! = Waiter!

Fräulein! = Waitress!

These are what you'd use to call the waiter or waitress over...

...and these are the names of the jobs.

waiter: der Kellner (-)
waitress: die Kellnerin (-nen)

Darf ich bitte die Karte haben? = May I have the menu, please?

the menu of the day: die Tageskarte

See page 49 on 'hotels' for asking where things are.

the phone: das Telefon

Wo ist die Toilette, bitte? = Where's the toilet, please?

Ich hätte gern... — I'd like...

This stuff could be used in other situations too, like shops — so learn it well.

Haben Sie Bockwurst? = Do you have boiled sausage?

fried sausage: Bratwurst

the chicken: das Hähnchen
the lamb: das Lamm

Ich hätte gern das Schnitzel mit Pommes. = I'd like the schnitzel with chips.

rice: Reis
pickled cabbage: Sauerkraut

See page 13 for more food vocab.

Wie schmeckt es? — What does it taste like?

You might want to know what something's like before you scoff it all — so be sure to learn this:

Wie schmeckt Sauerkraut? = What does Sauerkraut taste like?

sausage in curry sauce: Currywurst

Sind Sie fertig? — Are you finished?

There's no getting away from having to know this. You can't leave without paying.

Die Rechnung, bitte. = The bill, please.

Darf ich bitte zahlen? = May I pay, please?

The bill, sir.

The day of Rechnung — it's time to pay...

A little tip for you: 'Fräulein' is considered a bit sexist nowadays, and not just for addressing a waitress. 'Herr Ober' is a tad old-fashioned too. Your exam board doesn't seem to mind about all this though, so you still need to know it. The rest of this stuff's pretty useful, so get it learnt.

At a Restaurant

All this restaurant stuff's not hard — but your exam could well be if you don't make an effort to memorise it.

Haben Sie einen Tisch frei? — Do you have a table free?

This part's easy, so it's definitely worth learning.

Einen Tisch für vier Personen, bitte. = A table for four, please.

two: zwei   *three:* drei

See page 1 for more about numbers.

Ich bin nicht zufrieden — I'm not satisfied

You might find you want to make a complaint — in which case, this little lot might come in handy...

too hot: zu heiß   *too salty:* zu salzig

Das Rindfleisch ist zu kalt. = The beef is too cold.

The steak: Das Steak
The pork: Das Schweinefleisch
The soup: Die Suppe
The sausage: Die Wurst

See page 13 for more food vocab.

It is a bit nippy actually...

Die Speisekarte — The Menu

A few other bits and pieces for you to learn...

Ist die Bedienung inbegriffen? = Is service included?

If you see these words or their abbreviations on a menu, it means service is 'included'.

inbegriffen
inklusive
(or inkl.)

It's always handy to know which bit of the menu you're looking at.

COURSES: DIE GÄNGE
starter: die Vorspeise (-e)
main course: das Hauptgericht (-e)
dessert: der Nachtisch (-e)

Herr Ober! — Es gibt eine Fliege in meiner Suppe...

Being at a restaurant could easily come up somewhere, so you need to know all about it.
If you've learnt all the stuff on this page, then it'll be easy. So no skiving out of anything.

Talking About Your Holiday

When you've been on <u>holiday</u> you want to bore everyone by <u>telling</u> them all about it.
After this page you'll be able to bore people in <u>German</u> too... and get good <u>marks</u>.

Wohin bist du gefahren? — *Where did you go?*

Talking about your holiday is a great place to use the <u>perfect tense</u>.
Get it right and the examiners will be dead <u>impressed</u>. For help, see <u>page 104</u>.

Ich bin | vor zwei Wochen | nach | Amerika | gefahren.   = I went to <u>America</u> <u>two weeks ago</u>.

a week ago:	vor einer Woche
last month:	letzten Monat
in July:	im Juli
in the summer:	im Sommer

Spain:	Spanien
France:	Frankreich
Ireland:	Irland

When 'vor' means 'ago',
you need the dative case.
<u>See page 85</u>.

Other dates and times: <u>pages 2–3</u>.
Points of the compass: <u>page 60</u>.
A bigger list of countries: <u>page 43</u>.

Mit wem warst du im Urlaub?

— *Who did you go on holiday with?*

| *a fortnight:* | zwei Wochen |
| *a month:* | einen Monat |

Use the dative case after 'mit'. See <u>pages 85 and 96</u>.

Ich war | eine Woche | lang mit | meiner Familie | im Urlaub.   = I went on holiday with
<u>my family</u> for <u>a week</u>.

For past tenses, see
<u>pages 104-105</u>.

| *my brother:* | meinem Bruder |
| *my friends:* | meinen Freunden |

For friends and family
— see <u>page 18</u>.

Wir sind | in einem Hotel | geblieben.   = We stayed <u>in a hotel</u>.

| *on a campsite:* | auf einem Campingplatz |
| *with friends:* | bei Freunden |

Was hast du gemacht? — *What did you do?*

You need to be able to say what you <u>did</u> on holiday — <u>learn</u> it well.

Ich bin | an den Strand | gegangen.   = I went <u>to the beach</u>.

| *to a disco:* | zu einer Diskothek |
| *to a museum:* | in ein Museum |

| *sunned myself:* | mich gesonnt |
| *played tennis:* | Tennis gespielt |

Ich habe | mich entspannt |.   = I <u>relaxed</u>.

I spent my holiday revising German — honest...

You need to be able to <u>talk</u> about holidays in your <u>speaking</u> and <u>writing</u> tasks, and <u>understand</u> other
people going on about <u>their holidays</u>. Cover up the page and see how much you can <u>remember</u>.

Talking About Your Holiday

This is the kind of stuff that'll really impress the examiner. So for lots more lovely marks, plough on...

Wie bist du dorthin gekommen? — How did you get there?

'Dorthin' means 'there' when you're going 'to' a place. It's a useful one.

Wir sind mit dem Auto **dorthin gekommen.** = We went there by car.

plane: dem Flugzeug
boat: dem Boot
bike: dem Fahrrad

For more types of transport, see pages 44–45.

You could also say: **Wir sind mit** dem Auto **gefahren.** = We travelled by car.

Wie war das Wetter? — How was the weather?

No description of your holiday would be complete without giving a run-down of the weather.

Es war sonnig und heiß . = It was sunny and hot.

cold: kalt   rainy: regnerisch

See page 56 for more on the weather.

Es hat geregnet . = It rained.

snowed: geschneit

Wie hat dir deine Reise gefallen?
— How was your journey?

Giving your opinion is a great way to impress those examiners.

Wie fandst du deinen Urlaub? = How was your holiday?

For more on giving opinions see pages 7-9.

Er hat mir gefallen. = I liked it.

Er hat mir nicht gefallen. = I didn't like it.

For more on talking about the past, see pages 104-105.

'Urlaub' is masculine — that's why it's 'er war', not 'es' or 'sie'.

Er war in Ordnung. = It was OK.

Still awake? — Perhaps you'd like to see my photos...

You need to know all this vocab for writing and talking about holidays. You can always make up a holiday you didn't have, if you know the German words for it. Smile — it could be worse. Just.

Talking About Your Holiday

You're not done yet — oh no. There's plenty more you can say about holidays. Just you wait and see...

Wohin wirst du fahren? — Where will you go?

You've got to be able to talk about the future — things that you will be doing...

These are all in the future tense...

| Where will you go?
Wohin wirst du fahren? |

| Who will you go on holiday with?
Mit wem wirst du im Urlaub fahren? |

| What will you do?
Was wirst du machen? |

| How will you get there?
Wie wirst du dorthin kommen? |

...and these are in the present future tense...

| I'm going to America in two weeks.
Ich fahre in zwei Wochen nach Amerika. |

| I'm going on holiday for a month with my family.
Ich fahre einen Monat lang mit meiner Familie im Urlaub. |

| I'm going to the beach.
Ich gehe an den Strand. |

| I'm going there by car.
Ich komme mit dem Wagen dorthin. |

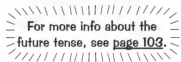

For more info about the future tense, see page 103.

Ein deutscher Austausch — A German Exchange

Finally, you might want to talk about an exchange visit you did with school.

Letztes Jahr bin ich mit der Schule nach Deutschland gefahren. = Last year I went to Germany with school.

Ich habe meinen Brieffreund besucht. = I visited my pen friend.

my pen friend (female): meine Brieffreundin
a German school: eine deutsche Schule

Es hat viel Spaß gemacht. = It was a lot of fun.

For more on talking about the past, see pages 104-105.

Finding a way to sneak the future tense in will always impress...

It's usual to use the accusative here, so it's 'diesen' not 'dieser'.

Diesen Sommer wird mein Brieffreund nach England kommen. = This summer my pen friend will come to England.

I've got a pen friend — his name's Parker...

So, that just about wraps up talking about your holiday. There's loads of stuff you can say, which makes this a really important topic. Make sure you know it well. I mean ultra-well.

The Weather

You may well have to talk about the <u>weather</u> yourself, or understand a <u>forecast</u> in your <u>listening</u> exam. But don't worry — just learn these few <u>easy sentences</u> and this bit of <u>vocab</u>.

Wie ist das Wetter? — What's the weather like?

These <u>short phrases</u> are the ones you definitely <u>can't do without</u> — luckily, they're <u>easy</u>.

Die Sonne scheint.

= The sun's shining.

It's snowing: Es schneit

Es regnet .

= It's <u>raining</u>.

Es ist kalt . = It's <u>cold</u>.

hot:	heiß	overcast:	bedeckt	warm:	warm
windy:	windig	wet:	nass	cool:	kühl
sunny:	sonnig	dry:	trocken	foggy:	nebelig

Wie ist die Temperatur? = What's the temperature?

You can also say '<u>Wie viel Grad ist es?</u>' — it means the same thing.

Es ist siebzehn Grad Celsius. = It is 17 °C.

Es ist windig.

Wie wird das Wetter morgen?

You'll be dead <u>impressive</u> if you know this — and it's fairly easy. Ideal.

— What will the weather be like tomorrow?

Morgen wird es schneien . = <u>Tomorrow</u> it will <u>snow</u>.

Next week:	Nächste Woche	rain:	regnen	be hot:	heiß sein
On Tuesday:	Am Dienstag	be sunny:	sonnig sein	be cold:	kalt sein
		be windy:	windig sein	thunder:	donnern

Morgen gibt es Hagel . = Tomorrow there will be <u>hail</u>.

rain:	Regen	thunder:	Donner
snow:	Schnee	lightning:	Blitz

Morgen wird es sonnig sein.

That's what you said yesterday.

See <u>pages 2–3</u> for more on times and dates, and <u>page 103</u> for using 'werden' to talk about the future.

Die Wettervorhersage — The weather forecast

This is the <u>crunch</u> — a <u>real</u> weather forecast. You <u>won't know all the words</u>, but you don't need to. Look at the bits of words you <u>do know</u> and have a guess.

Work through this one, and see if you can <u>figure out</u> what each bit means. Any words you <u>don't</u> know will be in the <u>dictionary</u> at the back of the book.

today:	heute
in the south:	im Süden
in the north:	im Norden

<u>Der Wetterbericht für heute</u>
Heute wird es in Deutschland warm sein.
Morgen wird es im Süden windig und im Norden bedeckt sein. An der Küste wird es regnen.

When you've translated it as well as you can, check it against this:

Today's Weather Report
Today it will be warm in Germany. Tomorrow it will be windy in the South and overcast in the North. It will rain on the coast.

Learn this page — Wetter you like it or not...

All I want to know is "Do I need a coat?" and "Will I get a tan?" Still, this stuff comes up in the exams so you've got to do it — luckily it's <u>not</u> that <u>hard</u>. All you need to do is <u>learn</u> the main <u>sentences</u> on this page and the <u>vocab</u>, and you'll be working for the Met Office in no time...

Revision Summary

These questions are here to make sure you really <u>know your stuff</u>. Work through them all, and <u>make a note</u> of the ones you couldn't do. Look back through the section to <u>find out</u> how to answer them. Try those problem questions again. Then look up any you still can't do. <u>Keep at it</u> until you can do them all — cos that'll mean you've really learnt it.

1) Write down five countries in German.
   How would you say that you came from one of these countries?

2) Ask for three return tickets to Dresden, second class.

3) Say in German that you go to school by car, but your friend walks.
   (Make sure you use the right verb for these.)

4) You've missed the bus to Frankfurt.
   Ask when the next bus leaves and when it arrives in Frankfurt.

5) You arrive in Tübingen and go to the tourist information office.
   Ask where the zoo is.

6) There's an excursion to a nearby museum. Ask for a leaflet about the excursion.

7) You get to a hotel in Germany. Ask them if they have any free rooms.

8) Say you want one double room and two single rooms. Say you want to stay five nights.
   Say you'll take the rooms.

9) Ask where the dining room is.

10) Ask when breakfast is served.

11) You get to your room and find that's it's dirty and the shower doesn't work.
    Tell the hotel staff this and say that you would like the room cleaned.

12) You're going out for a meal. Ask if you can have a table for two and ask where the toilet is.

13) Order roast chicken with potatoes.

14) Attract the waitress's attention and tell her that the potatoes are cold.

15) You've just been on holiday to Italy. You went for two weeks with your sister. You went there by plane. You relaxed and sunned yourself. The weather was hot and sunny.
    You enjoyed the holiday and are going to go to Spain next year.
    Phew — say that lot in German.

16) Your German pen friend wants to know what the weather is like where you are.
    Say that it is raining, but that tomorrow the sun will shine.

Names of Buildings

You'll be able to talk about your town much better if you know what buildings there are in it — and the examiners will think you're pretty cool too. Which means bucketloads of marks.

Die Gebäude — Buildings

These are the basic, bog-standard 'learn-them-or-else' buildings. (Building = das Gebäude.) Don't go any further until you know all of them.

the bank: die Bank (-en)

the baker's: die Bäckerei (-en)

the butcher's: die Metzgerei (-en)

the theatre: das Theater (-)

the post office: die Post (die Postämter)

the railway station: der Bahnhof (die Bahnhöfe)

the library: die Bibliothek (-en)

the cinema: das Kino (-s)

the supermarket: der Supermarkt (die Supermärkte)

the marketplace: der Marktplatz (die Marktplätze)

the castle: das Schloss (die Schlösser)

the church: die Kirche (-n)

Andere Gebäude — Other buildings

Remember, plurals are always 'die'.

OK, I'll come clean. There are absolutely loads of buildings you need to know...

TOURISTY BITS

the hotel:	das Hotel (-s)
the youth hostel:	die Jugendherberge (-n)
the restaurant:	das Restaurant (-s)
the tourist information office:	das Verkehrsamt (die Verkehrsämter)
the museum:	das Museum (die Museen)
the zoo:	der Zoo (-s)

SHOPS　See page 35 for more shops.

the shop:	das Geschäft (-e)
the pharmacy:	die Apotheke (-n)
the chemist's:	die Drogerie (-n)
the department store:	das Kaufhaus (die Kaufhäuser)
the cake shop:	die Konditorei (-en)
the market:	der Markt (die Märkte)

OTHER IMPORTANT PLACES

the hospital:	das Krankenhaus (die Krankenhäuser)	the swimming baths:	das Schwimmbad (die Schwimmbäder)
the town hall:	das Rathaus (die Rathäuser)	the indoor swimming pool:	das Hallenbad (die Hallenbäder)
the cathedral:	der Dom (-e)	the sports centre:	das Sportzentrum (die Sportzentren)
the park:	der Park (-s)	the stadium:	das Stadion (die Stadien)
the airport:	der Flughafen (die Flughäfen)	the school:	die Schule (-n)
the university:	die Universität (-en)		

There's a butcher's, a baker's, a lovely little candlestick place...

There are lots of words to learn here. The best way to do it is to turn over the page and see if you can write them all down, have a look and then have another go... It's boring, but it works. Just reading the page isn't enough — you wouldn't remember them tomorrow, never mind in an exam.

Asking Directions

You're probably going to get at least <u>one</u> question about asking <u>directions</u>. So this page is going to be really <u>important</u>. Start learning this stuff and get these phrases between your ears.

Wo ist... ? — Where is... ?

It's dead easy to ask <u>where</u> a place is — say '<u>Wo ist...</u>' and stick the <u>place</u> on the end.
No dodgy word order — say it how you would in English.

Wo ist die Post **, bitte?** = Where is <u>the post office</u>, please?

See <u>page 58</u> for more buildings.

Gibt es hier in der Nähe eine Bibliothek **?** = Is there <u>a library</u> near here?

Realising her mistake, Phoebe began frantically searching for a trouser shop.

Wie weit ist es? — How far is it?

The place you're looking for might be <u>too far</u> to walk — you might need a <u>bus</u> or <u>tram</u> instead. Here's how you check the <u>distance</u>, before you let yourself in for a 3-hour trek to the airport.

Wie weit ist es zum Kino **?** = How far is it <u>to the cinema</u>?

IMPORTANT BIT:
It's '<u>zur</u>' for '<u>die</u>' words and '<u>zum</u>' for '<u>der</u>' and '<u>das</u>' words.

Es **ist** zwei Kilometer **von hier.** = <u>It's two kilometres</u> from here.

It: Er/Sie/Es

a hundred metres: hundert Meter
not far: nicht weit

Wie komme ich zu...? — How do I get to...?

If you're not standing right <u>in front</u> of it, you'll need <u>directions</u>.
Here's how you <u>ask</u> for them...

Entschuldigen Sie bitte, wie komme ich zur Bank **?** = Excuse me please, how do I get <u>to the bank</u>?

IMPORTANT BIT:
Swap this for any place, using '<u>zum</u>' or '<u>zur</u>' like in the last section.

to the station: zum Bahnhof
to the library: zur Bibliothek
to the castle: zum Schloss

You'll need <u>all</u> this vocabulary to <u>understand</u> any directions you're given:

go straight on:	gehen Sie geradeaus
go right:	gehen Sie rechts
go left:	gehen Sie links
on the corner:	an der Ecke
round the corner:	um die Ecke
over there:	da drüben

right at the traffic lights:	rechts an der Ampel
straight on, past the church:	geradeaus, an der Kirche vorbei
take the first road on the left:	nehmen Sie die erste Straße links

Look at <u>page 1</u> for more stuff on 1st, 2nd, etc.

Everyone needs some direction in life...

This is another page of stuff you're almost <u>bound</u> to get in one of your papers, so it's time to <u>cover up</u> the page and see how much of the vocab you can <u>remember</u> — and <u>keep going</u> until you know it all. Use the phrases on <u>all</u> the buildings you can remember from <u>page 58</u>. No pain, no gain.

Where You're From

At some point, you're probably going to get asked about <u>where</u> you're from. And you're going to <u>have</u> to be able to <u>answer</u>. So it's a good job you're reading this page...

Woher kommst du? — Where do you come from?

Get this phrase learnt <u>off by heart</u> — if the country you're from isn't here, look at <u>page 43</u>, or go look it up in a dictionary.

Ich komme aus England **. Ich bin** Engländer(in) **.**   = I come from <u>England</u>. I am <u>English</u>.

Wales:	Wales
Northern Ireland:	Nordirland
Scotland:	Schottland
Great Britain:	Großbritannien

Welsh:	Waliser(in)
Northern Irish:	Nordirländer(in)
Scottish:	Schotte/Schottin
British:	Brite/Britin

IMPORTANT BIT: You must add '-in' on the end for <u>women and girls</u>.

With '<u>Schotte</u>' and '<u>Brite</u>' you also have to <u>remove</u> the '<u>-e</u>' from the end before you add on the '<u>-in</u>' to make the feminine versions.

Wo wohnst du?   = Where do you live?

Ich wohne in England **.**   = I live in <u>England</u>.

Wo wohnst du? — Where do you live?

You're <u>bound</u> to get asked this at some point — so get your answer ready.

Ich komme aus Mars. Ich bin Marsmensch.

Ich wohne in Barrow **.**   = I live in <u>Barrow</u>.

Barrow liegt in Nordwestengland **.**   = Barrow's <u>in the north-west of England</u>.

in the north: im Norden	*in the south:* im Süden	*in south-east England:* in Südostengland
in the east: im Osten	*in the west:* im Westen	*in north Scotland:* in Nordschottland

a city: eine Großstadt   *a village:* ein Dorf

Barrow ist eine Stadt **mit ungefähr 60 000 Einwohnern und viel Industrie.**   = Barrow is <u>a town</u> with about 60 000 inhabitants and a lot of industry.

See <u>page 85</u> for an explanation of the '-n' on the end of 'Einwohner'.

Ein wohner, zwei wohner — this'll take for ever...

This page is fairly <u>straightforward</u>, which — after all that asking for directions stuff — is quite <u>nice</u>. It's so straightfoward in fact that you'd be a <u>fool</u> not to <u>learn it</u>. So I suggest you get to it...

Talking About Where You Live

Whether you like where you live or not, you can still find plenty to say about it. Make sure you learn these phrases, then you can happily regurgitate them in your speaking and writing tasks without even thinking.

Die Gegend von Plymouth... — The Plymouth area...

Come up with this little lot and you'll knock those examiners for six...

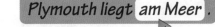

Plymouth liegt am Meer . = Plymouth is <u>by the sea</u>.

in the countryside:	auf dem Land	*on the coast:*	an der Küste
by a river:	neben einem Fluss	*in the mountains:*	in den Bergen
near London:	in der Nähe von London		

Dative plural — noun adds '-n'. See page 85.

Mein Haus

Die Landschaft um Plymouth ist sehr schön und grün. = The landscape around Plymouth is very beautiful and green.

Was für eine Stadt ist Hull? — What kind of town is Hull?

If you want a <u>really good</u> mark, make sure you're ready to give more <u>details</u>.
It's always best if you can give an opinion and then say <u>why</u>.

Die Stadt ist sehr interessant . = The town is <u>very interesting</u>.

See pages 7-9 for more on opinions.

boring:	langweilig
great:	klasse/prima
dirty:	schmutzig
clean:	sauber
quiet/peaceful:	ruhig/still

Es gibt viel **zu tun.** = There's <u>lots</u> to do.

nothing: nichts   *not much/little:* wenig

Put them all <u>together</u> and make a <u>longer</u> sentence — you'll get <u>extra marks</u> if you get it right.

Put the name of your town in here.

Ich wohne gern in Hull **, weil es immer viel zu tun gibt.** = I like living in <u>Hull</u>, because there's always lots to do.

'Weil' sends the verb to the end of the sentence. <u>See page 89</u>.

Ich wohne nicht gern in Hull **, weil es nichts zu tun gibt.** = I don't like living in <u>Hull</u>, because there's nothing to do.

Hull — it's a little bit like Paris actually...

If you think you come from a really dreary place which has <u>nothing</u> going for it, you can <u>make things up</u> (within reason) — but chances are there'll be <u>something</u> to say about a place near you. Start with <u>whereabouts</u> it is and see how much you can say about it <u>without</u> looking at the page.

Talking About Where You Live

More really important stuff — you'll need to be able to talk about the place where you live, where your home is and what it looks like.

In deiner Stadt — In your town

This sort of thing is easy marks. Make sure you can reel off those buildings at the drop of a hat.

Was gibt es in deiner Stadt? = What is there in your town?

See page 58 for more buildings.

You need the accusative case (see page 84) after 'Es gibt'.

Es gibt einen Markt . = There's a market.

a cathedral:	einen Dom	a university:	eine Universität
a park:	einen Park	a sports centre:	ein Sportzentrum

Wohnst du gern in Barrow? = Do you like living in Barrow?

don't like: nicht gern   **Ich wohne** gern **in Barrow.** = I like living in Barrow.

Beschreib dein Haus... — Describe your house...

Watch out — in German addresses, the house number comes after the street name, and the street name is joined to the word 'Straße'.

Ich wohne in der Magdalenstraße 24 in Lancaster. = I live at 24 Magdalen Street, in Lancaster.

Being able to talk about where you live is really important...

Ich wohne in einem kleinen , alten **Haus.** = I live in a small old house.

big:	großen	modern:	modernen
new:	neuen	cold:	kalten

See page 91 for more on adjective endings.

I LIVE... : ICH WOHNE...

in a house:	in einem Haus
in a flat:	in einer Wohnung
in a semi-detached house:	in einem Doppelhaus
in a detached house:	in einem Einfamilienhaus
in a terraced house:	in einem Reihenhaus

My house: Mein Haus

Meine Wohnung liegt in der Nähe von einem Park . = My flat is near a park.

See pages 85 and 96 for 'in' and 'von' with the dative.

the town centre:	der Stadtmitte	a shopping centre:	einem Einkaufszentrum
the motorway:	der Autobahn	a bus station:	einem Busbahnhof
the shops:	den Geschäften	a train station:	einem Bahnhof

These are all in the dative case.

I know where you live...

Bit creepy this — why are they interested in finding out where your house is... Still, you've got to learn it anyway, so cover the page, scribble it all down, and check how many you got right.

Inside Your Home

You've got to be able to <u>describe</u> what's in your house. Luckily, you don't need to say <u>everything</u> that's in it — just some things. This may not look <u>exciting</u>, but ignore it at your <u>peril</u>.

Wie ist dein Haus? — What's your house like?

Whether or not you need to ask where <u>rooms</u> are in your <u>exchange partner's</u> home, you <u>do</u> need to know this stuff for the exams. To make the first question a bit more <u>polite</u>, just add '<u>bitte</u>' on the end — <u>easy</u>.

Wie sieht die Küche **aus?**   = What does <u>the kitchen</u> look like?

the living room:	das Wohnzimmer (-)
the bathroom:	das Badezimmer (-) / das Bad (die Bäder)
the dining room:	das Esszimmer (-)
the bedroom:	das Schlafzimmer (-)

Ist die Küche groß **?**   = Is the kitchen <u>big</u>?

small: klein

Wo ist die Küche **?**   = Where is <u>the kitchen</u>?

<u>Get learning</u> the words below for what's in your room — and <u>remember</u> that if your room <u>doesn't</u> have any of these things in it, you can always <u>lie</u> — as long as you get the <u>vocab right</u>.

Was für Möbel gibt es in deinem Schlafzimmer?   = What kind of furniture is there in <u>your bedroom</u>?

In meinem Schlafzimmer gibt es ein Bett **,** zwei Stühle **und** einen kleinen Tisch **.**   = In my bedroom there is <u>a bed</u>, <u>two chairs</u> and <u>a small table</u>.

You can use any of these words in the white boxes above, but you need to get the <u>right endings</u> for '<u>ein</u>' — the <u>accusative case</u> is used after 'es gibt'. See <u>pages 84 & 90</u> for more info.

THINGS IN THE HOME

armchair:	der Sessel (-)	*cupboard:*	der Schrank (die Schränke)	*bed:*	das Bett (-en)
sofa:	das Sofa (-s)	*wall:*	die Wand (die Wände)	*curtains (plural):*	die Vorhänge
lamp:	die Lampe (-n)	*carpet:*	der Teppich (-e)		
table:	der Tisch (-e)	*ceiling:*	die Decke (-n)		
chair:	der Stuhl (die Stühle)	*wardrobe:*	der Kleiderschrank (die Kleiderschränke)		

Remember, plurals are always 'die'.

Hast du einen Garten? — Have you got a garden?

More stuff which will help you to do <u>really well</u>...

Mein Haus hat einen Garten.   = <u>My house</u> has a garden.

My flat: Meine Wohnung

Wir haben Blumen **in unserem Garten.**   = We have <u>flowers</u> in our garden.

a tree: einen Baum (die Bäume)
a lawn: einen Rasen

Who would live in a house like this...

This is stuff they could easily chuck at you. If the <u>list</u> of things in your room looks a bit <u>grisly</u>, <u>start off</u> with just a <u>few</u> — but make sure you can <u>understand</u> all the words if you <u>read</u> or <u>hear</u> them.

Celebrations

Time to get the <u>party poppers</u> out — this page is gonna be a hoot...
Now where did I put my balloon animals...

Wann feierst du? — When do you celebrate?

There are <u>loads</u> of things you can celebrate — any excuse for a <u>party</u> and all that.
Here are just a few:

Put the <u>date</u> you celebrate here. For more on dates see <u>page 3</u>.

Wir feiern Weihnachten am fünfundzwanzigsten Dezember.

= We celebrate <u>Christmas</u> on the <u>25th of December</u>.

New Year's Eve:	Silvester	Hanukkah:	Chanukka
New Year:	Neujahr	Ramadan:	Ramadan
my birthday:	meinen Geburtstag	Easter:	Ostern

Mit wem feierst du? — Who do you celebrate with?

Remember: '<u>mit</u>' is followed by the <u>dative case</u>. See <u>page 96</u> for more info.

Ich feiere meinen Geburtstag mit meiner Familie.

= I celebrate my birthday with <u>my family</u>.

| my friends: | meinen Freunden | in the restaurant: | im Restaurant |
| my parents: | meinen Eltern | at a hotel: | in einem Hotel |

Normalerweise habe ich eine Party zu Hause.

= Normally I have a party <u>at home</u>.

Wie feierst du? — How do you celebrate?

These examiners want to know <u>everything</u>, the nosy beggars...

Zu Weihnachten ...

= At Christmas...

...we have a tree:	...haben wir einen Baum
...we send cards:	...senden wir Karten
...we give presents:	...geben wir Geschenke

Zu Silvester ...

= At New Year...

...we have fireworks:	...haben wir Feuerwerk
...we dance:	...tanzen wir
...we have fun:	...machen wir Spaß

Celebrate — you've reached the end of the page...

Well that was fun... Admittedly not as fun as <u>actually</u> celebrating something, but still...
There's <u>loads</u> you can say about festivals and the like — just make sure you've <u>cracked</u> this lot first.

The Environment

Things get <u>serious</u> when the environment comes up, and you're supposed to have an opinion.
It's a chance for you to write or say what you <u>think</u> about something real and <u>important</u>
— not just what colour <u>velour jumpsuit</u> you'd like to buy in the sale.

Ist die Umwelt wichtig für dich..?

Is the environment important to you..?

Ja, ich halte die Umwelt für total wichtig.
= Yes, I think the environment is very important.

Always give a <u>reason why</u> — it makes the examiners go all tingly inside...

Ich habe große Angst um die Umwelt wegen des Treibhauseffekts .
= I'm really worried about the environment <u>because of the greenhouse effect</u>.

because of the hole in the ozone layer: wegen des Ozonloches
because we don't recycle enough: weil wir nicht genug recyceln

Wir müssen die Umwelt schützen.
= We must protect the environment.

Hast du Angst um die Umwelt..?

Do you worry about the environment..?

Nein, ich interessiere mich nicht dafür.
= No, I'm not interested in it.

Well, don't just leave it at that for Pete's sake...

Ich bin sehr beschäftigt und ich habe keine Zeit zu recyceln.
= I am very busy and I don't have time to recycle.

Blumen und die Natur sind langweilig. Ich mag lieber Computerspiele.
= Flowers and nature are boring. I prefer computer games.

If you're really up on <u>green</u> matters then you could get well stuck into this, but if you're not
then say so. You'll get as many marks for saying <u>why</u> you're not interested as you would for
<u>enthusing</u> about Greenpeace.

This sort of stuff could easily be <u>sneaked</u> into a <u>reading</u> comprehension or a <u>listening</u> conversation,
so make sure you're familiar with it.

Ah, a nice warm bed — my ideal environment...

There are so many <u>different aspects</u> of the environment you could <u>choose</u> to talk about — or not
talk about if you really couldn't give a monkey's. As always, <u>be wise</u> and learn the <u>basics</u> —
there's more of this on the next page, so <u>make sure</u> you learn this lot before turning over...

The Environment

Yep, more on the environment I'm afraid. It is a pretty <u>big topic</u> after all.
There's <u>lots</u> more vocab to be learnt on this page, so <u>be prepared</u>...

Es gibt schwere Umweltprobleme...
— There are serious environmental problems...

You might <u>get asked</u> about, or hear people talking about, <u>problems</u> with the environment.
Here are some of the biggies...

Es gibt zu viel | Verschmutzung |. = There is too much <u>pollution</u>.

> **IMPORTANT:**
> 'Umwelt<u>freundlich</u>' means
> 'environmentally <u>friendly</u>'
> — 'umwelt<u>feindlich</u>' means
> 'environmentally <u>unfriendly</u>'.
> Don't mix them up.

water pollution: Wasserverschmutzung
consumption: Verbrauch

Wir produzieren zu viel Müll. = We produce too much rubbish.

Verschmutzung macht saurer Regen. = Pollution causes acid rain.

Pestizide und Insektizide | schaden die Umwelt.

= <u>Pesticides and insecticides</u> damage the environment.

greenhouse gases: Treibhausgase
CFCs: FCKWs

Roy wasn't too fussed about global warming — it made holidays in Aberdeen that much nicer.

Wie kann man mehr umweltfreundlich sein?
— How can you be more environmentally friendly?

So, you know what the problems are — what can you do about them?

Wir sollten ...

= We should...

travel on the bus: mit dem Bus fahren
recycle waste paper: Altpapier recyceln
recycle packaging: Verpackung recyceln
use less water: weniger Wasser benutzen

Bist du Umweltfreundlich? = Are you environmentally friendly?

Ja, ich recyceln und ich fahre immer mit dem Rad in die Schule.

= Yes, I recycle and I always go to school by bike.

The greenhouse effect — my tomatoes love it...

If you get asked a question about the environment in your <u>speaking assessment</u>, look on it as an opportunity to really <u>show off</u>. There's some pretty <u>mark-worthy</u> vocab on this page — so <u>learn it</u>.

Revision Summary

The thing with doing GCSE German is that it's mainly about learning a few phrases, being able to change a few words in them, and stringing some of those phrases together. But if you don't <u>know the phrases</u>, you've got a problem. These questions will check you know what you need to know about this section. <u>Keep trying</u> them until you can do them <u>all</u>.

1) You've just arrived in Heidelberg and are writing to your pen friend about the sights. How do you say that there is a castle, a swimming pool, a university, a zoo, a museum and a theatre?

2) You need to go to the pharmacy in Germany. Ask where it is, and how far away it is.

3) A German tourist has come to see your home town and is looking for the youth hostel. Tell him to go straight on and turn left at the traffic lights.

4) Tell your German pen friend where you live and whereabouts it is (which country and whether it's north-east etc.).

5) Say in German that you like living in your town, there's loads to do and it's quite clean. Say there's a sports centre and a cinema.

6) Say your address in German and describe the place where you live — is it a town or a village, is the landscape nice, and how many people live there?

7) Julia lives in a big house with a garden. It's near a shopping centre, a bus stop and a motorway. How would she say this in German?

8) Give the names of the rooms in your home in German and say how many bedrooms it has.

9) In his bedroom Tom has a bed, two lamps, a wardrobe and a cupboard. He doesn't have a sofa. How will he say all this in German?

10) Erika is telling you about her birthday. She tells you that it's on the 24th of July, and that she and her family celebrate with a big party at her house. How would she say this in German?

11) Your German pen friend is writing an article about the environment for his school newspaper. He wants to know whether or not the environment is important to you. In German, tell him whether it is or isn't and make sure you give a reason why.

12) Your German pen friend is really struggling with this newspaper article. Now he wants to know two environmental problems and two things that we can do to be more environmentally friendly.
Give him these in German. Honestly, you might as well be writing this thing for him...

I've told you Hermann, you're really going to have to write it yourself. Just put in a bit about recycling...

School Subjects

School and jobs — maybe not what thrills you most in life. But never mind — this stuff's really <u>important</u>, so learn it well and you'll have less to stress about.

Welche Schulfächer hast du?

— *What school subjects do you do?*

Go over each group of subjects until you can write them all out without looking.

NUMBERS AND STUFF

maths: Mathe(matik) (die)
ICT: Informatik (die)

LANGUAGES

German:	Deutsch (das)
French:	Französisch (das)
Spanish:	Spanisch (das)
Italian:	Italienisch (das)

HUMANITIES

English:	Englisch (das)
history:	Geschichte (die)
geography:	Erdkunde/Geografie (die)
religious studies:	Religion (die)
media studies:	Medienwissenschaften (die)

PHYSICAL EDUCATION

PE: Sport (der)

Not that I ever did <u>anything</u> this impressive in PE.

Normally these words are <u>adjectives</u>, so they don't have capitals (see <u>page 43</u>). When they're used as names of languages, they become <u>nouns</u> (see <u>page 86</u>) — so they need a capital letter.

SCIENCES

science:	Naturwissenschaften (die)
physics:	Physik (die)
chemistry:	Chemie (die)
biology:	Biologie (die)

THE ARTS

theatre studies:	Theaterwissenschaften (die)
art:	Kunst (die)
music:	Musik (die)

Welche Fächer sind dir lieber?

— *Which subjects do you prefer?*

OK, this stuff about school isn't all that exciting, but you <u>definitely</u> need to know it.

Was ist dein Lieblingsfach?   = What is your favourite subject?

Darn. I forgot my PE kit.

Ich mag Mathe .   = I like <u>maths</u>.

There's more on how to say what you like and don't like on <u>pages 7-9</u>.

Biologie *gefällt mir mehr.*   = I prefer <u>biology</u>.

Deutsch *ist mein Lieblingsfach.*   = <u>German</u> is my favourite subject.

Ich hasse Sport .   = I hate <u>PE</u>.

Make sure you learn these lessons...

Make sure you can <u>say</u> all the subjects you do, and at least <u>understand</u> the ones you don't do. You <u>don't</u> need to use 'der', 'die' or 'das' when you're talking about a school subject — phew. You should have seen pretty much all of this stuff before — just make sure it's firmly lodged in your brain.

The School Routine

This isn't the most thrilling set of sentences, but when it comes to the exams they're gold dust. Keep each sentence <u>small</u> and <u>perfectly formed</u> — that way it's harder to mess it up.

Wie kommst du in die Schule?

— How do you get to school?

This could come up in the reading or listening exam too, so make sure you learn <u>the lot</u>.

Ich fahre mit dem Auto **in die Schule.** = I go to school by <u>car</u>.

Use '<u>in die Schule</u>' for '<u>to school</u>'. '<u>Gehen</u>' means '<u>to go</u>' only for '<u>on foot</u>', so use 'fahren' if you have any kind of <u>transport</u>.

car: dem Auto/dem Wagen
bus: dem Bus
bike: dem Fahrrad

Ich gehe zu Fuß in die Schule. = I go to school on foot.

Der Stundenplan — The timetable

Write out all these sentences and slot in the <u>right times</u> and <u>numbers</u> for <u>your school</u> — then all you've got to do is <u>learn</u>, <u>learn</u> and <u>learn</u> some more, until you can reel them off like a robot.

For more on times, see <u>page 2</u>.

Die Schule fängt um neun Uhr **an.** = School begins at <u>9.00</u>.

Die Schule ist um halb vier **aus.** = School ends at <u>3.30</u>.

Um elf haben wir Pause . = We have <u>break</u> <u>at 11</u>.

Lunch break: Mittagspause

BREAK'S OVER!!

Watch out — 'Stunde' can mean 'lesson' or 'hour'. Sneaky.

Wir haben acht **Stunden pro Tag.** = We have <u>8</u> lessons per day.

Jede Stunde dauert vierzig Minuten . = Each lesson lasts <u>forty minutes</u>.

Wir machen eine Stunde **Hausaufgaben pro Tag.** = We do <u>one hour</u> of homework every day.

Die Ferien — The holidays

So you can talk about just how much <u>lovely</u> holiday you get, learn this lot:

Wir haben im Sommer sechs Wochen **Ferien.** = We have <u>six weeks'</u> holiday <u>in the summer</u>.

at Christmas: zu Weihnachten
at Easter: zu Ostern

eight weeks': acht Wochen   *five days':* fünf Tage

Timetable this lot into your revision...

Next time your mum asks what you've been doing at school all day, why not reply in German... Don't worry, she already thinks you're weird. But this <u>is</u> all <u>useful</u> stuff and you'll feel like a right lemon if you don't <u>know it</u> when you need to. Remember the handy phrase '<u>pro Tag</u>' — it'll come in useful.

Talking About School

This page is full of extra little bits that follow on from the basic school conversation. They can crop up in <u>both</u> the <u>exams</u> and things like the <u>speaking</u> and <u>writing tasks</u> — without them you'll miss out on some <u>easy marks</u>.

Die Regeln — The Rules

This is all a bit more <u>tricky</u>, but if you want a top mark, you need to <u>learn it</u>.

Die Regeln sind streng.	= The rules are strict.

Mum says that I'll grow into it.

Billy's new school uniform was a little on the large side.

For more on clothes and colours, see <u>page 38</u>. For adjective endings, see <u>page 91</u>.

In der Schule müssen wir eine Uniform tragen.	= We must wear a uniform at school.

Unsere Uniform ist ein roter **Pulli, eine** graue **Hose, ein** weißes **Hemd und ein** grüner **Schlips.**	= Our uniform is a <u>red</u> jumper, <u>grey</u> trousers, a <u>white</u> shirt and a <u>green</u> tie.

In meiner Schultasche... — In my school bag...

<u>Learn</u> this list of stuff you might find in your <u>school bag</u> — and I'm not talking about half-eaten sandwiches and an unwashed PE kit.

Remember, plurals are always 'die'.

English	German	English	German
ballpoint pen:	der Kugelschreiber (-) / der Kuli (-s)	felt-tip pen:	der Filzstift (-e)
		scissors:	die Schere (-n)
pencil:	der Bleistift (-e)	exercise book:	das Heft (-e)
sharpener:	der Anspitzer (-)	writing pad:	der Schreibblock (-s or die Schreibblöcke)
rubber:	der Radiergummi (-s)	calculator:	der Taschenrechner (-)
ruler:	das Lineal (-e)	school book:	das Schulbuch (die Schulbücher)
fountain pen:	der Füller (-)	chalk:	die Kreide (-n)

Wo ist die Bibliothek? — Where is the library?

You might need to <u>describe</u> your school, or <u>listen</u> to somebody talking about theirs.

Wo ist die Turnhalle **?**	= Where is <u>the gym</u>?

For more on asking where something is see <u>page 49</u>.

In meiner Schule gibt es eine Bibliothek **,** eine Kantine **,** einen großen Sportplatz **und viele** Klassenzimmer **.**	= In my school there is <u>a library</u>, <u>a canteen</u>, <u>a large sports field</u> and many <u>classrooms</u>.

These are <u>accusative</u> endings. See <u>pages 90-91</u> for more info.

You can put any of the 'Places in School' in the white boxes.

PLACES IN SCHOOL			
assembly hall:	die Aula	corridor:	der Korridor (-e)
library:	die Bibliothek	staff room:	das Lehrerzimmer
canteen:	die Kantine	gymnasium:	die Turnhalle (-n)
classroom:	das Klassenzimmer (-)	sports hall:	die Sporthalle (-n)
laboratory:	das Labor (-s/-e)	sports field:	der Sportplatz (die Sportplätze)
language lab:	das Sprachlabor (-s/-e)	school yard:	der Schulhof

School rules — not as far as I'm concerned...

There's a lot of <u>vocab</u> for this section — make sure you <u>learn</u> it. The more you can reel off about your school, the better — <u>close the book</u> and see how much you can <u>remember</u>. Any Germans you meet will love to hear about your uniform, since they don't have them — pretty unfair.

Classroom Language

This stuff is really <u>important</u> if you're not always word-perfect at understanding German.
It's really useful to be able to ask someone to <u>repeat</u> something, or <u>spell out</u> a word you're not sure about.

Ich verstehe nicht — I don't understand

These phases can be <u>vital</u> in your <u>speaking assessment</u>. Even if the worst happens, it's far better to say
'I don't understand' <u>in German</u> than to shrug, give a cheesy smile and mumble something in English.

Verstehst du? = Do you understand? **Ich verstehe (nicht).** = I (don't) understand.

Ich verstehe nicht.

Wie spricht man das aus? = How do you pronounce that?

Wie sagt man das auf Deutsch? = How do you say that in German?

Wie buchstabiert man das? = How do you spell that?

Kannst du dieses Wort erklären? = <u>Can you</u> (informal) explain this word?

Können Sie das bitte wiederholen? = <u>Can you</u> (formal) repeat that, please?

Ist das richtig? = Is that right? **Das ist falsch.** = That's wrong.

Setzt euch! — Sit down!

These phrases are all in the <u>imperative</u>. For more info see <u>page 106</u>.

Learn these three short phrases to avoid the wrath of a scary teacher.

Steht auf! = Stand up! **Setzt euch!** = Sit down! **Seid ruhig!** = Be quiet!

Wie lange...? — How long...?

This isn't here because I like it. It's here because it could crop up somewhere. So <u>learn it</u>.

Wie lange lernst du schon Deutsch? = How long have you been learning German?

Be careful to use the present tense — you don't say 'I have been' as in English.

Ich lerne seit drei Jahren **Deutsch.** = I've been learning German for <u>three years</u>.

The word '<u>seit</u>' is really useful. It means '<u>since</u>' — this sentence literally translates as 'I am learning
German <u>since</u> three years'. You use 'seit' and the <u>present tense</u> to say how long you've been doing
anything — and you have to follow it with the <u>dative case</u> (see <u>pages 85 & 96</u>).

Mind your language...

Learn <u>all</u> these <u>dead useful</u> phrases for your speaking — even if you haven't a <u>clue</u> what your
teacher just said, you'll get credit for asking them to <u>repeat</u> something — and you'll save yourself
from an embarrassing silence at the same time. <u>Don't panic</u> — things like that happen to everyone.

More School Stuff

You're expected to know a little bit about how <u>German schools</u> work — you know,
broaden your <u>horizons</u> and all that. It's really quite <u>interesting</u> actually. No, honestly.

Meine Noten sind sehr gut — My grades are very good...

The German marking system works a bit <u>differently</u> to ours.
Instead of A, B, C etc., they have the numbers <u>1-6</u>.
It's pretty simple — just make sure you're familiar with it...

Quite frankly, if we'd had a 7 you'd have got it.

GERMAN GRADES	
1 = very good:	1 = sehr gut
2 = good:	2 = gut
3 = satisfactory:	3 = befriedigend
4 = adequate:	4 = ausreichend
5 = (fail) inadequate	5 = mangelhaft
6 = (fail) unsatisfactory	6 = ungenügend

Deutsche Schulen — German Schools...

At first glance, the German school system
seems <u>mind-bogglingly</u> complicated. <u>Don't</u>
panic — again, just make sure you're
<u>familiar</u> with the different terms.

FOR LITTLE ONES

der Kindergarten — *voluntary nursery school for 3-6 year olds*
die Grundschule — *primary school*

SECONDARY SCHOOLS

das Gymnasium — *takes the most academic pupils and prepares them for* das Abitur *('A-levels') and university*
die Hauptschule — *focuses on vocational and practical training*
die Realschule — *somewhere between a Gymnasium and a Hauptschule, covers a broader range of subjects*
die Gesamtschule — *combines all three of the schools above in one (like a comprehensive school in the UK)*
die Oberstufe — *sixth form, usually part of a Gymnasium*

Talk about your extracurricular activities

Time to admit to all those weird and wonderful hobbies — or pretend you do something that's <u>easy to say</u>.

Was machst du nach der Schule?   = What do you do after school?

For more on hobbies, see <u>pages 27-28</u>.

I'm a member of a theatre group: bin ich Mitglied einer Theatergruppe
I play in a band: spiele ich in einer Band

Nach der Schule spiele ich Sport .

= After school, <u>I play sport</u>.

It's easier to just
keep quiet about
some hobbies.

Das Gymnasium — not a school for gymnasts...

Now, there's quite a bit of school-related <u>vocab</u> on this page, so make sure you <u>learn</u> it. It may
be duller than a big dull thing, but if it comes up in an exam you'll be blummin' <u>grateful</u> for it.

Problems at School

OK, it's time to get it all off your chest — in German of course. This page'll help you to pour out your own troubles as well as listen with a sympathetic ear to someone else's. Lovely jubbly.

Wie geht es in der Schule? — How are things at school?

Es geht gut in der Schule, danke. = It's going well at school, thank you.

Es geht nicht so gut. = It's not going so well.

Schule kann sehr stressig sein. = School can be very stressful.

Was für Probleme gibt es in der Schule? — What sort of problems are there at school?

Come on now, you can tell me...

Ich habe Angst um meine Prüfungen. = I'm worried about my exams.

grades: Noten
results: Resultaten

Ich will nicht durchfallen. = I don't want to fail.

Manchmal finde ich die Arbeit schwierig. = Sometimes I find the work difficult.

lessons: den Unterricht

'Weil' sends the verb to the end of the sentence. See pages 9 and 89.

Ich kann nicht mit meinen Freunden ausgehen, weil ich zu viel Hausaufgaben habe.

= I can't go out with my friends because I have too much homework.

For more on issues that could affect you at school (like bullying and racism) see page 21.

Meine Eltern sind sehr streng. Ich muss schwer studieren.

= My parents are very strict. I must study hard.

It's a hard-knock life...

Those exam boards do like to get you talking through your troubles. Just think of it as free therapy. Now you could encounter other people talking about this little lot too. What a nice cheery interlude to the exam that'll be. Cover this page up and see how much of it you remember.

Work Experience

These two pages <u>encourage</u> you to think about your <u>future</u> in even more <u>detail</u> — heck, it's nearly a public service. If you can't quite manage to see your future without the aid of a crystal ball then get exercising your <u>imagination</u>.

Wo hast du das Arbeitspraktikum gemacht?
— Where did you do your work experience?

Work experience is quite simply <u>joyous</u> — I remember my week spent bored to death in a certain high street bank. At least it helped me <u>decide</u> there was no way on this Earth that banking was for me.

Put the place you worked in here.

Ich habe das **Arbeitspraktikum** bei **Siemens** gemacht.

work experience: das Betriebspraktikum

= I did my <u>work experience</u> at <u>Siemens</u>.

Ich habe **anderthalb Wochen** dort gearbeitet.

= I worked there for <u>a week and a half</u>.

one week: eine Woche
two weeks: zwei Wochen

Hat dir die Arbeit gefallen? — Did you like the work?

More <u>opinions</u> wanted — own up, did you or did you not like it..?

Die Arbeit hat mir gefallen. = I liked the work.

Die Arbeit hat mir nicht gefallen.

= I didn't like the work.

Die Arbeit **hat Spaß gemacht** . = The work <u>was fun</u>.

was stressful: war stressig
was interesting: war interessant

at home: zu Hause

Ich fühlte mich **einsam** . = I felt <u>lonely</u>.

Meine Kollegen waren **unfreundlich** .

= My colleagues were <u>unfriendly</u>.

very friendly: sehr freundlich
interesting: interessant

Are you experienced...

If you <u>haven't</u> done any work experience then you'd better <u>learn</u> how to say that in <u>German</u> in case you're asked — it's just 'ich habe <u>kein</u> Arbeitspraktikum gemacht', in case you're interested.

Plans for the Future

If you know what you're doing after school, great — if you haven't got a clue, <u>make it up</u>.   Job's a good 'un.

Was möchtest du nach der Schule machen?

— What would you like to do after school?

This stuff could easily come up — so you'd be daft not to learn it, really.

Ich möchte das Abitur machen.   = I would like to do 'A-levels'.

Abitur is the German equivalent of A-levels — except that they do more subjects than we do.

Ich möchte auf die Universität gehen.   = I would like to go to university.

Ich möchte Geografie studieren.   = I would like to study geography.

Ich möchte Lehrer werden.   = I would like to become a teacher.

Give short, sharp reasons for your answers

Work out an explanation for the answer you've given above.
Keep your explanations <u>short</u>, <u>clear</u> and <u>simple</u>.

For all the different school subjects see <u>page 68</u>.

maths: Mathe
music: Musik

Ich möchte Englisch studieren,
weil es interessant ist .

= I would like to study <u>English</u>,
because it <u>is interesting</u>.

is my favourite subject: mein Lieblingsfach ist
is fun: Spaß macht

a vet: Tierarzt
a pharmacist: Apotheker   For other jobs, see <u>page 76</u>.

Ich möchte Schauspieler werden,
weil ich das Theater mag.

= I would like to become <u>an actor</u>
because I like <u>the theatre</u>.

animals: Tiere
chemistry: Chemie

Use 'werden' (to become) to say what job you'd like to do.

Future plans — I'd like to build a time machine...

Things like the stuff on this page come up <u>year after year</u> — so if you've learnt it all, you'll be laughing. Use words like '<u>weil</u>' for extra marks. Being able to explain <u>why</u> is dead <u>impressive</u>.

Types of Job

There are more jobs here than you can shake a stick at — and you do need to be able to <u>recognise</u> <u>all</u> of them because any of the little blighters could pop up in your <u>listening</u> and <u>reading</u> exams.

You usually add an '-in' to make a job *feminine*

<u>Masculine/Feminine</u>
For most jobs, you add '-<u>in</u>' to the end to make it <u>feminine</u>. If the job ends in '-<u>mann</u>', change it to '-<u>frau</u>' for a women. Watch out for exceptions like 'Friseur/ Friseuse', and for places where you have to add an <u>umlaut</u> as well the <u>feminine ending</u>.

Architekt (m) **Architektin (f)** = architect

Hausmann (m) **Hausfrau (f)** = house husband/wife

Arzt (m) **Ärztin (f)** = doctor

The *gender* of a job depends on who's doing it...

You'll need to be able to <u>say</u> and <u>write</u> any of the jobs you and your family do — and <u>recognise</u> the rest when you see or hear them.

GREY-SUIT-TYPE JOBS

secretary:	Sekretär(in)
manager:	Manager(in)
civil servant:	Beamter/Beamtin

ARTY JOBS

actor/actress:	Schauspieler(in)
musician:	Musiker(in)
painter:	Maler(in)
singer:	Sänger(in)

Bill had come a long way from his days as a plumber.

MEDICAL JOBS

dentist:	Zahnarzt/Zahnärztin
pharmacist:	Apotheker(in)
nurse:	Krankenschwester (f), Krankenpfleger (m)
doctor:	Arzt/Ärztin
vet:	Tierarzt/Tierärztin

Don't worry Sir, we'll get that out for you...

As you'd expect, the gender of the job is always masculine for a man and feminine for a woman.

GET-YOUR-HANDS-DIRTY JOBS

mechanic:	Mechaniker(in)
electrician:	Elektriker(in)
plumber:	Klempner(in)
chef:	Koch/Köchin
butcher:	Metzger(in)
baker:	Bäcker(in)
farmer:	Bauer/Bäuerin
builder:	Bauarbeiter(in)

A LOAD MORE JOBS

engineer:	Ingenieur(in)
salesperson:	Verkäufer(in)
teacher:	Lehrer(in)
head teacher:	Direktor(in)
computer scientist:	Informatiker(in)
hairdresser:	Friseur/Friseuse
policeman/woman:	Polizist(in)
firefighter:	Feuerwehrmann/-frau
postman/woman:	Briefträger(in)
air steward(ess):	Steward(ess)
soldier:	Soldat(in)

OTHER JOB SITUATIONS

student:	Student(in)
work experience:	das Arbeitspraktikum
housewife/husband:	Hausfrau/-mann

Ingenieur — quite a job to pronounce...

<u>Don't</u> be put off by the long lists. Start off with the jobs you find <u>easiest</u>, and remember that you'll only need to <u>say</u> the ones people in your family do — but you should <u>understand</u> the rest. Make sure you know the <u>female</u> version of each job title — and watch out for those odd ones.

Jobs: Advantages and Disadvantages

Pretty <u>self-explanatory</u> this, really. You might have to talk about the <u>pros</u> and <u>cons</u> of <u>different jobs</u>, what <u>you</u> would or wouldn't like to do in the future and <u>why</u>, that sort of thing. So let's get cracking...

Was für Beruf möchtest du?

— *What sort of job would you like?*

Ich will im Freien *arbeiten.*   = I want to work <u>outdoors</u>.

with animals: mit Tieren
with people: mit Leuten
in a hospital: in einem Krankenhaus

Ich möchte selbständig sein.

= I'd like to be self-employed.

Ich möchte nicht gern... — I wouldn't like...

OK, so what <u>don't</u> you want to do?

Ich will nicht in einem Büro *arbeiten.*   = I don't want to work <u>in an office</u>.

with children: mit Kindern

a soldier: Soldat(in)   *a police officer:* Polizist(in)

Ich hätte nicht gern Lehrer(in) *sein.*   = I wouldn't like to be <u>a teacher</u>.

Das Gehalt ist gut, aber die Arbeit ist stressig .   = The pay is good, but the work is <u>stressful</u>.

difficult: schwer
boring: langweilig

Die Arbeitszeit ist zu lang.   = The working hours are too long.

Ich bin lieber... — I'd prefer to be...

Ich möchte einen Beruf, der interessanter *ist.*   = I'd like a job that's <u>more interesting</u>.

more creative: kreativer
not so stressful: nicht so stressig

\\\\\ ||||||||| /////
For more jobs, see <u>page 76</u>.
If you're a <u>girl</u>, you'll need
to use the <u>feminine form</u>.
///// ||||||||| \\\\\

Ich bin lieber Architekt(in) .   = I'd prefer to be <u>an architect</u>.

a musician: Musiker(in)

Advantage one: will be able to buy new trainers...

This page kinda relies on you having an <u>opinion</u>. The more <u>interesting</u> things you can think of to say, the more <u>marks</u> you'll get. Which is really the <u>whole point</u> after all. So get your <u>thinking-cap</u> on...

Working Abroad

Working abroad is the perfect opportunity to put all your finely-honed German skills to good use.
And a little jaunt in a Berlin Bäckerei will jazz up your CV nicely...

Arbeiten im Ausland... — Working abroad...

First up, a mite of work experience...

Nächstes Jahr, möchte ich ein Arbeitspraktikum in Deutschland machen.

= Next year, I would like to do a work experience placement in Germany.

Ich werde in einem Hotel **arbeiten.**   = I will work in a hotel.

a restaurant: einem Restaurant
an office: einem Büro

For more about work experience, see page 74.

Ich hätte gern mein Deutsch verbessern.   = I would like to improve my German.

Möchtest du im Ausland arbeiten?

— Would you like to work abroad?

Me? Work abroad? With all that sun, sand and sea? No thank you.
But just in case that appeals to you, here's how to tell people all about your plans...

For more on plans for the future, see page 75.

Austria: nach Österreich
Switzerland: in die Schweiz

Nach meinem Abitur werde ich nach Deutschland **fahren.**

= After my 'A-levels', I will go to Germany.

See page 43 for more countries.

You know, I think we're a little overdressed for the office.

Ich möchte ...   = I would like ...

... *to work in a hotel:*   in einem Hotel arbeiten
... *to travel:*   reisen
... *to meet new people:*   neue Leute kennen lernen

Es wird viel Spaß machen.   = It will be a lot of fun.

Mind the gap...

Obviously you need to know what to say if someone asks you whether you'd like to work abroad, but this is the sort of thing that crops up in reading and listening exams all the time, so you're likely to get to hear about other people's opinions on the matter too. You have been warned. Learn it.

Getting a Job

Everybody needs a job. This page is all about how to nab yourself one.
Don't say you never learn anything useful...

Stellenangebote... — Job vacancies...

You might see (and be asked questions about) adverts like these in the reading exam...

Stellenangebot:
Wir suchen Kellner/Kellnerin.
Samstag und Sonntag Abende
19.00-22.00

Sind Sie kreativ?
Möchten Sie mit Kindern arbeiten?
Wir brauchen Sie!
Telefonieren: 01 23 45

Wir suchen einen(e)Verkäufer/Verkäuferin.
Fünf Stunden pro Woche.
Sie müssen fleißig sein.
Näheres erfahren Sie unter Telefonnummer:
54 32 10

= Job offer:
We're looking for a waiter/waitress.
Saturday and Sunday evenings
7-10 pm

= Would you like to work
with children?
We need you!
Telephone: 01 23 45

= We are looking for a shop assistant.
5 hours a week.
You must be hard-working.
Telephone: 54 32 10

Mein Lebenslauf... — My C.V. ...

Well you can't apply for that dream job without one...

LEBENSLAUF

Name: Marie Dalton
Adresse: 12 Pemberton Way, Loxley, Barnshire, BA22 3PM
Tel: 01234 567 765
E-mail: E-mail: m.dalton@wahooworld.co.uk

Ausbildung:
2007: A-Levels: Philosophie (A), Mathe (B), Deutsch (B)

Berufstätigkeit:
Seit 2007: Verkäuferin für Loxley Leisure

Sonstige Kenntnisse: Erste-Hilfe-Qualifikation
Führerschein
Ich spreche Englisch, Deutsch und Italienisch

CURRICULUM VITAE

Name: Marie Dalton
Address: 12 Pemberton Way, Loxley, Barnshire, BA22 3PM
Tel: 01234 567 765
E-mail: E-mail: m.dalton@wahooworld.co.uk

Education:
2007: A-Levels: Philosophy (A), Maths (B), German (B)

Employment:
Since 2007: Sales assistant for Loxley Leisure

Other Skills: First aid qualification
Driving licence
I speak English, German and Italian

Stellenbewerbung... — Job application...

You'll need a covering letter to go with that CV of yours, so here's a nice little example for you.
For more on writing formal letters, see page 11.

Dear Mr Meyer,

With regard to your advert in the Berliner Zeitung,
I would like to apply for the position of sales
manager. I enclose my CV.

I hope to hear from you soon,

Marie Dalton.

Marie Dalton
12 Pemberton Way
Loxley
Barnshire
BA22 3PM

Loxley, den 28.5.2009

Herr Meyer
Meyer Moden
Charlottenstraße 261
10234 Berlin

Sehr geehrter Herr Meyer,

in Bezug auf Ihren Stellenangebot in der Berliner Zeitung
möchte ich mich um die Stelle als Verkaufsleiterin bewerben.
Ich lege meinen Lebenslauf bei.

Ich hoffe, bald wieder von Ihnen zu hören,

Marie Dalton.

Wanted: chocolate taster, no experience necessary...

This page is pretty darn important, so make sure you're familiar with it. You could get given
this sort of thing in the reading exam, or you might have to write something similar yourself.

Getting A Job

Right, here are examples of answers to the basic questions you could expect to be asked in a job interview. You don't have to learn these sentences parrot-fashion. Use them to make up some answers for yourself.

Ein Interview — An Interview

A lot of the stuff in your GCSEs will be addressed to you informally — you'll be called 'du' and not 'Sie'. In a job interview you would always be 'Sie'. Better get used to it.

| Wie heissen Sie? | = What is your name? | Wie alt sind Sie? | = How old are you? |

Sie interessieren sich für welche Stelle?
— Which position are you interested in?

Ich möchte gern bei der Touristeninformation in Münster arbeiten.

= I'd like to work in the tourist information office in Münster.

Warum möchten Sie diese Stelle?
— Why do you want this job?

Ich möchte gern mein Deutsch verbessern.   = I'd like to improve my German.

Ich interessiere mich für Tourismus.   = I'm interested in tourism.

qualifications: Qualifikationen

Ich habe die nötige Erfahrung und ich bin sehr fleißig.

= I have the necessary experience and I'm very hardworking.

Was haben Sie in der Schule gemacht?
— What did you do at school?

Ich habe eine Gesamtschule in Fareham besucht.   = I went to a comprehensive in Fareham.

In der Schule waren Deutsch und Französisch meine Lieblingsfächer.   = German and French were my favourite subjects at school.

"Selling Yourself" — sounds dodgy...

Most of this stuff isn't new, but get used to dealing with it in this context. There's loads of clever stuff to say here and you can use a lot of it when you're writing job applications too (see page 79).

Telephones

Phone calls come up <u>all the time</u>. So make sure you <u>learn</u> this page. You need to know what to say when you <u>call</u> someone, how to <u>answer</u> the phone, and about passing a <u>message</u> on.

Telefonieren — Telephoning

Was ist deine Telefonnummer? = What is <u>your</u> telephone number?

Use '<u>deine</u>' if you're talking to someone you know well. You might hear '<u>Ihre</u>' used in more formal conversations.

Meine Telefonnummer ist achtundzwanzig, neunzehn, vierundfünfzig .

See page 1 for more numbers.

= My telephone number is <u>281954</u>.

Please call me (informal):
Rufst du mich an, bitte.

Rufen Sie mich an, bitte. = Please call me (formal).

Hallo, ist Lisa da? — Hello, is Lisa there?

Say this when you <u>answer</u> the phone: **Hallo! Reginald am Apparat.** =Hello! <u>Reginald</u> speaking.

These are for when <u>you</u> phone someone:

Hallo! Hier spricht Andreas. = Hello! Andreas speaking.

Kann ich mit Lisa sprechen? = Can I speak to Lisa?

Der Anrufbeantworter — The answering machine

You have to understand phone <u>messages</u>, and be able to leave one. This is your <u>bog-standard</u> phone message:

Hallo, hier spricht Gabriele. Meine Telefonnummer ist neunundfünfzig, neunzehn, sechsundfünfzig. Kann Bob mich um 20 Uhr zurückrufen? Danke. Auf Wiederhören.

= Hello, Gabriele speaking.
My phone number is 59 19 56.
Can Bob call me back at 8 pm?
Thanks, bye.

You say 'Auf Wieder<u>hören</u>' not 'Auf Wieder<u>sehen</u>' when you're on the phone.

Ich höre zu... — I'm listening...

More stuff you might hear on the phone...

Darf ich etwas ausrichten? = May I take a message?

Sie haben die falsche Nummer. = You've got the wrong number.

Sorry, wrong number.: Es tut mir Leid, falsch verbunden.

Telefonieren — what a load of phoney rubbish...

Whether you end up having to <u>talk</u> on the phone in a <u>speaking assessment</u>, or <u>listen</u> to a phone conversation in your <u>listening exam</u>, this stuff is pretty <u>crucial</u>. Get learning those set phrases.

The Business World

This page covers all those little consumer-y type problems you might find yourself with. Which is nice.

Können Sie mir helfen, bitte? — Can you help me please?

Here's how to ask for information:

Entschuldigung, wo kann ich einen Klempner finden?

= Excuse me, where can I find a plumber?

a hairdresser:	einen Friseur
a dentist:	einen Zahnarzt
a chemist:	einen Drogist

Sie sollten im Telefonbuch suchen.

= You should look in the phone book.

on the internet:	im Internet
in the post office:	in der Post
in the tourist information office:	im Verkehrsamt

Es gibt ein Problem mit meiner Bestellung...
— There's a problem with my order...

Here's an example of a phone conversation between a vendor and a customer:

Verkäuferin:

'Hallo, ComputerWelt. Erika am Apparat.'
Hello, ComputerWelt. Erika speaking.

'Also, kann ich Ihren Name haben, bitte?'
OK, can I have your name please?

'Danke schön. Ich habe Ihre Bestellung gefunden. Was für Problem gibt es?'
Thank you. I've found your order. What's the problem?

'Es tut mir Leid, mein Herr. Morgen früh werden wir Ihnen die Tastatur schicken.'
I'm sorry sir. We'll send the keyboard to you tomorrow morning.'

'Bitte schön. Sonst noch etwas?'
You're welcome. Will there be anything else?

'Auf Wiederhören.'
Goodbye.

Kunde:

'Hallo. Letzte Woche habe ich einen Computer bestellt, aber es gibt ein Problem mit er.'
Hello. I ordered a computer last week, but there's a problem with it.

'Ja. Mein Name ist Hans Klaus.'
Yes. My name is Hans Klaus.

'Sie haben den Computer und den Bildschirm geschickt, aber die Tastatur ist noch nicht angekommen.'
You've sent the computer and the monitor, but the keyboard hasn't arrived yet.

For more computer vocab, see page 33.

'Das ist toll. Danke schön.'
That's great. Thank you.

'Nein danke, das ist alles. Auf Wiederhören.'
No thanks, that's everything. Goodbye.

Business World — Britain's dullest theme park...

The phone conversation above is the sort of thing you might have to listen to in an exam. Obviously there are loads of different possible scenarios, but they'll all use vocab you should already be familiar with. The important thing is not to get thrown by hearing it in a different context.

Revision Summary

You really need to know this stuff. Go through these questions — if you can answer them all without looking anything up, then give yourself a pat on the back and <u>smile widely</u>. If there are some you can't do, <u>look them up</u>. Then try again. And again. Keep going till you can do 'em all.

1) Say what all your GCSE subjects are in German (or as many as possible).
   I guess one of them will be Deutsch...

2) Roland goes to school by bike, but Sonia goes by car.
   How would each of them tell the other in German how they get to school?

3) How would you say in German that your lunch break begins at 12:45 pm and lasts one hour?

4) Marie wants to know what your school is like.
   Tell her in German that there's an assembly hall, a canteen, a library and a large sports field.

5) Your teacher has just said a long sentence in German and you don't understand.
   How would you ask her to repeat it?

6) How do you say in German that you've been learning French for five years
   and German for four years?

7) Your German friend Michael is looking a bit down. You ask him if he has any problems at
   school and he tells you that he finds the work difficult and he's worried about his exams.
   Write down what he's told you in German.

8) Write a full German sentence explaining where you did your work experience.
   If you haven't done work experience then write that down.

9) Write the German for whether you liked your work experience and why.

10) Monika wants to study physics.
    How does she say that she wants to do the Abitur and become a teacher?

11) Write down the German names of four occupations that you might possibly do in the future and
    four that you would never ever want to do. Say why you wouldn't want to do one of the jobs.

12) Your friend Nadja wants to go abroad next year to work in a hotel and improve her German.
    How would she say this in German?

13) How would you write a reply in German to a job advert for an assistant in a bookshop?
    Explain why you want the job and why you think you're suitable.

14) Your brother's friend leaves a message on the answering machine. He says that it's James
    and that his telephone number is 94 84 27. He also asks if your brother can ring him back
    at 2 pm. Before deleting the message, you decide to wind your brother up by writing it out
    in German. What would you put?

CASES: NOMINATIVE AND ACCUSATIVE | ## The Wonderful Truth About Cases

Cases are a pain in the neck. They can seem pretty <u>nasty</u>, but if you get the <u>four</u> cases <u>clear</u> in your head, it'll make the <u>rest</u> of this grammar stuff a lot <u>easier</u>. And that could make a <u>real</u> difference to your <u>marks</u>.

'Cases' <u>mean you have to change words</u> to fit

The <u>only</u> reason you need to <u>know</u> about cases is that some words have to be <u>spelt differently</u> depending on what case they're in.

EXAMPLE: | Der rote Hund | folgt | dem roten Hund | .   = <u>The red dog</u> follows <u>the red dog</u>.

<u>Both</u> these bits <u>mean</u> the <u>same</u> thing ('the red dog') but some of the <u>letters</u> in the words have <u>changed</u>, because the second bit is in a <u>different case</u> from the first bit.

This page and the next page are about <u>when</u> you use the different cases.
<u>How</u> you <u>change the words</u> to fit the case is on <u>pages 85-86</u>, <u>90-92</u> & <u>96-99</u>.

<u>The most often-used cases are</u>

<u>the</u> nominative <u>and the</u> accusative

<u>What case</u> a bit of the sentence is <u>depends</u> on what the words are <u>doing</u> in the sentence:

| Hermann | isst | Eis | .   = <u>Hermann</u> eats <u>ice cream</u>.

...this bit of the sentence is <u>who is doing it</u>...
(<u>Hermann</u> — or Harold, or Henry or the Queen of Sheba or whoever — is eating ice cream.)

This bit of the sentence is <u>what is going on</u>... it's the <u>verb</u>. (Hermann is <u>eating</u> ice cream, or buying it, or drinking it or whatever.)

...and this bit of the sentence is <u>who or what it is done to</u>. (Hermann is eating <u>ice cream</u>, or biscuits, or toast or whatever.)

= NOMINATIVE CASE

This is kind of the <u>normal common-or-garden</u> case. If you look up a word in the <u>dictionary</u>, it'll tell you what it is in the <u>nominative</u> case.

Her Majesty the Queen of Sheba

= ACCUSATIVE CASE

That's the secret of all this <u>mysterious-sounding</u> 'nominative' and 'accusative' cases business.
Or, in <u>two lines</u>...

The Golden Rules
<u>NOMINATIVE</u> = who (or what) is <u>DOING</u> it
<u>ACCUSATIVE</u> = who (or what) it's <u>DONE TO</u>

I learnt German grammar — just in case...

<u>Cases</u> are one of the <u>trickiest</u> things about GCSE German, so get this stuff <u>learnt</u> and you're well on your way to success. The <u>nominative</u> and <u>accusative</u> cases are an <u>absolute must</u> — go over this page till you can write down those <u>golden rules</u> from <u>memory</u>. For top marks, read on...

More Cases and Noun Endings

Top Tip Number 1 in a series of 1 — read page 84 before you tackle this page.
The genitive and the dative cases sound hard, but they're just as easy (☺) as the accusative.

The genitive case — things like Bob's, Sue's...

When you want to say things like Bob's, the milkman's, my mum's... you use the genitive case.

Der Wagen meines Vaters .

= My father's car.
(The car of my father.)

= GENITIVE CASE

Hermann isst das Eis des Mädchens .

= Hermann eats the girl's ice cream.
(Hermann eats the ice cream of the girl.)

= GENITIVE CASE

NB: Stuff like 'my dad's a doctor' isn't in the genitive — it's short for 'my dad is a doctor',
which has got nothing to do with a doctor belonging to your dad.

The dative case — to Bob, from Bob...

Make sure you totally understand the accusative case (see page 84), then look at these sentences:

Hermann schreibt einen Brief .

= Hermann writes a letter.

= ACCUSATIVE CASE

Hermann schreibt einem Freund .

= Hermann writes to a friend.

= DATIVE CASE

1. These sentences are different. The friend is not being written — he's being written to.
   So the letter is more directly involved in the action than the friend is. That's why they're in different cases.

2. Usually when you've got a word like 'on', 'at', 'from', 'of', 'for', 'in', 'by', 'with', 'to'...
   in the English translation, that's when you need to use the dative in the German.
   (Sometimes you need to use the accusative with words like this though — see page 96.)

"To Jane:
It's not you,
it's me..."

3. There are a few sneaky exceptions that don't have one of those words,
   but are in the dative case anyway — see page 97.

Nouns get these endings to fit the case

Words for people and objects (nouns — see page 86) sometimes have to change, depending
on what case they're in. You change them by adding on the right ending from this table.

You don't have to change them very often — that's why the table is mostly blank.

EXAMPLE:
Normally, 'apples' =
'Äpfel', but in the
dative plural it's 'Äpfeln'.

Ich singe den Äpfeln.

= I sing to the apples.

NB: If it already ends in 'n', you don't add an
extra 'n'. For example, streets = Straßen,
and in the plural dative it's still Straßen.

Watch out though. Some words don't follow this pattern
— if you've learnt some different endings for a word,
then make sure you use those instead.

Endings for nouns in different cases			
	Masculine	Feminine	Neuter	Plural
Nominative	–	–	–	–
Accusative	–	–	–	–
Genitive	-s	–	-s	–
Dative	–	–	–	-n

There are quite a few words where you have to add '-es' rather than
'-s' in the genitive — they tend to end in '-s', '-ß', '-x' or '-z'.

To Bob, Happy Birthday, from Bob...

Not my idea of fun, but you need to learn about the genitive and dative cases to know when to
change the endings on things like nouns and describing words. Make sure you know that table too.

NOUNS	# Words for People and Objects

Scary — it looks like there's a lot on this page, but it's all <u>pretty simple</u> stuff about words for <u>people</u> and <u>objects</u> — nouns. Just about <u>every</u> sentence has a noun in it, so this is <u>dead important</u>.

Every German noun starts with a capital letter

In English, words like Richard, London and January always have capital letters.
In German <u>absolutely every noun</u> (<u>object</u>, <u>person</u> or <u>place</u>) has a capital letter.

EXAMPLE: *apple:* der <u>A</u>pfel   *elephant:* der <u>E</u>lefant   *cow:* die <u>K</u>uh   *baby:* das <u>B</u>aby

I said USE A CAPITAL!!

Every German noun is masculine, feminine or neuter

It's no good just knowing the German words for things — you have to know whether each one's <u>masculine</u>, <u>feminine</u> or <u>neuter</u> too.

DER, DIE AND DAS
A <u>DER</u> in front means it's <u>masculine</u>
(in the <u>nominative</u> case).
<u>DIE</u> in front = <u>feminine</u>
(or a plural).
<u>DAS</u> in front = <u>neuter</u>.

The Golden Rule
Each time you <u>learn</u> a <u>word</u>, remember a <u>der</u>, <u>die</u> or <u>das</u> to go with it — don't think 'cow = Kuh', think 'cow = <u>die</u> Kuh'.

Whether a word is <u>masculine</u>, <u>feminine</u> or <u>neuter</u> affects loads of stuff. You have to use different words for 'the' and 'a', and you have to change adjectives (like big, red, shiny) to fit the word.

EXAMPLE: *a big apple:* <u>ein</u> großer Apfel (masculine)
a big cow: <u>eine</u> große Kuh (feminine)

See <u>pages 90-91</u> for more on this.

These rules help you guess what a word is

If you have to guess if a word is <u>masculine</u>, <u>feminine</u> or <u>neuter</u>, these are good rules of thumb.

Rules of Thumb for Masculine, Feminine and Neuter Nouns

MASCULINE NOUNS: nouns that end:	FEMININE NOUNS: nouns that end:	NEUTER NOUNS: nouns that end:
-el -us -ling -ismus -er also: male people, days, months, seasons	-ie -heit -tion -ei -keit -sion -ung -schaft -tät also: most female people	-chen -um -lein -ment also: infinitives of verbs used as nouns, e.g. das Turnen (gymnastics)

Weak nouns have weird endings

Some <u>masculine nouns</u> take <u>different endings</u> to the ones at the bottom of <u>page 85</u>. It's annoying, but as long as you learn which words they are then it's not too tricky — the endings are actually dead simple.

person: der Mensch
man: der Herr

Nominative	der Mensch / der Herr
Accusative	den Mensch<u>en</u> / den Herr<u>n</u>

Tobias lehnt gegen den Herr<u>n</u>.

= Tobias leans against the man.

Nouns ending in '<u>-e</u>' are usually <u>feminine</u>, so watch out for these sneaky <u>masculine nouns</u> that end in '<u>-e</u>':

name: der Name
boy: der Junge

Nominative	der Name / der Junge
Accusative	den Name<u>n</u> / den Junge<u>n</u>

Sie küsst den Junge<u>n</u>.

= She kisses the boy.

I didn't know about this gender thing — it's neuter me...

Blimey. This page is pretty full of stuff, but it <u>all</u> boils down to this — <u>every time</u> you learn a word in German, you <u>have</u> to learn whether it's <u>der</u>, <u>die</u> or <u>das</u>, and you have to learn what its <u>plural</u> is...

Words for People and Objects

The stuff on page 86 is fine if you've only got one of something. But if you've got more than one then it's not going to be much help to you. That's why you also need to know about plurals...

When you learn a German word, learn the plural too

In English you generally add an 's' to make things plural, e.g. boy + s = boys.
German is much trickier — there are nine main ways to make something plural. Yuck.

Nine Ways To Make Something Plural

No change, *der Metzger → die Metzger (butchers).*
Add an <u>umlaut</u> to the stressed syllable, *der Apfel → die Äpfel (apples).*
Add an '**e**' on the end, *der Tag → die Tage (days).*
Add an <u>umlaut</u> and an '**e**' on the end, *die Hand → die Hände (hands).*
Add an '**er**' on the end, *das Lied → die Lieder (songs).*
Add an <u>umlaut</u> and an '**er**' on the end, *das Haus → die Häuser (houses).*
Add an '**s**' on the end, *das Sofa → die Sofas (sofas).*
Add an '**n**' on the end, *die Straße → die Straßen (streets).*
Add an '**en**' on the end, *das Bett → die Betten (beds).*

Most feminine nouns do one of these two things.

Whatever gender a noun is, its plural is always a 'die' word (in the nominative and accusative cases, anyway).

*Top tip for plurals:
Each time you learn a word, learn how to make it into a plural too.*

1 When you look them up in a dictionary, you get the plural in brackets like this: 'Bett (-en)', which means 'Betten', or 'Hand (¨e)', which means 'Hände'.

2 A compound noun is a noun made up of two or more words stuck together. When you add an umlaut, it goes on the stressed syllable of the 'root word' (the last bit of the compound noun). E.g. the plural of 'die Bratwurst' is 'die Bratwürste', not 'die Brätwurste'.

Some adjectives can be used as nouns

In English you can use some adjectives (see pages 91-92) as nouns — e.g. the good, the bad and the ugly.
Well, it's the same in German...

A noun is an object, person or place.

Der Deutsche *ist sehr freundlich.*

The old man: Der Alte
The pretty girl: Die Hübsche

= The German (man) is very friendly.

You can do this with any adjective.

Because the adjective is now a noun, it has to have a capital letter.

You don't always have to say whether you're talking about a man or a woman in German, because it's clear from whether you use der (for a man) or die (for a woman).

The noun has the same ending that it would have if it was still an adjective (see page 91 for the tables of endings).

Nouns the time to get those plurals learnt...

Nouns, nouns, nouns — you just can't move for them, they're absolutely everywhere. It's a pain, but if you can get your head round them now then you're on to a winner. You know what to do...

WORD ORDER	# *Word Order*

You need to write proper sentences — so I'm going to tell you where to stick your words...

The *five commandments* for German word order

❶ Put the verb second

The <u>verb</u> (the action word) almost <u>always</u> goes <u>second</u> in a German sentence.

E.g. **Ich** *spiele* **Fußball.** = I <u>play</u> football.

Get thy words in the right order.

The word order in simple sentences like this is the same as in English.
The person or thing <u>doing the action</u> goes <u>first</u>, and the <u>verb</u> comes <u>second</u>.

The word order for questions and instructions is different. See <u>pages 4 and 106</u> for more details.

❷ <u>Keep</u> the verb second

As long as you <u>keep</u> the verb <u>second</u>, you can be fairly <u>flexible</u> with the word order in German.

E.g. If you want to say 'I play football at the weekend', you can say...

Ich *spiele* **am Wochenende Fußball.** = (I <u>play</u> at the weekend football.)

OR

Am Wochenende *spiele* **ich Fußball.** = (At the weekend <u>play</u> I football.)

<u>Swap</u> the verb and the person doing the action around, so that the verb is still the <u>second 'bit'</u> in the sentence (although in this case, <u>not</u> the second <u>word</u>).

❸ If there are two verbs, send one to the end

If you've got two verbs, treat the <u>first</u> one as <u>normal</u> and send the <u>second</u> one to the <u>end</u> of the sentence.

E.g. **Ich** *werde* **nach Deutschland** *fahren*. = (I <u>will</u> to Germany <u>go</u>.)

❹ Remember — WHEN, HOW, WHERE

At school, you might have heard the phrase 'Time, Manner, Place' — it just means that if you want to describe <u>WHEN</u>, <u>HOW</u> and <u>WHERE</u> you do something, that's <u>exactly</u> the order you have to say it in.

E.g. **Ich gehe** *heute Abend* *mit meinen Freunden* *ins Kino*.
　　　　　 <u>WHEN</u> (Time)　　　 <u>HOW</u> (Manner)　　 <u>WHERE</u> (Place)

= (I go <u>this evening with</u> <u>my friends to the cinema</u>.)

❺ Watch out for 'joining words' — they can change word order

Some <u>conjunctions</u> (joining words) can mess up the word order by sending the verb to the <u>end</u> of the sentence. Watch out though — they <u>don't all</u> do this. See <u>page 89</u> for more info.

E.g. **Ich schwimme,** *weil* **ich sportlich** *bin*. = (I swim because I sporty <u>am</u>.)

'<u>Weil</u>' ('because') is a joining word which sends the verb ('<u>bin</u>') to the end of the sentence.

W then O then R then D — That's word order...

This word order malarkey might <u>seem</u> mightily confusing at first glance, but trust me — if you <u>follow these rules</u> you won't go far wrong. When you're writing anything in German, always keep this lot in mind — and give your work a <u>quick squiz</u> afterwards to check you've got it all right.

Words to Join Up Phrases

These words help you to join phrases together to make more interesting sentences.
The examiners will be looking for things like this — show them how clever you are.

Und = And

Ich spiele gern Fußball. **AND** Ich spiele gern Rugby. = Ich spiele gern Fußball _und_ Rugby.

= I like playing football. = I like playing rugby. = I like playing football _and_ rugby.

Oder = Or

Er spielt jeden Tag Fußball. **OR** Er spielt jeden Tag Rugby. = Er spielt jeden Tag Fußball _oder_ Rugby.

= He plays football every day. = He plays rugby every day. = He plays football _or_ rugby every day.

Aber = But

Ich spiele gern Fußball. **BUT** Ich spiele nicht gern Rugby. = Ich spiele gern Fußball, _aber_ ich spiele nicht gern Rugby.

= I like playing football. = I don't like playing rugby. = I like playing football _but_ I don't like playing rugby.

Some joining words affect the word order

The words below work in the same way as the stuff above, but with one difference —
if there's a verb (see page 100) after them, then that verb gets sent to the end of the sentence.

Weil = Because

Bob geht ins Kino, _weil_ Hermann ~~geht ins Kino~~ geht.

= Bob is going to the cinema, because Hermann is going to the cinema.

There's another way to say 'because' — you don't see it as often as
'weil', but it's dead useful because it doesn't change the word order:

Denn = Because

Hermann geht einkaufen, _denn_ Bob geht ins Kino.

= Hermann is going shopping, because Bob is going to the cinema.

All these joining words (and
'aber' above) need a comma
before them in a sentence.

MORE JOINING WORDS

although:	obwohl
if/when:	wenn
before:	bevor
until:	bis
that:	dass
when:	als

I can do joined-up letters, but joined-up phrases...

At last, a fairly easy page. You use 'and', 'or' and 'but' all the time when you're speaking English
— if you don't use them when you speak German, you'll sound a bit weird. Which no-one wants.

ARTICLES — 'The' and 'A'

'The' and 'a' are really important words — you use them all the time.
They're tricky in German, because there are different ones for <u>masculine</u>, <u>feminine</u> or <u>neuter</u> words
(see <u>page 86</u>), and for different <u>cases</u> (nominative, accusative or whatever — see <u>pages 84-85</u>).

'The' — start by learning der, die, das, die

1) In English there's just <u>one</u> word for 'the' — simple.
2) In German, you need to know whether you want the <u>masculine</u>, <u>feminine</u> or <u>neuter</u>, and what <u>case</u> you want (<u>nominative</u>, <u>accusative</u>, <u>genitive</u> or <u>dative</u>).
3) Start by learning the <u>first line</u> — <u>der</u>, <u>die</u>, <u>das</u>, <u>die</u>. You <u>absolutely</u> have to know those ones.

Table of the German words for 'THE'

	masculine	feminine	neuter	plural
nominative	der	die	das	die
accusative	den	die	das	die
genitive	des	der	des	der
dative	dem	der	dem	den

This table is pretty scary, but you <u>have</u> to know it <u>all</u> to get everything right in your writing tasks. Cover the page, and <u>write</u> the table out. When you can get it <u>right</u> every time, you'll <u>know</u> which word to use when you're <u>writing</u> or <u>speaking</u> in German.

EXAMPLES

Masculine, nominative:

Der Apfel ist rot.

= <u>The</u> apple is red.

Plural, nominative:

Die Äpfel sind rot.

= <u>The</u> apples are red.

Masculine, dative:

Ich singe dem Apfel ein Lied.

= I sing a song <u>to the</u> apple.

Plural, dative:

Ich singe den Äpfeln ein Lied.

= I sing a song <u>to the</u> apples.

For why the last one is <u>Äpfeln</u> instead of <u>Äpfel</u>, see <u>page 85</u>.

'A' — start by learning ein, eine, ein

1) Like the German for 'the', the word for 'a' is different for <u>masculine</u>, <u>feminine</u> or <u>neuter</u>, and for different <u>cases</u> (<u>nominative</u>, <u>accusative</u>, <u>genitive</u> or <u>dative</u>).
2) Start by learning the <u>first line</u> — <u>ein</u>, <u>eine</u>, <u>ein</u>. When you've got that sorted, move on to the other ones.

Table of the German words for 'A'

	masculine	feminine	neuter
nominative	ein	eine	ein
accusative	einen	eine	ein
genitive	eines	einer	eines
dative	einem	einer	einem

EXAMPLES

Masculine, nominative:
Ein Hund. = <u>A</u> dog.

Feminine, nominative:
Eine Katze. = <u>A</u> cat.

Masculine, accusative:
Ich habe einen Hund.
= I have <u>a</u> dog.

Feminine, accusative:
Ich habe eine Katze.
= I have <u>a</u> cat.

Der-die-das — sounds like German trainers...

It's stuff like this that makes me glad I speak English — just one word for 'the', and one word* for 'a'... But there's no getting round it, you <u>need</u> all this stuff to be able to write in <u>German</u>. You have to be able to <u>cover up</u> the page and write out <u>both tables</u> — keep on practising till you can.

* Well, two words actually — let's not forget about 'an'.

Words to Describe Things

ADJECTIVES

Make your sentences a lot more interesting (which means more marks) with some describing words (adjectives).

Adjectives that go after the noun don't change

When the describing word (the adjective — e.g. red) is somewhere after the word it's describing (e.g. apple), it doesn't change at all.

Der Apfel ist rot. = The apple is red.

Das Haus ist rot. = The house is red.

Die Lampe ist rot. = The lamp is red.

For how to add things like 'very' and 'a bit', see page 93.

You just use the basic describing word, without any endings.

Endings for when the adjective comes before the noun

In the sentences below, red comes before apples, so you have to give it the right ending from this table:

Plural, accusative: *Ich habe rote Äpfel.* = I have red apples.

These endings are also used if the describing word comes after a number bigger than one, or after viele (many), wenige (few), einige (some), etwas (something), or nichts (nothing).

Plural, nominative: *Zwei rote Äpfel.* = Two red apples.

Ich habe viele große Äpfel. = I have many big apples.

Endings for adjectives before the noun

	masculine	feminine	neuter	plural
nominative	roter	rote	rotes	rote
accusative	roten	rote	rotes	rote
genitive	roten	roter	roten	roter
dative	rotem	roter	rotem	roten

You almost never need to use the ones shaded in grey.

There are special endings after 'the'

You've got to add these endings if the describing word comes after 'the' (der, die, das etc.), 'dieser' (this), 'jeder' (each/every), 'beide' (both) 'welcher' (which) and alle (all).

Masculine, nominative:

Der rote Apfel. = The red apple.

Dieser kleine Apfel ist gut. = This small apple is good.

Endings for adjectives after definite articles

	masculine	feminine	neuter	plural
nominative	rote	rote	rote	roten
accusative	roten	rote	rote	roten
genitive	roten	roten	roten	roten
dative	roten	roten	roten	roten

There are special endings after 'a' and belonging words

You need these endings when the describing word comes after ein (a, or one) or kein (no, or none), or after belonging words like mein, dein, sein, ihr...

Masculine, nominative:

Der rote Apfel. = The red apple.

Mein roter Apfel ist gut. = My red apple is good.

Endings for adjectives after indefinite articles

	masculine	feminine	neuter	plural
nominative	roter	rote	rotes	roten
accusative	roten	rote	rotes	roten
genitive	roten	roten	roten	roten
dative	roten	roten	roten	roten

This is a roten way to spend an evening...

But at least once you know this stuff, you know it. Lots of the words end in '-en', which makes it easier. Learn the nominative and accusative part of each table first — they're the ones you'll need most often.

Section 7 — Grammar

ADJECTIVES | _**Words to Describe Things**_

Here are 20 <u>describing words</u> to whet your appetite. You need to know how to say <u>my</u>, <u>his</u>, <u>your</u>... too.

20 TOP DESCRIBING WORDS

big/tall:	groß	_sad:_	traurig	_beautiful:_ schön		_fast:_	schnell
small/short:	klein	_easy:_	einfach	_ugly:_	hässlich	_slow:_	langsam
long:	lang	_difficult:_	schwierig	_old:_	alt	_interesting:_	interessant
wide:	breit	_good:_	gut	_young:_	jung	_boring:_	langweilig
happy:	glücklich	_bad:_	schlecht	_new:_	neu	_normal:_	normal
			(or schlimm)				

See <u>page 38</u> for colours.

<u>My, your, our</u> — _**words for who it belongs to**_

You have to be able to <u>use</u> and <u>understand</u> these words to say that something <u>belongs</u> to someone:

But <u>watch out</u> — they need the right <u>ending</u> to go with the <u>object</u> you're talking about (they're the same as the ein/eine/ein table — see <u>page 90</u> — except there's an extra 'plurals' column):

THE POSSESSIVE ADJECTIVES

mein:	_my_	unser:	_our_
dein:	_your (informal singular)_	euer:	_your (informal plural)_
sein:	_his_	Ihr:	_your (formal singular & plural)_
ihr:	_her_		
sein:	_its_	ihr:	_their_

Table of endings for 'mein'

	masc	fem	neut	plural
nominative	mein	meine	mein	meine
accusative	meinen	meine	mein	meine
genitive	meines	meiner	meines	meiner
dative	meinem	meiner	meinem	meinen

Here's an example sentence for each <u>case</u>, using the <u>right ending</u> for '<u>mein</u>'.

<u>Meine</u> Tasche ist blau. = My bag is blue.

Ich mag <u>mein</u> Fahrrad. = I like my bike.

Das Auto <u>meines</u> Vaters ist rot. = My father's car is red. (The car of my father is red.)

Ich schreibe <u>meinen</u> Eltern. = I write to my parents.

This is the neat bit — <u>all</u> of them use the <u>same endings</u> as 'mein' does.

E.g.

<u>Deine</u> Tasche ist blau. = Your bag is blue.

<u>Seine</u> Tasche ist blau. = His bag is blue.

<u>Unsere</u> Tasche ist blau. = Our bag is blue.

<u>Welcher, dieser</u> <u>and jeder</u> — _**Which, this and every**_

3 dead handy words that you need to be able to <u>use</u>.

Welche Schokolade schmeckt besser?

Which apple: Welcher Apfel
Which bread: Welches Brot

= <u>Which chocolate</u> tastes better?

The <u>endings</u> follow the same pattern as '<u>der</u>' — look at the <u>last letter</u> for each word in the first table on <u>page 90</u>, e.g. the last line would be diese<u>m</u>, diese<u>r</u>, diese<u>m</u>, diese<u>n</u>.

Actually I think you'll find that Camilla belongs to me.

Diese Katze gehört Camilla. = This cat belongs to Camilla.

Jeder Lehrer ist blau. = Every teacher is blue.

**The happy student revised the interesting German...**

You need words like '<u>my</u>' all the time — for talking about your family, friends, describing yourself... The 20 top <u>describing words</u> are a good start, but you'll need loads more — <u>learn</u> each new one you come across. And remember, '<u>welcher</u>' = which, '<u>dieser</u>' = this and '<u>jeder</u>' = each or every.

Making Sentences More Interesting | ADVERBS

The two pages before this are about describing objects e.g. 'the red bus'. This page is about describing things you do, e.g. 'I speak German perfectly', and about adding more info, e.g. 'I speak German almost perfectly'.

Make your sentences better by saying how you do things

In English, you don't say 'We speak strange' — you add an '-ly' onto the end to say 'We speak strangely'.
In German, you don't have to do anything — you just stick the describing word in as it is.

EXAMPLE: Ich fahre langsam. = I drive slowly (slow).

badly (bad): schlecht
quickly (fast): schnell

'Langsam' is just the German word for 'slow' — you can use any other suitable describing word here.

Ich singe. = I sing.

Ich singe laut. = I sing loudly.

Ich singe schlecht. = I sing badly.

La la la laAAAA

Use one of these words to give even more detail

Stick one of these words in front of the describing word in a sentence to add detail and impress your teacher:

You can use them for sentences saying how something is done...

Ich fahre sehr langsam.
= I drive very slowly.

quite: ganz/ziemlich
slightly: etwas/ein wenig
a bit: ein bisschen
too: zu
a lot: viel

...and for sentences about what something is like.

Bob ist ganz glücklich.
= Bob is quite happy.

These words give extra detail about time and place

You'll get even more marks if you can add information about when you do something...

sometimes: ab und zu
now and then: dann und wann
as soon as possible: so bald wie möglich
last week: letzte Woche
next weekend: nächtes Wochenende

Ich gehe oft ins Kino. = I often go to the cinema.

Manchmal isst sie Birnen. = Sometimes she eats pears.

The word order changes because the verb has to come second. See page 88.

...and where it is.

Ich wohne hier. = I live here.

Ich wohne nicht gern dort. = I don't like living there.

I speak German good (but English less good)...

For once, saying something in German is easier than saying it in English. To say how you do something, you just stick in a describing word — no endings, no faffing, brilliant. Practise taking a few German sentences and adding extra detail... then use 'em in the assessments.

COMPARATIVES AND SUPERLATIVES

Comparing Things

A lot of the time you don't just want to say that something is <u>big</u>, or <u>red</u> or whatever, you want to say that it's the <u>biggest</u>, or <u>bigger than</u> someone else's...

How to say smaller, smallest

In <u>English</u> you say small, small<u>er</u>, small<u>est</u>.
It's <u>almost</u> the <u>same</u> in German:

So here the adjective acts as the <u>noun</u>, just like in English — and of course all German nouns get a <u>capital letter</u>.

Anna ist klein .	Hermann ist kleiner .	Sina ist der Kleinste .
= Anna is <u>small</u>.	= Hermann is <u>smaller</u>.	= Sina is the <u>smallest</u>.

Stem	*Stem + '-er'*	*Stem + 'der', 'die' or 'das' and '-(e)ste'*
old: alt	⟹ older: älter	⟹ oldest: der/die/das Älteste
interesting: interessant	⟹ more interesting: interessanter	⟹ most interesting: der/die/das Interessanteste

For most words, '-ste' is added, but sometimes it's '-<u>este</u>', to make it easier to pronounce.
(You <u>can't</u> miss out the <u>der</u>, <u>die</u> or <u>das</u> — you <u>CAN'T</u> say 'Ethel ist Interessanteste'.)

You can do this with almost any <u>describing word</u>. A lot of <u>short</u> ones get an added <u>umlaut</u> like 'alt' does. Check out the top of <u>page 92</u> for more describing words.

Anna   Hermann   Sina

Just like in English, there are <u>odd ones out</u> — for example, you <u>don't</u> say good, gooder, goodest...

good: gut ⟹ better: <u>besser</u> ⟹ the best: der/die/das <u>Beste</u>

big (or tall): groß ⟹ bigger: <u>größer</u> ⟹ the biggest: der/die/das Größ<u>te</u> ⟹ | Liz ist die Größte . |

high: hoch ⟹ higher: <u>höher</u> ⟹ the highest: der/die/das Höchste

= Liz is <u>the tallest</u>.

much/a lot: viel ⟹ more: <u>mehr</u> ⟹ the most: der/die/das Meiste

near: nah ⟹ nearer: <u>näher</u> ⟹ the nearest: der/die/das Nächste

You <u>don't</u> need to use a <u>capital</u> if the adjective goes <u>before</u> a noun e.g. 'the tallest tree' would be 'der größte Baum'.

Describing words that end in '-er' (like 'älter') are <u>comparative adjectives</u>.
If you use them <u>before</u> a noun, they need <u>adjective endings</u>, like on <u>page 91</u>.

Learn these four great ways of comparing things

Jo ist älter als Ed.	Jo ist weniger alt als Ed.	Jo ist so alt wie Ed.	Jo ist ebenso alt wie Ed.
= Jo is older <u>than</u> Ed.	= Jo is <u>less</u> old <u>than</u> Ed.	= Jo is <u>as</u> old <u>as</u> Ed.	= Jo is <u>just as</u> old <u>as</u> Ed.

You can compare how people do things

It's all relative you know...

If you're talking about how someone <u>does</u> something, it's almost <u>the same</u> as the stuff above:

Einstein fährt schnell .	Bob fährt schneller .	Ethel fährt am schnellsten
= Einstein drives <u>quickly</u>.	= Bob drives <u>more quickly</u>.	= Ethel drives <u>the quickest</u>.

Here's one more <u>odd one out</u> you need to know:

The bit that's different is the <u>last one</u>.
You add '<u>am</u>' and '<u>-(e)sten</u>'.
(Instead of 'der', 'die' or 'das', and '-(e)ste'.)

willingly: gern ⟹ preferably: <u>lieber</u> ⟹ best of all: <u>am liebsten</u>

| Ich spreche lieber Deutsch. | = I <u>prefer</u> speaking German. |

'Best' is also slightly different: To say someone does something <u>best</u>, it's '<u>am besten</u>'.

Sneaky Wee Words

This stuff looks horrendous, but you've got to learn it if you want good marks.

TO — zu, or nach

Where we use 'to', German speakers often use 'zu':

(zum = zu dem — see page 96)

Komm zu mir. = Come to me.

zum Bahnhof gehen = to go to the station

For 'the train to London' (and other towns), it's 'nach':

der Zug nach London = the train to London

For things like to go, to do, use the infinitive — see page 100. E.g. gehen = to go, machen = to make.

They sometimes use 'an', 'auf' or 'in' too.

AT — an, bei, um or zu

Where we use 'at', in German it's usually 'an': an der Universität = at university

Sometimes 'bei' is used: bei einer Party = at a party

For 'at home', it's 'zu': zu Hause = at home   For times it's 'um': um acht Uhr = at 8 o'clock

ON — an, auf

Where we use 'on', in German it tends to be 'an':

am = an dem — see page 96.

an der Wand = on the wall

am Montag = on Monday

For 'on foot', it's 'zu': zu Fuß = on foot

Die Katze ist auf dem Elch.

For on top of something, it's 'auf': Das Buch ist auf dem Tisch. = The book is on the table.

FROM — von or aus

When we use 'from' in English, they usually use 'von' in German, including for where someone/thing has come from recently:

Der Zug ist von London gekommen. = The train has come from London.

For where someone/thing is from originally, it's 'aus': Ich komme aus England. = I come from England.

For 'made from' — see 'made of' on page 96.

IN — in or an

Where we use 'in', German speakers also tend to use 'in':

in Deutschland = in Germany   im Bett. = in bed   (im = in dem — see page 96)

For in the morning/evening, it's 'an': am Morgen. = in the morning   (am = an dem — see page 96)

This page is a gift to you, from me...

It may seem like a pain in the neck having to remember where and when to use all these little words, but trust me — if you get it right, it'll bag you loads of lovely marks in your writing assessment.

Sneaky Wee Words

Yep, more sneaky wee words (or <u>prepositions</u> as they're known by grammar fanatics).
Make sure you learn <u>which</u> words to use and <u>where</u> — it's not always obvious from the English.

OF — 'von', 'aus' or left out

Where we use 'of', the German is usually '<u>von</u>':

ein Freund von mir   = a friend of mine

For 'made of', it's '<u>aus</u>':

aus Wolle   = made of wool

Es besteht aus Wolle.

You <u>leave it out</u> of dates: *der erste März*   = the first of March   See <u>page 3</u> for more on dates.

It's often <u>left out</u> in <u>genitive</u> sentences too: *einer der Besten*   = one of the best

FOR — für, or seit

Where we use 'for', German speakers usually use '<u>für</u>':

ein Geschenk für mich   = a present for me

For time amounts in the past, it's '<u>seit</u>':

Ich habe sie seit zwei Jahren nicht gesehen.   = I haven't seen her for two years.

An dem ⇒ am — short forms

Some of the words on these two pages get <u>shortened</u>
when they go with dem, das or der. For example:

an dem ersten Januar ⇒ *am ersten Januar*

= on the first of January

SHORT FORMS

an dem = am	bei dem = beim
an das = ans	von dem = vom
in dem = im	zu der = zur
in das = ins	zu dem = zum

To be 100% right, you have to use the right case

When they're in a sentence, these words <u>change the case</u> (pages 84-85) of the stuff that comes <u>after</u> them.
To be sure <u>what case</u> to use, you have to <u>learn</u> these lists.

Some words change the case to <u>genitive</u> — you won't have to use them, but you should <u>recognise</u> them.

ACCUSATIVE

bis = *till, by*
durch = *through*
für = *for*
gegen = *against, about*
ohne = *without*
um = *round, around, at*

DATIVE

aus = *from, out of, made of*
bei = *at, near*
gegenüber = *opposite, facing*
mit = *with*
nach = *to, after*
seit = *since, for*
von = *from, of*
zu = *to, at*

DATIVE OR ACCUSATIVE

an = *to, on, in, at*
auf = *on, to, at*
entlang = *along*
hinter = *after, behind*
in = *in, to*
neben = *next to, beside*
über = *via, above, over*
unter = *under, among*
vor = *before, ago, in front of*

GENITIVE

außerhalb = *outside of*
statt = *instead of*
trotz = *despite*
während = *during, while*
wegen = *because of*

For prepositions which use <u>either</u> the dative <u>or</u> accusative case, use the <u>accusative</u>
when what you're talking about is <u>moving</u> and the <u>dative</u> if there's <u>no movement</u>.

E.g. *Die Katze schläft hinter* dem *Sofa.*   = The cat sleeps behind <u>the</u> (dative) sofa. ⟵ The cat <u>isn't</u> moving.

Die Katze läuft hinter das *Sofa.*   = The cat runs behind <u>the</u> (accusative) sofa. ⟵ The cat <u>is</u> moving.

In, out, shake it all about...

The <u>take-home message</u> here? To get the most marks, you have to use the <u>right case</u>. If you're
not sure about cases, go and <u>look them up</u> (on <u>pages 84-85</u>) — they're pretty darned important.

I, You, Him, Them...

Dead handy page, this. <u>Pronouns</u> are everywhere, and they can make your German sound much more natural.

Pronouns _replace_ nouns

<u>Pronouns</u> are words like '<u>you</u>', '<u>she</u>' or '<u>them</u>'.

'<u>He</u>' is a <u>pronoun</u>. It means you don't have to say '<u>Dave</u>' again.

> Dave has a new job at the poodle parlour. (He) likes shaving poodles.

You use different sets of pronouns for different cases.
If you're not sure about this case stuff, look at <u>pages 84-85</u>.

You use _ich (I) in the_ nominative _case_

You need 'I', 'you', 'he', etc. the most often — for the <u>main person/thing</u> in a sentence (the subject).
Learn them all, or you'll be <u>totally scuppered</u> in the exams.

THE NOMINATIVE CASE			
_I:_	ich	_we:_	wir
you (informal sing.):	du	_you (inf. plu.):_	ihr
_he:_	er	_you_	
she:	sie	_(formal sing. & plu.):_	Sie
_it:_	es	_they:_	sie

> Der Hund beißt den Kamm. = The dog bites the comb.

> (Er) beißt den Kamm. = <u>He</u> bites the comb.

The <u>nominative</u> case is explained on <u>page 84</u>.

Remember — in English there's only one word for '<u>you</u>', but in German there are <u>loads</u>.

The <u>nominative</u> words for <u>you</u> are:
<u>du</u> = you (informal singular) — for talking to <u>one person</u> you know well, or another young person
<u>ihr</u> = you (informal plural) — the same as 'du' but for talking to <u>more than one person</u>
<u>Sie</u> = you (formal singular and plural) — for talking to <u>one or more</u> older people who you don't know well or who you should be polite to

You use _mich (me) in the_ accusative _case_

These are for the person/thing in a sentence that's <u>having the action done to it</u> (the direct object).
This is the <u>accusative</u> case.

THE ACCUSATIVE CASE			
_me:_	mich	_us:_	uns
you (informal sing.):	dich	_you (inf. plu.):_	euch
him:	ihn	_you (formal sing. & plu.):_	Sie
her:	sie	_them:_	sie
_it:_	es		

> Dave kitzelt den Hund. = Dave tickles the dog.

> Dave kitzelt (ihn). = Dave tickles <u>him</u>.

<u>Accusative</u> case — see <u>page 84</u>.

There are special words for _to me, to her, to them_

For things that need 'to', 'by', 'with' or 'from' — like writing <u>to someone</u> — the <u>dative</u> case is used.

> Der Hund gibt Dave den Kamm. = The dog gives the comb to Dave.

> Der Hund gibt (ihm) den Kamm. = The dog gives the comb <u>to him</u>.

THE DATIVE CASE			
_to me:_	mir	_to us:_	uns
to you (inf. sing.):	dir	_to you (inf. plu.):_	euch
to him:	ihm	_to you (formal sing. & plu.):_	Ihnen
to her:	ihr	_to them:_	ihnen
_to it:_	ihm		

See <u>page 85</u> for more on the <u>dative</u> case.

These examiners are really taking the mich now...

So, <u>grammar's not much fun</u> — big deal. <u>You're</u> the one who wants to make it through your GCSE, and to do that <u>you</u> need to learn this stuff — sorry, but there's <u>no escape</u>. Shut the book, write down each lot of pronouns, then write a German sentence using each one.

PRONOUNS

Someone, No One, Who? & What?

You need to know things like 'one' or 'someone' and ask questions like 'who?' or 'what?'.
So you'd better get stuck in. <u>This bit's dead easy</u>, so don't whinge — just do it.

The German word 'man' means 'one', not 'man'

Get this in your skull now — '<u>man</u>' means '<u>one</u>'. It <u>doesn't</u> mean the English word 'man'.
German speakers use 'man' more than we use 'one' in English — it isn't posh at all.

| Wie sagt | man | das auf Deutsch? |

= How does <u>one</u> say that in German?
(How do you say that in German?)

In English, we usually say 'you' instead of 'one' in everyday conversation.

Someone, anyone — *jemand*

The word for '<u>someone</u>' is the same as for '<u>anyone</u>' — '<u>jemand</u>'.

| Kann | jemand | helfen? |

= Can <u>someone</u> help?

| ... wenn | jemand | mitmachen will... |

= ... if <u>anyone</u> wants to join in...

No one — *niemand*

'<u>Niemand</u>' means '<u>no one</u>'. It's a bit like 'jemand', so don't get them mixed up.
Remember — '<u>n</u>iemand' begins with an '<u>n</u>' for no one.

| Warum ist | niemand | gekommen? |

= Why has <u>no one</u> come?

Warum ist niemand gekommen?

Wer? — Who? / Was? — What? / Was für? What sort of?

Get learning these useful <u>question words</u>...

| Wer | sitzt auf der Katze? |

= <u>Who</u> is sitting on the cat?

Meow?

| Was | is das? |

= <u>What</u> is that?

| Was für | eine Katze ist es? |

= <u>What sort of</u> cat is it?

Look at <u>page 4</u> for more about questions.

'<u>Who</u>' changes for the <u>different cases</u> — you'll see 'wer' the most, but make sure you recognise all three.

'Who' in the different cases		
nominative	*who*	wer
accusative	*whom*	wen
dative	*to whom*	wem

| Wer | ist das? | = <u>Who</u> is that?

| Wen | liebst du? | = <u>Whom</u> do you love?

| Zu | wem | höre ich? | = <u>To whom</u> am I listening?

Man, this is interesting...

Shut the book and scribble down the words for '<u>one</u>', '<u>someone</u>'/ '<u>anyone</u>', '<u>no one</u>', '<u>who</u>',
'<u>what</u>' and '<u>what sort of</u>' Keep going till you <u>know them all</u>. This wer/wen/wem malarkey is really
<u>top level</u> stuff — but you'll look <u>dead impressive</u> if you know what they mean. Wunderbar.

'That', 'Which', 'Whom' & 'Whose'

Tricky stuff this, but learn it and you'll nab yourself loads of juicy marks.

Relative pronouns — 'that', 'which', 'whom', 'whose'

Words like 'that', 'which', 'whom' and 'whose' are relative pronouns — they relate back to the thing you're talking about. This is the kind of thing I mean:

The dog, which had dug up my sprouts, looked guilty.

The 'which' refers back to the dog.

In German the relative clause (the bit with the relative pronoun in) is separated from the rest of the sentence by commas.

Relative pronouns change the word order. They send the verb to the end of the relative clause (the bit inside the commas).

The pronoun refers to 'der Mann'. The verb goes to the end of the clause.

Der Mann, der in der Ecke sitzt, ist ganz klein.

= The man who sits in the corner is quite small.

You've got to use the right one...

It's a bit tricky working out which relative pronoun you need to use in German, but as you'd probably expect, it just depends on the noun (page 86) and its case (pages 84-85).

In the nominative case, the relative pronoun is just 'der', 'die' or 'das':

Die Katze, die mich gebissen hat, war schwarz.

= The cat that bit me was black.

It's 'die Katze', so the pronoun is also 'die'.

Der Hund, der mich gebissen hat, war schwarz.

= The dog that bit me was black.

It's 'der Hund', so the pronoun is also 'der'.

It all depends on the case...

Don't panic: you don't have to be able to use these in your writing — just recognise them if they come up.

In the accusative case — the relative pronoun can be 'den', 'die', or 'das':

Der Mann, den ich gesehen habe, war witzig.

= The man whom I saw was funny.

In the genitive case — the relative pronoun is either 'dessen' or 'deren':

Das Pferd, dessen Bein gebrochen ist, ist traurig.

= The horse whose leg is broken is sad.

In the dative case — the relative pronoun can be 'dem', 'der' or 'denen':

Die Jungen, denen er eine Frage stellt, verstehen nicht.

= The boys (to) whom he asks a question don't understand.

'Was' can be used as a relative pronoun too

'Was' can be used as a relative pronoun — for example, you use it after 'alles', 'nichts', 'etwas' 'vieles' and 'weniges'.

E.g. Alles, was der Lehrer sagte, war interessant.

= Everything that the teacher said was interesting.

The chair that is broken is mine — typical...

This is really grim stuff, but you only need to be able to use relative pronouns in the nominative case. You should be able to recognise the others though if they come up in a reading exam or the like.

VERBS, TENSES
AND THE INFINITIVE

| VERBS, TENSES AND THE INFINITIVE | # The Lowdown on Verbs |

<u>Verbs</u> are pretty darn <u>important</u>. Make sure you know all this stuff — it'll make your life a whole lot <u>easier</u> over the next few pages.

Verbs are action words — they tell you what's going on

Ethel | plays | football every Saturday.

**
This is a <u>verb</u>.
/////////////

These are <u>verbs</u>.

Alex | wished | his grandma | preferred | knitting.

There's a load of stuff you need to know about verbs, but it all boils down to these next <u>two points</u>:

1) You have different words for *different times*

You say things differently if they happened last week, or aren't going to happen till tomorrow.

HAS ALREADY HAPPENED
I went to Tibet last year.
I have been to Tibet.
I have gone to Tibet.

PAST

HAPPENING NOW
I go to Tibet.
I am going to Tibet.

PRESENT

HASN'T HAPPENED YET
I go to Tibet on Monday.
I will go to Tibet.
I will be going to Tibet.

FUTURE

**
These are in different <u>tenses</u>, in case you're interested.
///////////////////////

2) You have different words for *different people*

You <u>don't</u> say '<u>I plays</u> football' — it'd be daft. You change the verb to fit the person.

HAPPENING TO ME
I am miserable.

HAPPENING TO YOU
You are miserable.

HAPPENING TO HER
She is miserable.

**
I bet you love these cheery examples.
///////////

OK, you get the picture — verbs are dead important. You use them all the time, so you need to learn all this stuff. That's why I go on about them so much.

The word you look up in the dictionary *means 'to...'*

When you want to say '<u>I dance</u>' in German, you start by looking up '<u>dance</u>' in the dictionary. But you can't just use the <u>first word</u> you find — there's more to it than that...

When you look up a verb <u>in the dictionary</u>, this is what you get:

to go: gehen
to dance: tanzen

For grammar fans, this is called the <u>infinitive</u>.

You're <u>not supposed</u> to just use the verb in its <u>raw state</u> — you have to <u>change</u> it so it's right for the <u>person</u> and <u>time</u> you're talking about. The different verb forms are covered on the next few pages.

Action words round the edge — a verbacious border...

I'm not kidding — this is <u>mega-important</u> stuff. Over the next few pages I've given you <u>loads of stuff</u> on verbs because there's loads you <u>need to know</u>. Some of it's easy, some of it's tricky — but if you <u>don't understand</u> the things on <u>this page</u> before you start, you'll have <u>no chance</u>.

Verbs in the Present Tense

If you want <u>loads of marks</u>, you've got to make your German sound <u>natural</u>. One <u>sure-fire way</u> to lose marks is to say something <u>daft</u> like '<u>I likes to gone swimming</u>.' Here's how you can avoid it...

The present tense is what's happening now

The <u>present tense</u> is the <u>easy</u> one — and you use it more than anything else, so it's <u>dead important</u>. The <u>endings are the same</u> for all <u>regular verbs</u>. 'Machen' is regular, so here it is with its endings...

The first bit ('<u>mach</u>') doesn't change.

inf. = informal
frml. = formal
sing. = singular
plu. = plural

MACHEN = TO DO OR MAKE	
I make =	ich mach**e**
you (inf. sing.) make =	du mach**st**
he makes =	er mach**t**
she makes =	sie mach**t**
it makes =	es mach**t**
we make =	wir mach**en**
you (inf. plu.) make =	ihr mach**t**
you (frml. sing. & plu.)	
make =	Sie mach**en**
they make =	sie mach**en**

So if you want to say something like 'He <u>makes</u> me happy', it's dead easy:

1) Start by <u>knocking off</u> the '<u>-en</u>': mach~~en~~

2) Then <u>add on</u> the <u>new ending</u>: mach<u>t</u>

3) And — <u>ta da</u>...

> **Er macht mich glücklich.**

> = He makes me happy.

Here are some more <u>regular verbs</u> — these verbs all follow the same pattern as '<u>machen</u>'. Learn it and you've learnt them all.

to ask:	fragen	*to book:* buchen		*to explain:*	erklären
to believe:	glauben	*to buy:* kaufen		*to dance:*	tanzen

Watch out — There's a catch...

Some regular verbs don't end in '-en' — they end in '<u>-rn</u>' or '<u>-ln</u>'.
Still, it's no problem — they follow nearly the same rules. Just watch out for missing '-e's.

'-rn' verbs:

You <u>miss</u> <u>out</u> the '<u>-e</u>' before the '-r' for ich.

FEIERN = TO CELEBRATE			
ich	feir**e**	*wir*	feier**n**
du	feier**st**	*ihr*	feier**t**
er	feier**t**	*Sie*	feier**n**
sie	feier**t**	*sie*	feier**n**
es	feier**t**		

You only add '<u>-n</u>' instead of '-en' for wir, Sie and sie.

'-ln' verbs:

<u>Lose</u> the '<u>-e</u>' before the 'l' for ich.

SEGELN = TO SAIL			
ich	segl**e**	*wir*	segel**n**
du	segel**st**	*ihr*	segel**t**
er	segel**t**	*Sie*	segel**n**
sie	segel**t**	*sie*	segel**n**
es	segel**t**		

Add '<u>-n</u>' not '-en' for wir, Sie and sie.

Just learn one of these types, and you can use the same rules for the other. Great stuff.

Instead of 'I go swimming', say 'I go to swim'

You sometimes need to say '<u>I go swimming</u>' rather than just 'I swim' — so you need <u>two</u> verbs. For the <u>first</u> verb, you need to put it in the <u>right form</u> for the <u>person</u>, but for the <u>second</u>, you just need the <u>infinitive</u>.

to swim = *schwimmen*

I <u>go</u> = *Ich gehe*

 *Ich gehe schwimmen* . = I go <u>swimming</u>.

bowling:	kegeln	*jogging:* joggen	*dancing:* tanzen	*camping:*	zelten
hiking:	wandern	*running:* laufen	*fishing:* angeln	*skiing:*	Ski fahren / Ski laufen

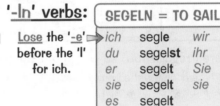

Great, I love presents...

OK, this is pretty easy stuff. <u>Learn the endings</u> for normal, regular '<u>en</u>' verbs, and remember that they go a <u>bit weird</u> for '<u>-rn</u>' and '<u>-ln</u>' ones. And when you say '<u>I go swimming</u>', the 'go' works like normal and the '<u>swimming</u>' part needs to be the <u>infinitive</u> (the one you look up <u>in the dictionary</u>).

PRESENT TENSE

Verbs in the Present Tense

You could be conned into thinking nearly all verbs are regular (see page 101). But in fact, loads aren't.

Sein, haben, fahren **and** essen **are** irregular

Verbs that don't follow the same pattern as regular verbs are called 'irregular verbs' (how original). Most of the really useful verbs are irregular — d'oh. Anyway, here are four that you'll need most...

inf. = informal
frml. = formal
sing. = singular
plu. = plural

'Sein' means 'to be' — it's probably the most important verb in the world... ever. So learn it.

① SEIN = TO BE

I am =	ich	bin	wir	sind	= we are
you (inf. sing.) are =	du	bist	ihr	seid	= you (inf. plu.) are
he is =	er	ist	Sie	sind	= you (frml. sing. & plu.) are
she is =	sie	ist	sie	sind	= they are
it is =	es	ist			

② HABEN = TO HAVE

I have =	ich	habe	wir	haben	= we have
you (inf. sing.) have =	du	hast	ihr	habt	= you (inf. plu.) have
he has =	er	hat	Sie	haben	= you (frml. sing. & plu.) have
she has =	sie	hat	sie	haben	= they have
it has =	es	hat			

You'll need this verb loads — 'haben' ('to have'). It's easy to learn, so there's no excuse.

'Fahren' means 'to go or drive'. You need it loads for travel and holidays (section 4).

③ FAHREN = TO GO, TO DRIVE

I go =	ich	fahre	wir	fahren	= we go
you (inf. sing.) go =	du	fährst	ihr	fahrt	= you (inf. plu.) go
he goes =	er	fährt	Sie	fahren	= you (frml. sing. & plu.) go
she goes =	sie	fährt	sie	fahren	= they go
it goes =	es	fährt			

④ ESSEN = TO EAT

I eat =	ich	esse	wir	essen	= we eat
you (inf. sing.) eat =	du	isst	ihr	esst	= you (inf. plu.) eat
he eats =	er	isst	Sie	essen	= you (frml. sing. & plu.) eat
she eats =	sie	isst	sie	essen	= they eat
it eats =	es	isst			

These are the weird bits.

'Essen' ('to eat') nearly follows the rules. But not quite...

All these verbs are irregular too, so watch out for them:

to be called (he is called): heißen (er heißt)   *to give (he gives):*   geben (er gibt)
to know (he knows):   wissen (er weiß)   *to wear, carry (he wears, carries):* tragen (er trägt)

Some verbs **make you use the** dative case

You normally only need the dative case when you're saying 'to something or someone'.

Diese Zähne gehören **mir**, nicht **dir**.   = These teeth belong to me, not to you.

But some German verbs always need the dative case. You'd think 'I help the elephants' would be 'ich helfe die Elefanten' — but it isn't. 'Helfen' ('to help') is one of the awkward verbs that need the dative case, so you say:

You use 'den' because 'Elefanten' is plural and 'helfen' needs the dative.

Ich helfe **den** Elefanten.   = I help the elephants.

These verbs all need the dative case:

to thank: danken   *to hurt:* wehtun   *to believe:* glauben   *to answer:* antworten
to follow: folgen   *to write to:* schreiben   *to congratulate:* gratulieren

No fahrt jokes please...

People talk about German being easy, because it's got loads of rules to follow. But it's a right pain that loads of words don't follow the rules. And of course it's all the really important stuff that doesn't — how typical. (So the only way forward is simply to learn all this stuff. Sorry.)

Talking About the Future

You'll need to talk about things that are <u>going to happen</u> at some point in the <u>future</u>. There are <u>two ways</u> you can do it — and the first one's a <u>piece of cake</u>, so I'd learn that first if I were you.

1) You can use the present tense to talk about the future

Wahey — an easy bit. All you need to do to say something is <u>going</u> to happen in the <u>future</u>, is to say it <u>does happen</u> and then say <u>when</u> it's going to happen. Brilliant.

HAPPENING NOW ➤ **Ich fahre nach Wales.** = I am going to Wales.

GOING TO HAPPEN ➤ **Ich fahre** *nächstes Jahr* **nach Wales.** = I am going to Wales <u>next year</u>.

This tells you <u>when</u> it's going to happen.

You can stick the time bit anywhere in the sentence, as long as you don't break the rules of word order — see <u>page 88</u>.

See <u>pages 101-102</u> for all the stuff on the present tense.

Next week: Nächste Woche   On Monday: Am Montag
Tomorrow: Morgen   This summer: Diesen Sommer

Nächstes Jahr *fahre ich nach Wales.* = <u>Next year</u> I'm going to Wales.

"When you said you wanted to 'see Wales', this is not what I had in mind."

2) You can use 'werden' — 'to be going to do...'

This part's slightly trickier. '<u>Ich werde</u>' means '<u>I will</u>'.
You put the right form of '<u>werden</u>' for the person, and the <u>infinitive</u> of the other verb <u>at the end</u>.

Ich werde *nächstes Jahr nach Wales* **fahren** . = <u>I will go</u> to Wales next year.

WERDEN = TO BE GOING TO DO

I will =	ich	werde	wir	werden =	we will
you (inf. sing.) will =	du	wirst	ihr	werdet =	you (inf. plu.) will
he will =	er	wird	Sie	werden =	you (frml. sing. & plu.) will
she will =	sie	wird	sie	werden =	they will
it will =	es	wird			

inf. = informal
frml. = formal
sing. = singular
plu. = plural

Look at <u>page 100</u> to find out about the <u>infinitive</u>.

'<u>Werden</u>' is an <u>irregular</u> verb. That's why the endings are all a bit weird.

Another example:

Eines Tages *wirst du* **in die Schule** *gehen* . = One day <u>you will go</u> to school.

To infinitive, and beyond...

I reckon the top one's easier, because you only have to <u>learn the words</u> for <u>times in the future</u> and bung them in a <u>bog-standard sentence</u>. '<u>Werden</u>' is a bit trickier, but you should be able to use that too.

PERFECT TENSE | # Talking About the Past

Sometimes they'll want you to talk about stuff that's <u>already happened</u> — so you need to say '<u>I have done</u>...' or '<u>I did</u>...', instead of '<u>I do</u>...'. (It's the <u>perfect</u> tense, if you're interested.)

Was hast du gemacht? — What have you done?

The past tense looks a bit fiddly, I agree, but it's easy once you've learnt the basics.

You usually start with '<u>I have</u>'.

Then you have to put the <u>past tense</u> bit on the end.

Ich habe einen Sessel gekauft.

= <u>I (have) bought</u> an armchair.

See <u>page 102</u> for all the endings for 'haben'.

THE PAST TENSE BIT

It looks a bit weird — but for <u>regular verbs</u> it's a doddle to work out.

① Add 'ge' to the start. ② Knock off the 'en'. ③ Add 't' on the end.

ge ⟹ kaufen ⟸ t
gekauft

Here are some more examples — they all work the same way.

Er hat mich nichts gefragt. = <u>He has asked</u> me nothing.

to do, make:	machen ⟹	gemacht:	done, made
to ask:	fragen ⟹	gefragt:	asked
to book:	buchen ⟹	gebucht:	booked
to clean:	putzen ⟹	geputzt:	cleaned

Sie haben in den Ferien viel gemacht.

= <u>They did</u> lots in the holidays.

Irregular verbs don't follow the pattern

OK, great — that's easy... then you get to the ones that <u>don't</u> follow the pattern (<u>irregular</u> verbs). Marvellous. Still, no way round it — you've just got to drum these into that brain of yours.

to sleep:	schlafen ⟹	geschlafen	to see:	sehen ⟹	gesehen
to take:	nehmen ⟹	genommen	to sing:	singen ⟹	gesungen
to eat:	essen ⟹	gegessen	to break:	brechen ⟹	gebrochen
to drink:	trinken ⟹	getrunken	to receive:	bekommen ⟹	bekommen
to give:	geben ⟹	gegeben	to forget:	vergessen ⟹	vergessen
to bring:	bringen ⟹	gebracht	to understand:	verstehen ⟹	verstanden

} Watch out — no 'ge' on the front.

For grammar fans — these are past participles.

Ist sie gegangen — Has she gone?

Some verbs need '<u>I am</u>' instead of '<u>I have</u>' to make them <u>past tense</u>. It's kind of like you're saying '<u>I am gone</u>' instead of '<u>I have gone</u>'.

She is: Sie ist
They are: Sie sind ⟹ Ich bin gegangen. = <u>I have gone / I went</u>.

See <u>page 102</u> for different forms of 'sein'.

It's mostly <u>movement verbs</u> that need '<u>I am</u>'. Here's a list of some common ones that do — you have to <u>remember which they are</u> and <u>learn the past tense bits</u>, because most of them are irregular.

to go, drive:	fahren ⟹	gefahren	to follow:	folgen ⟹	gefolgt	to be:	sein ⟹	gewesen
to run:	laufen ⟹	gelaufen	to come:	kommen ⟹	gekommen	to happen:	geschehen ⟹	geschehen
to climb:	steigen ⟹	gestiegen	to stay:	bleiben ⟹	geblieben	to happen:	passieren ⟹	passiert

That's all perfectly clear...

OK, this page ain't easy — no sirreee. But it's dead important — at some point you'll definitely need to <u>talk or write</u> about something that's <u>happened in the past</u>. Make sure you <u>get to grips</u> with the <u>easy stuff</u> at the top, then you won't find the tricky stuff anywhere near as bad. Honest.

Talking About the Past

You might be a bit fed up of the past tense by now — but this stuff is really handy, so it's worth the pain.

Ich hatte — I had / Ich war — I was

These little words are absolute gold dust — you'll soon find yourself using them all the time.

Sie hatte einen Hund. = She had a dog.

ICH HATTE — I HAD

ich hatte	wir hatten
du hattest	ihr hattet
er/sie/es hatte	Sie/sie hatten

This is the imperfect tense of the verb 'haben' — 'to have'.

This is called the imperfect tense, or the simple past.

Ich war sehr müde. = I was very tired.

ICH WAR — I WAS

ich war	wir waren
du warst	ihr wart
er/sie/es war	Sie/sie waren

This is the imperfect tense of the verb 'sein' — 'to be'.

James wasn't really listening when his teacher told him to 'consider the imperfect tense'.

More verbs in the imperfect tense

You use this when you're talking about things that happened in the past, without using 'haben' or 'sein' (that would be the perfect tense, see page 104). So, you use it to say things like 'I drank' or 'they jumped'.

All regular verbs take these endings (in bold):

Look for the extra 't' in the middle of a verb — that's your clue that it's the imperfect tense.

ICH MACHTE — I MADE

ich machte	wir machten
du machtest	ihr machtet
er/sie/es machte	Sie/sie machten

Was machtest du? = What did you do?

These are the most common irregular verbs. They use the same endings as 'war' in the box above. You probably won't need to use these, but you do need to make sure you recognise them, in case they come up in a reading exam.

Verb	Imperfect	English						
kommen	ich kam	I came	essen	ich aß	I ate	laufen	ich lief	I ran
denken	ich dachte	I thought	trinken	ich trank	I drank	sein	ich war	I was
fahren	ich fuhr	I drove	sehen	ich sah	I saw	haben	ich hatte	I had
gehen	ich ging	I went	singen	ich sang	I sang	geben	ich gab	I gave
			schreiben	ich schrieb	I wrote	helfen	ich half	I helped

Past tense? I'm always tense...

I'm not just telling you about this because of some strange whim of mine — if you don't know this stuff, then you won't be able to say things like 'I was happy' or 'I had eaten lots'. And that'd be a terrible shame, because they're great things to say. So cover the page and get learning.

More Verb Forms

Just one more form of the <u>past tense</u> to go, then you can move on to <u>bossing people about</u>. Much more fun.

I *had bought / gone etc...*

This is when you use <u>two past tense verbs</u> together.
It's made from the <u>imperfect</u> tense of haben/sein and the <u>perfect</u> tense of another verb.

E.g.   **Ich** hatte **ein Buch** gekauft **.**   = I <u>had</u> <u>bought</u> a book.

You won't have to use this tense yourself, but you do need to recognise it.

I HATTE GEKAUFT — I HAD BOUGHT

ich hatte gekauft	*wir hatten gekauft*
du hattest gekauft	*ihr hattet gekauft*
er/sie/es hatte gekauft	*Sie/sie hatten gekauft*

Just like with the <u>perfect</u> tense, with some verbs you have to use '<u>sein</u>' instead of '<u>haben</u>'.

I turned around...
und er war gegangen.

Ich war gegangen **.**   = I <u>had</u> <u>gone</u>.

ICH WAR GEGANGEN — I HAD GONE

ich war gegangen	*wir waren gegangen*
du warst gegangen	*ihr wart gegangen*
er/sie/es war gegangen	*Sie/sie waren gegangen*

Komm herein! — Come in!   Setz dich hin! — Sit down!

This is known as the <u>imperative</u>. It's used to <u>give instructions</u> and is really useful
when you're bossing people about. Here's how to turn a verb into an imperative:

EXAMPLE — TELLING PEOPLE TO GO:

Verb	Imperative	English
du gehst	*Geh!*	Go! (informal, singular)
ihr geht	*Geht!*	Go! (informal, plural)
Sie gehen	*Gehen Sie!*	Go! (formal, sing. & plu.)
wir gehen	*Gehen wir!*	Let's go!

The 2nd column shows what you turn the <u>verb</u> into to get the <u>imperative</u>.

You can use these endings for most verbs.
Luckily, the <u>only</u> form that ends differently from the <u>normal present tense</u> is the 'du' form. It loses its ending (the '-st').
A word of warning — some verbs lose the '-st' in the 'du' form, but <u>gain</u> an '<u>-e</u>'.

Just go!

Make sure you <u>learn</u> these:

Come in!	Komm herein!
Help me!	Hilf mir!
Take the book.	Nimm das Buch.
Bring the dog along.	Bring den Hund mit.
Ask the man there.	Frag den Mann da.
Sit down.	Setz dich hin.

Revise!

The pluperfect tense looks like a nightmare, but if you know the imperfect and the perfect then
it's not too tricky at all. The bottom half of this page is dead important too — you need to know
this stuff because they'll expect you to <u>understand</u> things like <u>signs</u> and <u>instructions</u>.

Myself, Yourself, etc.

This page tells you how to say 'myself', 'yourself', 'themselves', etc. It's dead important that you learn all this stuff, because some verbs just don't make sense without them.

Talking about yourself — 'sich'

'Sich' means 'oneself'. All the different ways to say 'self' are in the box on the right.

You can tell which verbs need 'self' by checking in the dictionary. If you look up 'to wash oneself', it'll say 'sich waschen'.

SICH = ONESELF			
myself:	mich	ourselves:	uns
yourself (inf.):	dich	yourselves (inf. plu.):	euch
himself:	sich	yourself, yourselves (frml.):	sich
herself:	sich	themselves, each other:	sich
itself:	sich		

Ich wasche mich — I wash myself

You need to talk about your 'daily routine'. So if you don't know how to say 'I wash myself', everyone'll think you smell.

Remember — these verbs don't make sense without the 'sich' bit.

SICH WASCHEN = TO WASH ONESELF

I wash myself =	ich wasche mich	wir waschen uns =	we wash ourselves
you wash yourself (informal) =	du wäschst dich	ihr wascht euch =	you wash yourselves (informal)
he washes himself =	er wäscht sich	Sie waschen sich =	you wash yourself, yourselves (formal)
she washes herself =	sie wäscht sich	sie waschen sich =	they wash themselves
it washes itself =	es wäscht sich		

There are lots of these verbs, but here are a few of the most useful ones. Learn these:

to dress oneself:	sich anziehen	to excuse oneself:	sich entschuldigen
to feel:	sich fühlen	to sit oneself down:	sich setzen
to get changed:	sich umziehen	to sun oneself:	sich sonnen

inf. = informal
frml. = formal
sing. = singular
plu. = plural

... and learn how they work:

Ich **fühle mich** schlecht. = I feel bad (ill).

The 'mich' goes straight after the verb.

With separable verbs (page 108), 'mich' goes between the two bits.

Ich **ziehe mich an**. = I dress myself.

Ich putze mir die Zähne — I clean my teeth

Some verbs need you to use 'to myself' or 'to yourself'. This is the dative case, by the way.
These are the three most important ones:

to clean one's teeth:	sich die Zähne putzen
to want/wish for ... :	sich ... wünschen
to imagine ... :	sich ... vorstellen

MIR = TO MYSELF			
to myself:	mir	to ourselves:	uns
to yourself (inf.):	dir	to yourselves (informal):	euch
to him/her/itself:	sich	to yourself, yourselves (frml.):	sich
		to themselves:	sich

This is how you put them in a sentence...

Ich wünsche **mir** ein Pferd. = I want a horse.

These are the bits you change for each person.

Ich habe mich gewaschen — I have washed myself

The perfect tense of these verbs is pretty much the same as normal (see page 104) except they all go with 'haben', not 'sein'.

Sie hat sich schlecht gefühlt. = She felt bad (ill).

Put the 'sich' straight after 'haben'.

I'm sich of talking about myself...

Learn how to say 'I wash myself', 'you wash yourself', etc. for each person — once you've got that, it's the same for almost all 'sich' verbs. Keep at it till it's firmly planted in that brain. Then have a go at the same thing for 'I clean my teeth'. Sorted. Then it's probably time to have a biscuit.

Separable Verbs

Separable verbs are made up of two bits

Some verbs are made up of two bits: the main verb and a bit stuck on the front, that can split off.

abfahren = to depart

Ignore 'ab' for now and use 'fahren' as a normal verb — then send 'ab' to the end of the sentence:

Ich fahre um neun Uhr ab. = I depart at 9 o'clock.

When you come across one of these verbs, think of it as two separate words. It's much easier.

Sie nimmt ihre Katze ins Kino mit . = She takes her cat into the cinema with her.

Here are some more of them — I've underlined the bits that split off.

to wash up:	abwaschen	to take with you:	mitnehmen
to arrive:	ankommen	to go away:	weggehen
to stop:	aufhören	to go out:	ausgehen

The past tense is a bit weird with these verbs

To make the past (perfect) tense of a separable verb, you split it up then put it back together. You leave the front bit as it is, then turn the main bit into the past tense.

aufhören = to stop ➡ **aufgehört** = stopped

So you end up with the 'ge' in the middle of the word.

You put the 'haben' (or 'sein') bit in the normal place, then shove the past tense bit at the end.

Here's an example: **Er hat endlich aufgehört .** = He has finally stopped.

Here's how to spot separable verbs anywhere

In your reading or listening paper, you've got to be able to spot these verbs, so you know what's going on. Check each sentence to see if there are two bits of a separable verb hiding in there. Watch out though — they could be the wrong way round. Here are a few examples with 'zurückfahren' ('to go back'):

Er will zurückfahren . = He wants to go back.

Wenn er zurückfährt , werde ich weinen. = If he goes back, I will cry.

Sie fuhr nach Berlin zurück . = She went back to Berlin. ← This is the past (imperfect) tense of 'fahren'. There's more about this on page 105.

Morgen fahre ich zurück . = Tomorrow, I go back. ←

Ich werde morgen zurückfahren . = I will go back tomorrow. ← These are talking about the future — see page 103.

I love my verbs — we're inseparable...

The best way to remember this is that a separable verb is really just two separate words. They're usually split up in the present tense, and you only make them into one word if they're right next to each other. Learn this page, then cover it up and test yourself by writing (in German) 'I arrive at 9:00'.

How to Say 'No', 'Not' and 'Nobody'   NEGATIVES

This is one of those bits where if you <u>learn</u> just a <u>couple of things</u>, you can <u>say loads more</u>.

Nicht — Not

This stuff is <u>pretty easy</u>. And it's bound to come up somewhere in the <u>exam</u>.

I shan't and I won't. You can't make me.

> **Der Vogel singt nicht.**   = The bird does not sing.

NEGATIVE WORDS:

not:	nicht
no longer:	nicht mehr
not even:	nicht einmal
never:	nie
not yet:	noch nicht
nowhere:	nirgendwo

> **Ich lese nie Bücher.**   = I never read books.

I just don't do that sort of thing any more.

> **Das mache ich nicht mehr.**   = I don't do that any more.

If you want to say a joke is <u>neither</u> clever <u>nor</u> funny, then it's a bit different: *neither ... nor:*   weder ... noch

> **Ihre Haare sind** weder **blond** noch **braun.**   = Her hair is <u>neither</u> blonde <u>nor</u> brown.

Ich habe keine Bratkartoffeln — I have no roast potatoes

'<u>Kein</u>' means '<u>no</u>' — as in '<u>I have no roast potatoes</u>'. When you use it in the singular, you need to change the ending depending on the gender, but in the plural (and the nominative case) it's just '<u>keine</u>' for <u>all the genders</u>.

I beg to differ...

> **Ich habe keinen Kartoffelsalat.**   = I have no potato salad.

> **Keine Hunde sind grün.**   = No dogs are green.

'Kein' also has other forms for different cases. In fact it takes exactly the same endings as 'mein' — see page 92.

Niemand — Nobody...

You need to be able to say '<u>nobody</u>' and '<u>nothing</u>'. It's not much to learn, so there's no excuse.

> **Ich habe** niemand **gesehen.**   = I've seen <u>nobody</u>.

nothing: nichts

This is ridiculous. I can't see anything.

SOME HANDY VARIATIONS:

nothing yet:	noch nichts
nothing left/nothing more:	nichts mehr
nobody yet:	noch niemand
nobody else/nobody any more:	niemand mehr

> **Ich sehe** gar nichts .   = I see <u>nothing at all</u>.

You can put '<u>gar</u>' in front of '<u>nicht</u>' or '<u>nichts</u>' to emphasise it — like saying '<u>nothing at all</u>'.

Being able to say 'nothing' sounds easy...

This stuff <u>doubles</u> what you can say — for anything you could already say, you can now say the <u>opposite</u>. '<u>Nicht</u>', '<u>nichts</u>', '<u>niemand</u>' and '<u>kein</u>' are really basic essential words, but if you want a decent mark, learn the others too. Cover the page, scribble them down, and see what you know.

MODAL VERBS

Modal Verbs

Geesh — there's loads of this grammar stuff. Still, the quicker you learn it, the quicker you can put this book down and get on with the rest of your life. Here's a nice bit about <u>modal verbs</u>...

Ich muss diese Verben lernen... I must learn these verbs...

Instead of saying 'I <u>learn</u> judo', you might want to say 'I <u>should learn</u> judo' or 'I <u>want to learn</u> judo'. Here are <u>six really handy verbs</u> you can use to give your opinions about doing something.

① WOLLEN = TO WANT

ich	will	wir	wollen
du	willst	ihr	wollt
er	will	Sie	wollen
sie	will	sie	wollen
es	will		

'Ich will' = 'I want'

② MÖGEN = TO LIKE

ich	mag	wir	mögen
du	magst	ihr	mögt
er	mag	Sie	mögen
sie	mag	sie	mögen
es	mag		

'Ich mag' = 'I like'

(For 'I <u>would</u> like' — 'ich möchte', see <u>page 111</u>.)

③ DÜRFEN = TO BE ALLOWED TO

ich	darf	wir	dürfen
du	darfst	ihr	dürft
er	darf	Sie	dürfen
sie	darf	sie	dürfen
es	darf		

'Ich darf' = 'I may'

④ KÖNNEN = TO BE ABLE TO

ich	kann	wir	können
du	kannst	ihr	könnt
er	kann	Sie	können
sie	kann	sie	können
es	kann		

'Ich kann' = 'I can'

⑤ SOLLEN = TO BE SUPPOSED TO

ich	soll	wir	sollen
du	sollst	ihr	sollt
er	soll	Sie	sollen
sie	soll	sie	sollen
es	soll		

'Ich soll' = 'I should'

⑥ MÜSSEN = TO HAVE TO

ich	muss	wir	müssen
du	musst	ihr	müsst
er	muss	Sie	müssen
sie	muss	sie	müssen
es	muss		

'Ich muss' = 'I must'

Modal verbs are dead useful...

This is how you use them:

Ich **muss** einen Brief **schreiben** . = I <u>must</u> <u>write</u> a letter.

Help! I really must write this letter...

You need the <u>right form</u> of the <u>modal verb</u> ('I want' or 'he wants') because that's the main verb...

...and you need the <u>infinitive</u> of the <u>other verb</u> (see <u>page 100</u> if you're not sure what that is). You stick this at the <u>end of the sentence</u>.

Du **sollst** deine Hausaufgaben **machen** . = You <u>should</u> <u>do</u> your homework.

Sie **können** sehr gut **singen** . = They <u>can</u> <u>sing</u> very well.

I prefer modal aeroplanes really...

A lot to learn here, but these modal verbs are <u>absolutely crucial</u>. They crop up <u>everywhere</u>, so it's really worth spending some time learning them now. The main things to remember are that the other verb has to be in the <u>infinitive</u>, and it has to go to the <u>end of the sentence</u>.

Modal Verbs

OK, I'll admit it. This <u>is</u> tricky. But it is <u>important</u>, so if you want top marks you need to <u>learn</u> it.

You can use modal verbs in the past tense too

If you want to say something like 'I wanted to wash the car', then you have to use the <u>past tense</u> of the <u>modal verb</u>. Here's what happens with '<u>können</u>':

KÖNNEN = TO BE ABLE TO

ich	konnte	wir	konnten
du	konntest	ihr	konntet
er	konnte	Sie	konnten
sie	konnte	sie	konnten
es	konnte		

Just <u>take off</u> the '<u>-en</u>', and the <u>umlaut</u>, and <u>add</u> the endings in red.

Follow this pattern for 'wollen', 'dürfen', 'müssen' and 'sollen' too.

WOLLEN = TO WANT

ich	wollte	wir	wollten
du	wolltest	ihr	wolltet
er	wollte	Sie	wollten
sie	wollte	sie	wollten
es	wollte		

DÜRFEN = TO BE ALLOWED TO

ich	durfte	wir	durften
du	durftest	ihr	durftet
er	durfte	Sie	durften
sie	durfte	sie	durften
es	durfte		

MÜSSEN = TO HAVE TO

ich	musste	wir	mussten
du	musstest	ihr	musstet
er	musste	Sie	mussten
sie	musste	sie	mussten
es	musste		

SOLLEN = TO BE SUPPOSED TO

ich	sollte	wir	sollten
du	solltest	ihr	solltet
er	sollte	Sie	sollten
sie	sollte	sie	sollten
es	sollte		

WATCH OUT:
'<u>Mögen</u>' is a bit different. It changes to '<u>mochten</u>' in the past tense. It takes the <u>same endings</u> as all the others though.

MÖGEN = TO LIKE

ich	mochte	wir	mochten
du	mochtest	ihr	mochtet
er	mochte	Sie	mochten
sie	mochte	sie	mochten
es	mochte		

Use them as you would in the present tense (see <u>page 110</u>). Here are a couple of examples:

Ich **musste** einen Apfel kaufen. = I <u>had</u> to buy an apple.

Ich **wollte** den Kuchen essen. = I <u>wanted</u> to eat the cake.

Ich möchte — I would like

Dead useful verb, this, so get it <u>learnt</u>.

<u>Don't</u> confuse with '<u>mochten</u>' the <u>past tense</u> of '<u>mögen</u>'. There's an <u>umlaut</u> on the '<u>o</u>'.

ICH MÖCHTE — I WOULD LIKE

ich	möchte	wir	möchten
du	möchtest	ihr	möchtet
er/sie/es	möchte	Sie/sie	möchten

(There are. I promise.)

Ich **möchte** fünfzig Tassen Tee, bitte.

= I <u>would like</u> fifty cups of tea, please.

Ich **möchte** Chinesisch **lernen**.

= I <u>would like</u> to <u>learn</u> Chinese.

The <u>other verb</u> has to be in the <u>infinitive</u>, and go at the <u>end</u>.

I know this is pretty complicated grammar, but you should already be familiar with 'möchten' — it's part of the basic shopping vocab (see <u>page 36</u>).

I would like a biscuit now...

Get all this stuff right in your <u>writing assessments</u> and you'll be in Marksville, Arizona.
Same goes for the <u>speaking assessments</u> actually...

Odds and Ends

With some verbs you have to stick an '<u>es</u>' (which means 'it') in.
1) Whatever is <u>doing</u> the action becomes something that's <u>having something done</u> to it.
2) So instead of saying something like 'I don't feel good' you'd say: 'It feels to me not good'. Crazy stuff.

Wie geht es dir? — How are you?

It looks strange, but you <u>have</u> to learn it — and <u>never</u> say 'ich bin gut' for 'I'm fine'.

Mir geht's gut.   = I'm fine.   *Es geht mir nicht so gut.*   = I don't feel so good.

This is just short for 'geht es'.

Other useful phrases that use 'es'

Here are some more of these awkward phrases. They're <u>easy</u> once you've <u>learnt</u> them <u>properly</u>.

Es regnet.   = It's raining.   This'll come in handy for talking about
the weather — see <u>pages 54 and 56</u>.   *Es tut weh.*   = It hurts.

Es gibt *viel zu tun.*   = <u>There is</u> lots to do.   *Es gefällt mir* *in München.*   = <u>I like it</u> in Munich.

(more literally, 'it gives lots to do')   (literal translation: 'it pleases to me')

Es tut mir Leid *, aber heute bin ich nicht frei.*   = <u>I'm sorry</u>, but I'm not free today.

(literally, 'it does sorrow to me')

Here are a few more miscellaneous things that you need to be able to understand...

Um... zu — in order to

'<u>Um... zu</u>' means '<u>in order to</u>'.

The verb that's in the infinitive comes <u>after</u> the 'zu'.

Um *diesen Satz* *zu verstehen* *, muss man Deutsch sprechen können.*

= <u>In order to understand</u> this sentence, you must be able to speak German.

Ignore 'zu' before a verb if there's no 'um'

When verbs <u>link</u> with an infinitive in the sentence, you sometimes find '<u>zu</u>' before the infinitive.
You only need to <u>understand</u> it, not use it — you can pretty much <u>ignore it</u> when you see it.

Ich *versuche* *den besten Satz in der Welt* *zu schreiben* *.*   = I'm <u>trying to write</u> the best
sentence in the world.

Die Stunde *beginnt* *langweilig* *zu werden* *.*   = The lesson is <u>beginning to get</u> boring.

Wie geht es dir? Not bad thanks, ducky...

This grammar stuff can be seriously scary. But if you <u>learn</u> all the phrases on these pages, it
becomes <u>a lot easier</u>. And don't worry too much about all the weirdy grammar names. Sorted.

Revision Summary

The stuff in this section really helps you to put words together to say what you want. The way to make sure you've learnt it is to check you can do <u>all these questions</u>. Try them all, and look up any you can't do. Then try them all again. And keep doing that until you can answer <u>every single one</u>.

1) In the sentence 'Lucas isst ein Eis' — *Lucas eats an ice cream*, is 'Lucas' in:
   a) the nominative b) the accusative?
2) When do you use the genitive case?
3) Which part of this sentence is in the dative case?
   'Ich spreche meiner Schwester' — *I speak to my sister*
4) How do you say *It is sunny* (sonnig) *but not warm* (warm) in German?
5) Rearrange the order of this sentence so it's correct:
   'Ich bin müde, weil ich hatte keinen Schlaf' — *I am tired because I haven't had any sleep.*
6) What are the words for 'the' and 'a' that go with each of these words in the nominative case?
   a) *Käse* (masculine)   b) *Baumwolle* (feminine)   c) *Messer* (neuter)
7) What are the words for 'the' and 'a' that go with the words in Q6 in the accusative case?
8) How do you say this sentence in German: *I have an ugly* (hässlich) *cat* (Katze)?
9) What are the German words for: a) *my* b) *his* c) *our*?
   For each answer, give the nominative for each gender.
10) How do you say *Now and then I am very funny* (lustig) in German?
11) How do you say *I am nearer* in German? How do you say *I am the nearest*?
12) What do these words mean in English? a) *nach*   b) *bei*   c) *seit*
13) Which case do these prepositions take? a) *für*   b) *mit*   c) *wegen*
14) What are the German words for 'I', 'you' (informal singular), 'he', 'she', 'it', 'we', 'you' (formal) and 'they' in: a) the nominative   b) the accusative   c) the dative?
15) How do you say 'who' in German?
16) Translate this sentence and pick out the relative clause:
   'Der Mann, der sehr dick ist, isst einen Kuchen.'
17) How do you say each of these in German?
   a) *he is* b) *they are* c) *you* (informal singular) *have* d) *I drive* e) *you* (informal plural) *eat*
18) How do you say *I will go to the shops* in German?
19) How do you say these sentences in German? Use the perfect tense.
   a) *They made a cake* b) *He booked a room*   c) *We drank coffee*   d) *They ran quickly*
20) How do you say these sentences in German? Use the imperfect tense.
   a) *She had four dogs* b) *They were friends*
21) Translate these phrases into English:
   a) *Geh!*   b) *Komm herein!*   c) *Nimm das Buch!*   d) *Setz dich hin!*
22) How do you say these phrases in German?
   a) *I wash myself* b) *He excuses himself* c) *They clean their teeth* d) *You washed yourself*
23) What do these words mean in English?
   a) *nicht einmal*   b) *kein*   c) *niemand*   d) *gar nichts*
24) How do you say these phrases in German?
   a) *I must eat vegetables*   b) *He can*   c) *They are supposed to go*   d) *I wanted*
25) How do you say these phrases in German?
   a) *I don't feel so good*   b) *There's lots to do*

Do Well in Your Exam

Here are some handy hints to help you in your exams. And only the tiniest smidgen of learning to do. Ahh.

Read the Questions carefully

Don't go losing easy marks — it'll break my heart.
Make sure you definitely do the things on this list:

> 1) Read all the instructions properly.
> 2) Read the question properly.
> 3) Answer the question — don't waffle.

Don't give up if you don't Understand

If you don't understand, don't panic. The key thing to remember is that you
can still do well in the exam, even if you don't understand every German word
that comes up. Just use one of the two methods below:

> If you're reading or listening — look for lookalikes

1) Some words look or sound the same in German and English.

2) These words are great because you'll recognise them when you see or hear them.

3) Be careful though — there are some exceptions you need to watch out for. Here are just a few
   examples of German words that look like an English word but have a totally different meaning:

sensibel:	*sensitive*	sympathisch:	*nice*
groß:	*big/tall*	die Fabrik:	*factory*
fast:	*almost*	die Marmelade:	*jam*
bald:	*soon*	das Rezept:	*prescription*
also:	*so*	Ich will...:	*I want...*
die Wand:	*wall*	das Gymnasium:	*grammar school*

> Words like these are
> called 'falsche Freunde'
> — false friends.

Make use of the Context

You'll likely come across the odd word that you don't know, especially in the reading exam.
Often you'll be able to find some clues telling you what the text is all about.

> 1) The type of text, e.g. newspaper article, advertisement, website
> 2) The title of the text
> 3) Any pictures
> 4) The verbal context

Say you see the following in the reading exam, and don't know what any of these words mean:

"...die Kleidung aus Polyester , aus Wolle , aus Baumwolle und aus Seide ."

1) Well, the fact that this is a list of things, all starting with 'aus ...' coming after the German word for
   'clothes' suggests they're all things that clothes can be made out of.

2) You can guess that 'Polyester' means 'polyester', and 'Wolle' means 'wool'.

3) So it's a pretty good guess that the two words you don't know are different types of fabric.
   (In fact, 'Seide' means 'silk' and 'Baumwolle' means 'cotton'.)

4) Often the questions won't depend on you understanding these more difficult words.
   It's important to be able to understand the gist though, and not let these words throw you.

False friends — my mum told me about them...

I can't emphasise enough how important it is to read the questions and instructions through properly.
It might seem obvious now, but it's amazing how many people get caught out in the exam...

Do Well in Your Exam

More ways to improve your marks — and not a drop of learning on the horizon...
It's almost as good as free cake.

Look for the Verb...

Here are a few tips to help you out if you're struggling with sentences in the reading exam.

1) The verb (or 'doing word') is probably going to give you the biggest clue as to what the sentence is about. Word order in German isn't always the same as it is in English, so you might have to go looking for one...

> First verb, 'must', is the second idea in the sentence.

Nach der Schule muss *ich mit meiner Mutter meine Großeltern* besuchen.

= After school, I must visit my grandparents with my mother.

> The second verb, 'to visit', is sent to the end of the sentence.

2) German is full of scarily long words. Don't be put off if you don't understand one at first glance though — they're often 'compounds' made up of two or three smaller words stuck together. Try breaking a word up to get at its meaning...

> A compound verb

zusammenkommen: 'zusammen' = *together,* 'kommen' = *to come:*   →   *to meet*
der Tiefkühlschrank: 'tief' = *deep,* 'kühl' = *cool,* 'der Schrank' = *cupboard:* →   *freezer*

> A compound noun

There is no need to resort to violence when breaking up words.

3) Don't ignore the little words — they can often make a big difference to the meaning of a sentence...

Ich spiele gern Sport, besonders *Tennis.*   = I like playing sport, especially Tennis.

Ich spiele gern Sport außer *Tennis.*   = I like playing sport, except Tennis.

4) Don't panic if you don't understand absolutely everything. Often, the important thing is to get the gist of what you're reading (or even listening to).

Take notes in the listening exam

1) You'll have 5 minutes at the start of the exam to have a quick look through the paper. This'll give you a chance to see how many questions there are, and you might get a few clues from the questions about what topics they're on, so it won't be a horrible surprise when the tape starts running.

2) You'll hear each extract twice. Different people have different strategies, but it's a good idea to jot down a few details that you think might come up in the questions, especially things like:

Dates   Numbers   Spelt-out names

3) But... don't forget to keep listening to the gist of the recording while you're making notes.

I hope you're taking notes...

Despite what some people might say, exams aren't meant to be easy. There are bound to be a few tricky bits, but you stand a good chance of working them out if you use your noggin. Don't leave blank spaces — at the end of the day a guess (preferably educated) is better than nothing.

How to Use Dictionaries

You're allowed to use a dictionary to help you in your <u>writing task</u>. 'Yippee!' I hear you cry — but using a dictionary <u>isn't</u> as easy as it seems. Finding the <u>right word</u> can be <u>dead tricky</u>, so here are some tips to help you make the most of one. And remember: if it <u>doesn't</u> make sense, you've got the <u>wrong</u> word.

Don't translate word for word *— it DOESN'T work*

Turn each word of this phrase into English, and you get <u>rubbish</u>.

Wie heißt du? ⟶ *How called you?*

It's the <u>same</u> the other way round — turn English into German word by word, and you get <u>gibberish</u> — <u>don't do it</u>.

What are you called? ⟶ *Was bist du geheißen?* **NO!**

If it doesn't *make* sense, you've got it *wrong*

Some words have several meanings — don't just pick the first one you see. Look at the <u>meanings</u> listed and <u>suss out</u> which one is what you're looking for.

If you read this... *Ich finde es sehr schwer, Deutsch zu sprechen.*

...you might look up '<u>schwer</u>' and find this:

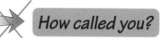

> **schwer**
>
> <u>a</u> heavy; (schwierig) difficult, hard; (schlimm) serious, bad //
> <u>ad</u> (sehr) very (much); (verletzt etc.) seriously, badly; <u>S-arbeiter</u> m manual labourer; <u>S-e</u> f weight, heaviness; (PHYS) gravity; <u>schwerelos</u> a weightless

So the sentence could mean:

I find it very <u>heavy</u> to speak German. ✗

I find it very <u>difficult</u> to speak German. ✔

I find it very <u>serious</u> to speak German. ✗

This is the only one that makes sense.

Ich finde es sehr schwer, Deutsch zu sprechen.

I think you're doing it wrong.

Look up bits *of* long words

Not <u>all</u> long German words are in all dictionaries. But you can look up <u>parts</u> of these words.

Say you need to know what <u>Wetterbericht</u> means...

1) If you tried to look up '<u>Wetterbericht</u>', you might only find the word '<u>Wetter</u>': weather.
2) So the whole word might be 'weather something'.
3) Look up the rest of it ('<u>Bericht</u>') and it turns out it means 'report'.
4) So 'Wetterbericht' means '<u>weather report</u>'.

Here's another example: '<u>Fachsprache</u>'. If you try to look it up, you might not find it, but you do find '<u>Fach-</u>' (which means technical or expert). So try to find the rest of the word — look up '<u>Sprache</u>' (which means language). '<u>Fachsprache</u>' means '<u>technical language</u>'.

The right words — 'food', 'TV', 'sleep'...

A word to the wise: <u>don't</u> go mad on the dictionary front or it'll all go <u>horribly wrong</u>. Instead of writing long <u>complicated</u> sentences where you have to look up <u>every word</u>, try to use the German you <u>already know</u>. Dictionaries can be really <u>helpful</u> — just make sure you can use them <u>properly</u>.

Hints for Writing

Here are a few general hints about how you should approach the writing tasks.

Write about what you know

1) You won't be asked to write about obscure German poetry.

2) You will need to cover certain specific things that the question asks you to, but there'll be plenty of scope to be imaginative.

3) Usually the writing tasks will give you some flexibility so you can base your answer on something you know about.

Examiners like to know When and Why...

1) Saying when and how often you did things gets you big bonus marks. Learn times and dates carefully (see pages 2-3).

2) Make sure you write about what you've done in the past (see pages 104-106) or what you will do in the future (page 103).

3) Give descriptions where possible, but keep things accurate — a short description in really good German is better than a long paragraph of nonsense.

4) Examiners also love opinions (see pages 7-9). Try to vary them as much as possible.

So where were you on the night of the 21st?

Er... Gestern war ich im Kino mit...

Johnny was having flashbacks to GCSE German.

...and Where and Who With...

The examiners really are quite nosy, and love as many details as you can give. It's a good idea to ask yourself all these 'wh-' questions, and write the bits that show your German off in the best light. Also, it doesn't matter if what you're writing isn't strictly true — as long as it's believable.

Vocab and grammar make you look good

1) The more correct grammar and vocab you can include, the better. But a correct simple sentence is much better than something complicated that doesn't make sense.

2) Your grammar doesn't have to be perfect — don't panic if you write something and then realise that it wasn't quite right. Obviously though, the better your grammar, the better your marks will be.

3) Make sure you pay attention to things like word order and adjective endings. There's a special grammar section in this book (see pages 84-113) to help you out.

Use your dictionary, but sparingly

1) DON'T try to use the dictionary to learn a completely new, fancy way of saying something.

2) Use it to look up a particular word that you've forgotten — a word that, when you see it, you'll know it's right.

3) Use it to check genders of nouns — that's whether words are masculine, feminine or neuter.

4) Check any spellings you're unsure of.

> Most importantly, don't use the dictionary to delve into the unknown. If you stick to what you know, you're far less likely to go wrong.

1) If right-handed, use right hand...

One of the most important things you can do when it comes to the writing task is plan ahead. Think about what you're going to write first and how you're going to cover all the points in the task. Then think about how you can show off your German. This could actually be fun you know...

Hints for Writing

Accuracy is really important in the writing assessment. Without it, your work will look like sloppy custard.

Start with the Verb

1) Verbs really are the cornerstone of any sentence.
   If you get the verb right, everything else should fall into place.

EXAMPLE:

> Last weekend, I played badminton with my friends.

You need 'haben', 'to have', as well as the past participle of the verb 'spielen', 'to play':

> Letztes Wochenende habe ich Badminton mit meinen Freunden gespielt.

You also need to think about word order and where the verbs appear in the sentence.

2) Be careful to get the whole expression that uses the verb, not just the verb itself.

EXAMPLE:

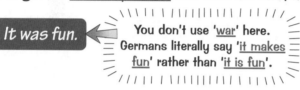

> It was fun.

You don't use 'war' here. Germans literally say 'it makes fun' rather than 'it is fun'.

> Es hat Spaß gemacht.

Check and re-check

No matter how careful you think you're being, mistakes can easily creep into your work.
Go through the checklist below for every sentence straight after you've written it.

1) Are the ENDINGS of the verbs right?

   Er spiele Tennis. ✘   Er spielt Tennis. ✓

2) Is the WORD ORDER right?

   Heute ich gehe ins Kino. ✘   Heute gehe ich ins Kino. ✓

3) Have you got the correct GENDERS for things?

   Die Kleid. ✘   Das Kleid. ✓

4) Is everything in the right CASE?

   Ich esse der Apfel. ✘   Ich esse den Apfel. ✓

5) Do your adjectives AGREE?

   Der groß Hund. ✘   Der große Hund. ✓

6) Have all your nouns got CAPITALS?

   Ich wohne in einer stadt. ✘   Ich wohne in einer Stadt. ✓

Then when you've finished the whole piece of work, have another read through with fresh eyes.
You're bound to pick up one or two more mistakes.

Check please...

Grammar. It might seem boring, but you've just got to know it. The more correct vocab and grammar you include in your work, the more lovely marks will fly your way. So get learning it.

Hints for Speaking

The speaking assessment fills many a student with <u>dread</u>. Remember though — it's your chance to show what you can <u>do</u>. It won't be nearly as bad as you think it's going to be. <u>Honest</u>.

Be Imaginative

There are two tricky things about the speaking assessment — one is <u>what to say</u>, and two is <u>how to say it</u>. No matter how good your German is, it won't shine through if you can't think of anything to say.

Say you're asked to talk about your <u>daily routine</u> (or to imagine someone else's daily routine). It would be easy to give a list of things you do when you get in from school:

> *"Ich mache meine Hausaufgaben. Ich sehe fern. Ich esse. Ich gehe ins Bett."*

> = I do my homework. I watch television. I eat. I go to bed.

It makes sense, but the problem is, it's all a bit <u>samey</u>...

1) Try to think of when this <u>isn't</u> the case, and put it into a <u>DIFFERENT TENSE</u>:

> *"Morgen werde ich Fußball nach der Schule spielen."*

> = Tomorrow I will play football after school.

2) Don't just talk about yourself. Talk about <u>OTHER PEOPLE</u> — even if you have to imagine them.

> *"Manchmal sehe ich mit meiner Schwester fern. Sie mag Zeichentrickfilme, aber ich sehe lieber die Nachrichten."*

> = Sometimes I watch TV with my sister. She likes cartoons, but I prefer to watch the news.

Imaginary friends are for speaking assessments — not real life.

3) Give loads of <u>OPINIONS</u> and <u>REASONS</u> for your opinions.

See <u>pages 7-9</u> for loads more on opinions.

> *"Ich mache meine Hausaufgaben vor dem Abendessen. Dann kann ich mich später entspannen."*

> = I do my homework before dinner. Then I can relax later on.

A couple of 'DON'T's...

1) <u>DON'T</u> try to <u>avoid</u> a topic if you find it difficult — that'll mean you won't get <u>any</u> marks at all for that bit of the assessment. You'll be surprised what you can muster up if you stay calm and concentrate on what you <u>do</u> know how to say.

2) <u>DON'T</u> make up a word in the hope that it exists in German unless you're really, really stuck (and you've tried all the other tricks on these pages). If it's your <u>last resort</u>, it's worth a try.

Once upon a time in a land far, far away...

... lived a little girl with a golden unicorn, and she... Er, OK, you don't have to be that imaginative. But <u>do</u> try to get plenty of <u>opinions</u>, <u>tenses</u> and <u>whatnot</u> in there. It's about <u>showing off</u>.

Hints for Speaking

Even with all that <u>careful planning</u>, sometimes things can still go a bit <u>wonky</u>.
Never fear though — here's how to come out the other side <u>smiling</u>...

Try to find another way of saying it

There may be a particular word or phrase that trips you up. There's always a <u>way round it</u> though.

1) If you can't <u>remember</u> a German word, use an <u>alternative</u> word or try <u>describing it</u> instead.

2) E.g. if you can't remember that '<u>strawberries</u>' are '<u>die Erdbeeren</u>' and you really need to say it, then describe them as 'small red fruit', or 'kleines rotes Obst'.

3) You can <u>fib</u> to avoid words you can't remember — if you can't remember the word for '<u>dog</u>' then just say you've got a <u>cat</u> instead. Make sure what you're saying makes <u>sense</u> though — saying you've got a <u>pet radio</u> isn't going to get you any marks, trust me.

4) If you can't remember the word for a <u>cup</u> (die Tasse) in your speaking assessment, you could say '<u>glass</u>' (das Glas) instead — you'll still make yourself <u>understood</u>.

You may just need to buy yourself some time

If you get a bit <u>stuck</u> for what to say, there's always a <u>way out</u>.

1) If you can't think of a way around it, you <u>can</u> ask for help in the speaking assessment — as long as you ask for it in <u>German</u>.

2) If you can't remember what a chair is, ask your examiner: "Wie sagt man 'chair' auf Deutsch?" It's <u>better</u> than wasting time trying to think of the word.

3) If you just need some <u>thinking time</u> in your speaking assessment or you want to check something then you can use these useful sentences to help you out:

Also...	So...	Können Sie das bitte wiederholen?	*Can you repeat that please?*
Ach so!	*Oh, I see!*	Ich verstehe nicht.	*I don't understand.*
Ja, natürlich...	*Yes, of course...*	Können Sie das erklären?	*Can you explain that?*
Ich bin nicht sicher.	*I'm not sure.*		

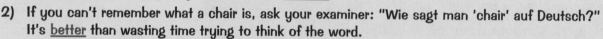
The added bonus of using phrases like these is that they make you sound more like a real German.

Have Confidence

1) Believe it or not, the teacher isn't trying to catch you out. He or she <u>wants</u> you to do <u>well</u>, and to be dazzled by all the excellent German you've learnt.

2) Speaking assessments can be pretty <u>daunting</u>. But remember it's the same for <u>everyone</u>.

3) <u>Nothing horrendous</u> is going to happen if you make a few slip-ups. Just try and focus on showing the teacher how much you've <u>learnt</u>.

4) Don't be afraid to make mistakes — even native German speakers make 'em. Don't let a silly error shake your <u>concentration</u> for the rest of the assessment.

Most importantly — DON'T PANIC...

That's easy for me to say I know, but seriously, <u>stay calm</u> and you stand a far better chance of <u>navigating</u> the bumpy bits. Well, that's it for now folks. Make sure you take this lot <u>on board</u> and <u>soar</u> through the assessments like a flying trapeze... <u>Viel Glück</u> — not that you'll need it of course.

KEY

m/f/n/pl: a masculine, feminine, neuter or plural noun — see p86/87
(-n), (-e) etc.: add whatever is in the brackets to make the plural
(-): plural is the same as singular (add nothing)
(¨): put an umlaut on the stressed vowel to make the plural, e.g. Apfel → Äpfel
v: a verb — see p100
v sep: separable verb — splits into two words in the present and some other tenses — see p108 (all verbs not labelled 'sep' are inseparable)
v ir: irregular verb (its forms are irregular in some tenses and persons, e.g. sein: ich bin)
adj: adjective — see p91/92 (has to agree with the noun it describes)
adv: adverb — see p93 (describes a verb or adjective)
prep: preposition — see p95/96 (connects the verb to a place, thing or person: 'to', 'for', 'with' etc.)
pron: pronoun — see p97-99 (replaces noun: e.g. 'he', 'me')
conj: conjunction — see p89 (connects two parts of a sentence, e.g. 'but')

prep + dat *from*
und zu *from time to time*
bestellen v sep *to cancel*
end m (-e) *evening*
endessen n (-) *dinner, evening meal*
ends adv *in the evening*
enteuerfilm m (-e) *adventure film*
er conj *but, however*
fahren v sep ir *depart*
fahrt f (-en) *departure*
fall m (no pl) *rubbish*
falleimer m (-) *rubbish bin*
fliegen v sep ir *to take off (plane)*
flug m (¨e) *take-off, departure*
gase n pl *exhaust gases, emissions*
gesehen von adv *apart from*
hängen von v sep ir *to depend on (something/one)*
hängig adj *dependent*
holen v sep *to collect, to meet*
itur n *equivalent of A-level(s)*
iturient/in m/f (-en/-nen) *A-level student*
schließen v sep ir *to shut/lock, to end (studies)*
schluss m (¨e) *end, final exams*
schlusszeugnis n (-se) *school leaving certificate*
spülen v sep *to wash up*
teil n (-e) *compartment*
teilung f (-en) *department, section*
trocknen v sep *to dry up*
waschen v sep ir *to wash up*
cker m (¨) *field*
DAC (= Allgemeiner Deutscher Automobil-Club) m *German version of AA/RAC*
der f (-n) *blood vessel*
dresse f (-n) *address*
erobics machen *to do aerobics*
ffe m (-n) *monkey*
frika n *Africa*
frikaner/in m/f (-/-nen) *African person*
rikanisch adj *African*
G (= Aktiengesellschaft) f *PLC/Ltd.*
ggression f (-en) *aggression*
nlich adj *similar*
hnung f (-en) *idea, suspicion, hunch*
IDS n *AIDS*
kte f (-n) *file, record*
ktentasche f (-n) *briefcase*
ktiv adj *active*
ktivität f (-en) *activity*
ktuell adj *current*
kzeptieren v *accept*
lkohol m (-e) *alcohol*
lkoholfrei adj *non-alcoholic*
lkoholiker/in m/f (-/-nen) *alcoholic*
lkoholisch adj *alcoholic*
lkoholismus m *alcoholism*
lle pron *all, everyone*
llee f (-n) *avenue*
llein adj *alone*
lles Gute *all the best*
llgemein adj *general*
lpen f pl *the Alps*
ls conj *as, than, when*
ls ob *as if, as though*
lso conj *so, therefore*
lt adj *old*

Altenheim n (-e) *old people's home*
Alter n *age*
älter adj *older*
altmodisch adj *old-fashioned*
Altpapier n *waste paper*
am Anfang *at the start*
am Apparat *speaking! (on telephone)*
Amerika n *America*
Amerikaner/in m/f (-/-nen) *American*
amerikanisch adj *American*
Ampel f (-n) *traffic lights*
amüsant adj *entertaining, amusing*
amüsieren sich v *to be amused, to have fun*
an prep + acc/dat *at, to, by*
an Bord m *aboard*
Ananas f (-/-se) *pineapple*
anbauen v sep *to build on, to grow*
anbieten v sep ir *to offer*
andere/r/s adj *other*
anders adj/adv *different(ly)*
anderswo adv *somewhere else*
anderthalb adj *one and a half*
Anfang m (¨e) *beginning*
anfangen v sep ir *to begin, to start*
Angebot n (-e) *offer*
angeln v *to fish*
Angelrute f (-n) *fishing rod*
angenehm adj *pleasant, enjoyable*
angenommen dass *assuming that*
Angestellte(r) *employee*
Angst haben *to be frightened*
ängstlich adj *anxious*
anhalten v sep ir *to stop (vehicles)*
anklopfen v sep *to knock*
ankommen v sep ir *to arrive*
Ankunft f (¨e) *arrival*
anmachen v sep *to put on / turn on*
Anmeldung f (-en) *reception (room)*
annehmen v sep ir *to accept, to suppose*
anonym adj *anonymous*
anprobieren v sep *try on (clothes)*
Anrufbeantworter m (-) *answerphone*
anrufen v sep ir *to phone*
anschauen v sep *to look at / watch*
ansehen v sep ir *to look at*
Ansichtskarte f (-n) *picture postcard*
Anspitzer m (-) *sharpener*
anspringen v sep ir *to start (cars)*
anspucken v sep *to spit at*
Antwort f (-en) *answer*
antworten v *to answer*
Anzeige f (-n) *advert (written)*
anziehen sich v sep ir *to put on, to get dressed*
Anzug m (¨e) *(men's) suit*
Apfel m (¨) *apple*
Apfelsine f (-n) *orange*
Apotheke f (-n) *pharmacy*
Apotheker/in m/f (-/-nen) *pharmacist*
Apparat m (-e) *machine, telephone*
Appetit m (-e) *appetite*
Aprikose f (-n) *apricot*
April m *April*
Arbeit f (-en) *work*
arbeiten v *to work*
Arbeiter/in m/f (-/-nen) *worker*
Arbeitgeber m (-) *employer*
Arbeitsbedingungen f pl *terms of employment*
Arbeitserfahrung f *work experience*
arbeitslos adj *unemployed*
Arbeitslosigkeit f *unemployment*
Arbeitspraktikum n *work experience*
Arbeitszeit f *working hours*
Arbeitszimmer n (-) *study*
Architekt/in m/f (-en/-nen) *architect*
ARD *German television company*
ärgerlich adj *annoying*
ärgern sich v *to get angry*
arm adj *poor*
Armband n (¨er) *bracelet*
Armbanduhr f (-en) *wristwatch*
Armee f (-n) *army*
Ärmelkanal m *the English Channel*
Armut f *poverty*
Art f (-en) *kind, sort, type*
artig adj *well-behaved*
Arzt/Ärztin m/f (¨e/-nen) *doctor*
Asien n *Asia*
atmen v *to breathe*
Atmosphäre f (-n) *atmosphere*
attraktiv adj *attractive*
auch adv *also*
auf prep + acc/dat *up, on*
auf dem Lande *in the country*
auf die Nerven gehen *to get on one's nerves*
auf diese Weise *in this way*
Auf Wiederhören! *Goodbye! (phone)*
Auf Wiedersehen! *Goodbye!*
Aufenthalt m (-) *stay*
Aufenthaltsraum m (¨e) *games room*
Aufgabe f (-n) *exercise / task*
aufgeben v sep ir *to give up*
aufhören v sep *to stop (doing something)*
aufmachen v sep *to open*
aufnehmen v sep ir *to pick up*
aufpassen v sep *to pay attention, watch out*
aufpassen auf v sep *to look after*
aufräumen v sep *to tidy up / clear away*
aufregend adj *exciting*
aufs Land *to the country*
Aufschnitt m (-e) *cold cut meat*
aufstehen v sep ir *to get up*
aufwachen v sep *to wake up*
Aufzug m (¨e) *lift (elevator)*
Auge n (-n) *eye*
Augenblick m (-e) *moment*
August m *August*
Aula f (Aulen) *school hall*
aus prep + dat *out of*
ausbilden v sep *to train*
Ausbildung f (-en) *training*
Ausfahrt f (-en) *departure / exit*
Ausflug m (¨e) *trip, excursion*
ausführen v sep *to take out*
ausfüllen v sep *to fill in (form)*
Ausgang m (¨e) *exit*
ausgeben v sep ir *to spend (money), to give out*
ausgehen v sep ir *to go outside*
ausgezeichnet adj *excellent*
auskommen mit v sep ir *to get on with*
Auskunft f (¨e) *information*
Ausland n *abroad*
Ausländer/in m/f (-/-nen) *foreigner*
ausländisch adj *foreign*
ausleihen v sep ir *to lend*
ausmachen v sep *to turn off*
auspacken v sep *unpack*
ausrichten v sep *pass on (message)*
ausruhen sich v sep *to have a rest*
Ausrüstung f (-en) *equipment*
aussehen v sep ir *to look (appearance)*
außen adv *outside*
außer prep + dat *except for*
außerdem adv *moreover, as well*
außerhalb prep + gen *outside*
aussetzen v sep *to abandon*
Aussicht f (-en) *view, prospect*
aussteigen v sep ir *to get out/off*
Ausstellung f (-en) *exhibition*
Austausch m (-e) *exchange*
Australien n *Australia*
Ausverkauf m (¨e) *sale*
ausverkaufen v sep *to sell out*
ausverkauft adj *sold out*
Auswahl f (-en) *choice, selection*
Ausweis m (-e) *ID card*
ausziehen sich v sep ir *to get undressed*
Auto n (-s) *car*
Autobahn f (-en) *motorway*
Autofähre f (-n) *car ferry*
Automat m (-en) *machine*
Autovermietung f (-en) *car rental firm*

B

babysitten v *to baby sit*
Bach m (¨e) *stream*
backen v ir *to bake*
Bäcker/in m/f (-/-nen) *baker*
Bäckerei f (-en) *bakery*
Backofen m (¨) *oven*
Backstein m (-e) *brick*
Bad n (¨er) *bath*
Badeanzug m (¨e) *swimming costume*
Badehose f (-n) *swimming trunks*
baden v *to have a bath, to bathe / swim*
Badeort m (-e) *seaside resort*
Badetuch n (¨er) *bath towel*
Badewanne f (-n) *bathtub*
Badezimmer n (-) *bathroom*
Badminton n *badminton*
Bahn f (-en) *railway*
Bahnhof m (¨e) *station*
Bahnsteig m (-e) *platform*
bald adv *soon*
Balkon m (-e or -s) *balcony*
Ball m (¨e) *ball*
Banane f (-n) *banana*
Band f (-s) *band, group*
Bank f (-en) *bank*
Bankkarte f (-n) *bank card*
Bär m (-en) *bear*
Bargeld n *cash*
Bart m (¨e) *beard*
basteln v *to make (craft)*
Batterie f (-n) *battery*
Bauarbeiter/in m/f (-/-nen) *building worker/labourer*
Bauch m (¨e) *stomach / tummy*
bauen v *to build*
Bauer/Bäuerin m/f (-n/-nen) *farmer*
Bauernhaus n (¨er) *farmhouse*
Bauernhof m (¨e) *farm*
Baum m (¨e) *tree*
Baumwolle f *cotton*
Bayern n *Bavaria*
Beamte(r) *official, civil servant*
beantworten v *answer*
bedecken v *to cover*
bedeckt adj *covered, overcast*
bedienen v *to serve*
Bedienung f (-en) *service*
bedrohen v *to threaten / endanger*
bedürftig adj *needy*
beeilen sich v *to hurry up*
beenden v *to end*
befehlen v ir *to order / command*
befinden sich v ir *to be located / situated*
befriedigend adj *satisfactory*
begegnen v *to meet*
Begeisterung f (-) *enthusiasm*
Beginn m *beginning*
beginnen v ir *to begin*
begleiten v *to accompany*
begrüßen v *to greet*
behalten v ir *to keep*
behandeln v *to treat*
Behandlung f (-en) *treatment*
bei prep + dat *near, with, next to*
beide pron *both*
beiliegend adj *enclosed*
Bein n (-e) *leg*
Beispiel n (-e) *example*
beitragen (zu) v sep ir *contribute (to)*
bekommen v ir *to receive, to be host to*
beleidigen v *to insult / offend*
Belgien n *Belgium*
Belgier/in m/f (-/-nen) *Belgian*
belgisch adj *Belgian*
beliebt adj *popular*
bemerken v *to notice, observe*
benachteiligen v *to put at a disadvantage, to discriminate against*
benutzen v *to use*
Benutzer/in m/f (-/-nen) *user*
Benzin n *petrol*
bequem adj *comfortable*
beraten v ir *to advise*
bereit adj *ready*
Berg m (-e) *mountain*
Bericht m (-e) *report*
Beruf m (-e) *job, occupation*
Berufsausbildung f *vocational training*
Berufsberater/in m/f (-/-nen) *careers advisor*
Berufsschule f (-n) *vocational school, technical college*
berufstätig adj *working*
berühmt adj *famous*
berühren v *to touch*
beschäftigt adj *busy*
beschließen v ir *to decide / resolve*
beschreiben v ir *to describe*
beschweren sich v *to complain*
besetzt adj *occupied, engaged*
besichtigen v *to visit, to see (sights)*
besitzen v ir *to own*
Besitzer/in m/f (-/-nen) *owner*
besonders adv *especially*
besprechen v ir *to discuss*
besser adj/adv *better*
Besteck n *cutlery*
bestehen v ir *pass (exam)*
bestehen aus v ir *to consist of*
bestellen v *to order*
bestimmt adv *definitely*
bestrafen v *to punish*
Besuch m (-e) *visit*
besuchen v *to visit*
Betreff m (-e) *subject (of letter/e-mail)*
betreten v ir *to enter, to step/walk on*
Betrieb m (-e) *firm, company*
Betriebspraktikum n *work experience*
betrunken adj *drunk*
Bett n (-en) *bed*
Betttuch n (¨er) *sheet*
Bettwäsche f *bed linen*
bevor conj *before, while*
bevorzugen v *to prefer*
bewegen v *to move*
bewerben sich um v ir *to apply for*
Bewerbung f *application*
bewölkt adj *cloudy*
Bewusstsein n *consciousness*
bezahlen v *to pay (for)*
Bezahlung f (-en) *payment*
Bezug m (¨e) *reference* (in Bezug auf = *with regard to, concerning*)
BH (= Büstenhalter) m *bra*
Bibliothek f (-en) *library*
Bibliothekar/in m/f (-e/-nen) *librarian*
Biene f (-n) *bee*
Bier n (-e) *beer*
bieten v ir *offer*
Bild n (-er) *picture*
Bildschirm m (-e) *screen*
billig adj *cheap*
Biologie f *biology*
biologisch adj *biological, organic*
Biomüll m *organic waste*
Birne f (-n) *pear, light bulb*
bis prep + acc *until*
bis bald/morgen/später *see you soon / tomorrow / later*
bisschen (ein) adj/adv *a little bit*
bitte *here you are, please*
bitte schön *you're welcome*
bitten v ir *to ask*
bitten um v ir *to ask for*
Blatt n (¨er) *leaf, sheet of paper*
blau adj *blue*
Blei n (-e) *lead (metal)*
bleiben v ir *to stay, to remain*
bleifrei adj *unleaded*
Bleistift m (-e) *pencil*
Blick m (-e) *look, glance, view*
Blitz m (-e) *lightning*
blitzen v *to flash with lightning*
Blockflöte f (-n) *recorder*
blöd adj *silly, stupid*
Blödsinn m *stupidity, rubbish*
Blume f (-n) *flower*
Blumenhändler/in m/f (-e/-nen) *florist*
Blumenkohl m *cauliflower*
Blumenladen m (¨) *florist's shop*
Bluse f (-n) *blouse*
Blut n *blood*
Bockwurst f (¨e) *boiled sausage*
Boden m (¨) *ground, floor*

nouns — **m**: masculine **f**: feminine **n**: neuter **pl**: plural **v**: verb **v sep**: separable verb **v ir**: irregular verb **adj**: adjective **adv**: adverb

Bodensee m *Lake Constance*
Bohne f (-n) *bean*
Bonbon n or m (-s) *sweet*
Boot n (-e) *boat*
böse adj *nasty, angry*
Bowling n *(ten-pin) bowling*
Brand m (¨e) *fire*
Braten m (-) *joint, roast meat*
braten v ir *to roast*
Bratkartoffeln f pl *fried potatoes*
Bratpfanne f (-n) *frying pan*
Bratwurst f (¨e) *fried sausage*
Brauch m (¨e) *custom*
brauchen v *need*
braun adj *brown*
BRD (= Bundesrepublik Deutschland) f *(Federal Republic of) Germany*
brechen v ir *to break*
breit adj *broad, wide*
Bremse f (-n) *brake*
bremsen v *to brake*
Brennstoff m (-e) *fuel*
Brief m (-e) *letter*
Brieffreund/in m/f (-e/-nen) *pen friend*
Briefkasten m (¨) *postbox*
Briefmarke f (-n) *stamp*
Brieftasche f (-n) *wallet*
Briefträger/in m/f (-/-nen) *postman/woman*
Briefumschlag m (¨e) *envelope*
Brille f (-n) *glasses*
bringen v ir *to bring*
Brite/Britin m/f (-n/-nen) *Briton*
britisch adj *British*
Broschüre f (-n) *brochure/leaflet*
Brot n (-e) *bread, loaf of bread*
Brötchen n (-) *bread roll*
Brücke f (-n) *bridge*
Bruder m (¨) *brother*
Brunnen m (-) *well, fountain*
Buch n (¨er) *book*
buchen v *to book*
Bücherei f (-en) *library*
Bücherregal n (-e) *bookcase*
Buchhandlung f (-en) *bookshop*
Büchse f (-n) *tin, can*
Buchstabe m (-n) *letter (of alphabet)*
buchstabieren v *to spell*
Bude f (-n) *stall, booth*
Bügeleisen n (-) *iron*
bügeln v *to iron*
Bühne f (-n) *stage*
Bundesstraße f (-n) *Federal road (= A-road)*
bunt adj *bright, multi-coloured*
Burg f (-en) *castle, fort*
Bürgersteig m (-e) *pavement*
Büro n (-s) *office*
bürsten v *to brush (e.g. hair)*
Bus m (-se) *bus*
Busbahnhof m (¨e) *coach station*
Bushaltestelle f (-n) *bus stop*
Büstenhalter m (-) *bra*
Butterbrot n (-e) *sandwich*

C

Café n (-s) *café*
Campingplatz m (¨e) *campsite*
Cent m (- or -s) *cent*
Champignon m (-s) *mushroom*
Charakter m (-e) *character*
chatten v *to chat (online)*
Chef/in m/f (-s/-nen) *boss*
Chemie f *chemistry*
chemisch adj/adv *chemical(ly)*
Chips m pl *crisps*
Chor m (¨e) *choir*
Cola f (-s) *cola*
Computer m (-) *computer*
Computerprogrammierer/in m/f (-/-nen) *computer programmer*
Computerspiel n (-e) *computer game*
Couch f (-s/-en) *couch*
Cousin(e) m/f (-s,-n) *cousin*
Currywurst f (¨e) *curried sausage*

D

da adv *there*
da drüben *over there*
Dach n (¨er) *roof*
dafür adv *instead*
dagegen adv *against it / that*
damals adv *then (at that time)*
Dame f (-n) *lady*
damit adv *so that, with that*
Dampfer m (-) *steamer, steamship*
danach adv *after that*
Däne/Dänin m/f (-n/-nen) *Dane*
Dänemark n *Denmark*
dänisch adj *Danish*
dankbar adj *grateful*
danke (schön) *thank you (very much)*
danken v *to thank*
dann adv *then*
das heißt (d.h.) *that is (i.e.)*
das pron *that*
das stimmt *that's right*
dass conj *that*
Datum n (Daten) *date*
dauern v *to last*
DB (= Deutsche Bundesbahn) *German railway company*
Decke f (-n) *roof, ceiling, blanket*
decken v *to lay (e.g. table), to cover*
Delikatessengeschäft n (-e) *delicatessen*
denken v ir *to think*
Denkmal n (¨er) *monument, memorial*
denn conj *then, than, because*
dennoch adv *nevertheless*
deshalb adv *therefore*
deswegen adv *therefore*
Detail n (-s) *detail*
deutsch adj *German*
Deutsch n *German (language)*
Deutsche(r)/Deutsche m/f *German (person)*
Deutschland n *Germany*
Dezember m *December*
d.h. (= das heißt) *i.e.*
dicht adj *dense, thick*
dick adj *fat, thick*
Dieb m (-e) *thief*
Diebstahl m (¨e) *theft*
Diele f (-n) *hallway*
Dienstag m *Tuesday*
diese/r/s pron *this*
Diesel m *diesel*
Ding n (-e) *thing*
Diplom n (-e) *degree, diploma*
direkt adj/adv *direct(ly)*
Direktor/in m/f (-en/-nen) *headteacher, director*
Disko f (-s) *disco*
Diskothek f (-en) *disco*
Diskriminierung f (-en) *discrimination*
diskutieren v *to discuss*
Disziplin f (-en) *discipline*
doch conj *yes (in opposition to what has been said before)*
Dokumentarfilm m (-e) *documentary*
Dom m (-e) *cathedral*
Donau f *the Danube*
Donner m (-) *thunder*
donnern v *to thunder*
Donnerstag m *Thursday*
doof adj *stupid*
Doppelbett n (-en) *double bed*
Doppelhaus n (¨er) *semi-detached house*
Doppelstunde f (-n) *double period*
Doppelzimmer n (-) *double room*
Dorf n (¨er) *village*
dort adv *there, in that place*
dort drüben adv *over there*
dorthin adv *there (to there)*
Dose f (-n) *tin, can*
Dosenöffner m (-) *tin opener*
Drama n (Dramen) *drama*
draußen adv *outside*
dreckig adj *dirty*
Dreieck n (-e) *triangle*
dreieckig adj *triangular*
drinnen adv *inside*
Drittel n (-) *a third*
drittens adv *thirdly*
Droge f (-n) *drug*
Drogenhändler m (-) *drug dealer*
Drogensüchtige(r) m/f *drug addict*
Drogerie f (-n) *chemist's*
drüben adv *over there*
Druck m (¨e) *pressure*
drucken v *to print*
drücken v *to press/push*
Drucker m (-) *printer*
dumm adj *stupid*
dunkel adj *dark*
dünn adj *thin*
durch prep + acc *through, by*
durchfallen v sep ir *to fail (exam)*
dürfen v ir *to be allowed to ("may")*
Durst m *thirst*
durstig adj *thirsty*
Dusche f (-n) *shower*
duschen v *to shower*
Dutzend n (-e) *dozen*
dynamisch adj *dynamic*
D-Zug m (¨e) *express train*

E

eben adj/adv *smooth; just, precisely*
ebenso adv (+ wie) *just as*
echt adj *real, genuine*
Ecke f (-n) *corner*
egal adj/adv *the same*
(Das ist mir egal = *I don't mind*)
egoistisch adj *selfish*
Ehefrau f (-en) *wife*
ehemalig adj *former, previous*
Ehemann m (¨er) *husband*
Ehepaar n (-e) *married couple*
ehrlich adj *honest, sincere*
Ehrlichkeit f *honesty*
Ei n (-er) *egg*
eigene/r/s adj *own*
eigentlich adj/adv *actual(ly)*
eilen v *to hurry*
eilig adj *in a hurry, hurried*
einander pron *each other, one another*
einatmen v sep *breathe in*
Einbahnstraße f (-n) *one-way street*
einfach adj *easy, single (ticket)*
Einfahrt f (-en) *entry, arrival (of train)*
Einfamilienhaus n (¨er) *detached house*
Eingang m (¨e) *entrance*
eingehen v sep ir *to enter*
einige pron *a few, some*
Einkäufe m pl *shopping (purchases)*
einkaufen v sep *to shop*
einkaufen gehen v sep *to go shopping*
Einkaufskorb m (¨e) *shopping basket*
Einkaufsliste f (-n) *shopping list*
Einkaufstasche f (-n) *shopping bag*
Einkaufswagen f (-) *shopping trolley*
Einkaufszentrum n (-zentren) *shopping centre*
einladen v sep ir *invite*
Einladung f (-en) *invitation*
einmal adv *once*
einnehmen v sep ir *to take, to earn, to take up (space)*
einpacken v sep *to pack*
einrichten v sep *to furnish, to fit out*
einsam adj *lonely*
einschlafen v sep ir *to go to sleep*
einschalten v sep *to switch on*
einsteigen v sep ir *get on/in (vehicle)*
einstellen v sep *to put in, to hire, to stop, to adjust*
Eintopf m (¨e) *stew*
eintreten v sep ir *to enter*
Eintritt m (-e) *entrance, admission charge*
Eintrittsgeld n (-er) *admission charge*
Eintrittskarte f (-n) *entrance ticket*
einverstanden adj *in agreement*
Einwanderer/Einwanderin m/f (-/-nen) *immigrant*
einwerfen v sep ir *break (window), post (letter)*
Einwohner/in m/f (-/-nen) *resident, inhabitant*
Einzelbett n (-en) *single bed*
Einzelkind n (-er) *only child*
einzeln adj *single*
Einzelzimmer n (-) *single room*
einzig adj *only, sole*
Eis n *ice, ice cream*
Eisbecher m (-) *ice cream sundae*
Eisbahn f (-en) *ice rink*
Eisdiele f (-n) *ice cream parlour*
Eisen n (-) *iron*
Eisenbahnlinie f (-n) *railway line*
Eishalle f (-n) *ice rink*
Eis laufen n *ice skating*
ekelhaft adj *disgusting*
Elektriker/in m/f (-/-nen) *electrician*
elektrisch adj *electric(al)*
Elektrogeschäft n (-e) *electrical shop*
Elektroherd m (-e) *electric cooker*
Eltern pl *parents*
E-Mail f (-s) *email*
Empfang m (¨e) *reception*
Empfänger/in m/f (-/-nen) *recipient*
Empfangschef/in m/f (-s/-nen) *head porter*
Empfangsdame f (-n) *receptionist*
empfehlen v ir *to recommend*
Ende n (-n) *end*
enden v *to end*
endlich adv *at last, finally*
Endspiel n (-e) *final (e.g. sport)*
Energie f (-n) *energy*
eng adj *narrow, tight*
England n *England*
Engländer/in m/f (-/-nen) *English person*
englisch adj *English*
Enkel/in m/f (-/-nen) *grandson/granddaughter*
Enkelkind n (-er) *grandchild*
enorm adj/adv *enormous(ly)*
Ente f (-n) *duck*
entfernt adj *distant*
entlang prep + acc/dat *along*
entscheiden sich v ir *to decide*
entschuldigen sich v *to apologise*
entschuldigen Sie! *excuse me!*
Entschuldigung f (-en) *apology, Excuse me!*
entsetzlich adj *horrible, terrible*
entsorgen v *to dispose of*
entspannen sich v *to relax*
entweder…oder *either… or*
entwerten v *to invalidate (a ticket)*
Erbse f (-n) *pea*
Erdbeere f (-n) *strawberry*
Erde f (-n) *earth*
Erdgeschoss n (-e) *ground floor*
Erdkunde f *geography*
Erdnuss f (¨e) *peanut*
erfahren adj *experienced*
Erfahrung f (-en) *experience*
Erfolg m (-e) *success*
erfolgreich adj *successful*
Erfrischungen f pl *refreshments*
erfüllen v *to fill / to fulfil*
erhalten v ir *to receive*
erinnern (sich) v *to remind of (to remember)*
erkälten sich v *to catch a cold*
Erkältung f (-en) *a cold*
erkennen v ir *to recognise*
erklären v *to explain, to declare*
erlauben v *to allow*
erleben v *to experience*
Ermäßigung f (-en) *reduction*
ermüdend adj *tiring*
ernst adj *serious*
erreichen v *reach, achieve*
erschöpft adj *exhausted*
erst adv *first, not before, only then*
erstaunt adj *astonished*
Erste Hilfe f *first aid*
erstens adv *firstly*
erster Klasse *first class*
Erwachsene(r) *adult*
erwarten v *to expect*
erzählen v *to tell*
Erzählung f (-en) *story*
Essecke f (-n) *eating area*
Essen n *food, meal*
essen v *to eat*
Essig m (-e) *vinegar*
Esszimmer n (-) *dining room*
Etage f (-n) *floor, storey*
Etagenbett n (-en) *bunk bed*
Etui n (-s) *case*
etwa adv *about, roughly, approximately*
etwas pron *something*
Euro m (-/-s) *euro*
Europa n *Europe*
Europäer/in m/f (-/-nen) *European*
europäisch adj *European*
Examen n (-/Examina) *examination*
Experiment n (-e) *experiment*

F

Fabrik f (-en) *factory*
Fach n (¨er) *subject*
Fähre f (-n) *ferry*
fahren v ir *to go, to drive*
Fahrer/in m/f (-/-nen) *driver*
Fahrgast n (¨e) *passenger*
Fahrgeld n (-er) *fare*
Fahrkarte f (-n) *ticket*
Fahrkartenautomat m (-en) *ticket machine*
Fahrkartenschalter m (-) *ticket offic*
Fahrplan m (¨e) *timetable*
Fahrpreis m (-e) *fare*
Fahrrad n (¨er) *bicycle*
Fahrradverleih m (-e) *cycle hire firm*
Fahrradweg m (-e) *cycle path*
Fahrschein m (-e) *ticket*
Fahrstuhl m (¨e) *lift (elevator)*
Fahrt f (-en) *journey, drive*
fallen v ir *to fall*
fallen lassen v ir *to drop*
falsch adj *wrong, false*
Familie f (-n) *family*
Familienmitglied n (-er) *member of the family*
Familienname m (-n) *surname*
fantastisch adj *fantastic*
Farbe f (-n) *colour*
Fasching m (-e/-s) *(pre-Lent) carniv*
fast adv *almost*
faszinierend adj *fascinating*
faul adj *lazy*
Fax n (-e) *fax*
FCKWs m pl *CFCs*
Februar m *February*
fehlen v *to go wrong, to fail, to miss*
Fehler m (-) *mistake, fault*
Feier f (-n) *party, celebration*
Feierabend m (-e) *evening (leisure time)*
feiern v *to celebrate*
Feiertag m (-e) *holiday*
Feld n (-er) *field*
Fenster n (-) *window*
Ferien pl *holidays*
Ferienhaus n (¨er) *holiday house*
Ferienwohnung f (-en) *holiday flat*
Fernsehapparat m (-e) *TV set*
Fernsehen n *TV*
fernsehen v ir sep *to watch TV*
Fernseher m *TV set*
Fernsehgerät n (-e) *TV set*
Fernsehraum m (¨e) *TV room*
fertig adj *ready, finished*
fest adj *solid, firm*
Fest n (-e) *festival, party*
Fett n (-e) *fat*
fettig adj *greasy*
feucht adj *damp*
Feuer n (-) *fire*
Feuerwehr f *fire brigade*
Feuerwehrmann/frau m/f (¨er/-en) *firefighter*
Feuerwerk n *fireworks*
Fieber n *fever, temperature*
Film m (-e) *film*
filtern v *to filter*
Filzstift m (-e) *felt-tip pen*
finden v ir *to find*
Finger m (-) *finger*
Firma f (Firmen) *firm, company*
Firmenchef/in m/f (-s/-nen) *company head*
Fisch m (-e) *fish*
Fischgeschäft n (-e) *fishmonger's*
Fitnesszentrum n (-zentren) *fitness centre*
flach adj *flat*
Flamme f (-n) *flame*
Flasche f (-n) *bottle*
Fleisch n *meat*
Fleischer/in m/f (-/-nen) *butcher*
Fleischerei f (-n) *butcher's*
fleißig adj *hard-working*
flexibel adj *flexible*
Fliege f (-n) *fly*
fliegen v ir *to fly*
fliehen v ir *to escape / flee*
Flöte f (-n) *flute*
Flug m (¨e) *flight*
Flughafen m (¨) *airport*

prep: preposition **pron: pronoun** **conj**: conjunction **bits in brackets**: plural ending **(¨)**: plural — add umlaut

GERMAN—ENGLISH DICTIONARY

ugzeug n (-e) *aeroplane*
ur m (-e) *corridor, hallway*
uss m (¨-e) *river*
ussufer n (-) *riverbank*
gen v *to follow*
relle f (-n) *trout*
rm f (-en) *form, shape*
rmular n (-e) *form (to fill in)*
rschen v *to research*
rtschritt m *progress*
ssil adj *fossil(ised)*
to n (-s) *photo*
toapparat m (-e) *camera*
tograf/in m/f (-en/-nen) *photographer*
tografieren v *take a photo*
age f (-n) *question*
agen v *to ask*
ankreich n *France*
anzose/Französin m/f (-n/-nen) *French person*
anzösisch n *French (language)*
anzösisch adj *French*
au f (-en) *Mrs, woman*
äulein(!) n (-) *Miss, young lady (waitress!)*
ech adj *cheeky*
ei adj *free*
eibad n (¨-er) *(open air) swimming pool*
eiheit f (-en) *freedom*
eitag m *Friday*
eiwillig adj *voluntary, optional*
eiwillige(r) m/f *volunteer*
eizeit f *free time*
eizeitaktivität f (-en) *leisure activity*
eizeitbeschäftigung f (-en) *free time/leisure activity*
eizeitpark m (-s) *amusement park*
eizeitzentrum n (-zentren) *leisure centre*
emdsprache f (-n) *foreign language*
essen v ir *(of animals) to eat*
eude f (-n) *joy*
euen sich v *to be pleased/happy*
euen sich auf v + acc *to look forward to*
euen sich über v + acc *to be pleased about*
eund/in m/f (-e/-nen) *friend*
eundlich adj *friendly*
eundschaft f (-en) *friendship*
ieren v ir *to freeze*
ikadelle f (-n) *meatball, rissole*
isch adj *fresh*
iseur/Friseuse m/f (-e/-n) *hairdresser*
iseursalon m (-s) *hairdresser's salon*
oh adj *happy*
rohe/Fröhliche Weihnachten! *Happy Christmas!*
ruchtsaft m (¨-e) *fruit juice*
üh adj *early*
üher adj/adv *former(ly)*
rühling m (-e) *spring*
rühstück n (-e) *breakfast*
ühstücken v *to have breakfast*
ühlen sich v *to feel*
ihren v *to lead*
ührerschein m (-e) *driving licence*
üllen v *to fill*
üller m (-) *(fountain) pen*
undbüro n (-s) *lost property office*
unktionieren v *to function, work*
ür prep + acc *for*
ir jetzt *for the moment*
urchtbar adj/adv *terrible/terribly*
uß m (¨-e) *foot*
ußball m (¨-e) *football*
ußboden m (¨) *floor*
ußgänger m (-) *pedestrian*
ußgängerzone f (-n) *pedestrian zone*
ußweg m (-e) *footpath*
ittern v *to feed (animals)*

G

abel f (-n) *fork*
ang m (¨-e) *corridor*
ans f (¨-e) *goose*
anz adv *completely, quite*
anztags adj *full-time*
anztagsjob m (-s) *full-time job*
Ganztagsstelle f (-n) *full-time job*
gar nicht adv *not at all*
Garage f (-n) *garage*
garantieren v *to guarantee*
Gardine f (-n) *curtain*
Garten m (¨) *garden*
Gärtner/in m/f (-/-nen) *gardener*
Gasherd m (-e) *gas cooker*
Gast m (¨-e) *guest*
Gastfreundschaft f *hospitality*
Gastgeber/in m/f (-/-nen) *host(ess)*
Gasthaus n (¨-er) *guest house, pub*
Gasthof m (¨-e) *inn*
Gaststätte f (-n) *restaurant, pub*
Gebäude n (-) *building*
geben v ir *to give*
Gebiet n (-e) *region, area*
Gebirge n (-) *mountain range*
geboren adj *born, née*
gebraten adj *roast*
Gebrauch m (¨-e) *use, custom*
gebrochen adj *broken*
Geburt f (-en) *birth*
Geburtsdatum n *date of birth*
Geburtsort m *place of birth*
Geburtstag m (-e) *birthday*
geduldig adj/adv *patient(ly)*
Gefahr f (-en) *danger*
gefährlich adj *dangerous*
gefallen v ir *to like, to please*
Gefühl n (-e) *feeling*
gegen prep + acc *against, towards*
Gegend f (-en) *region*
Gegenstand m (¨-e) *object*
Gegenteil n *the opposite*
gegenüber prep + dat *opposite*
Gegenwart f *present (time)*
Gehalt n (¨-er) *salary*
gehen v ir *to go (by foot)*
Gehirn n (-e) *brain*
gehören v *to belong to*
Geige f (-n) *violin*
gekocht adj *cooked*
gekochtes Ei n *boiled egg*
gelb adj *yellow*
Geld n *money*
Geldschein m (-e) *banknote*
Geldstück n (-e) *coin*
Geldtasche f (-n) *money purse, wallet*
Gelegenheit f (-en) *opportunity*
gelingen v ir *to succeed*
gemein adj *nasty, common*
gemischt adj *mixed*
Gemüse n *vegetables*
Gemüsehändler m *greengrocer's*
gemütlich adj *comfortable, cosy*
genau adj/adv *exact(ly)*
Genf n *Geneva*
genießen v ir *to enjoy*
genug adj *enough*
geöffnet adj *open(ed)*
Geografie f *geography*
Gepäck n *luggage*
Gepäckaufbewahrung f *left luggage*
geplant adj *planned*
gerade adj/adv *straight, precisely / just*
geradeaus adv *straight ahead*
Gerät n (-e) *piece of equipment / apparatus*
gerecht adj/adv *just(ly), fair(ly)*
Gericht n (-e) *dish, law-court*
gern adv *with pleasure, willingly*
gern geschehen! *you're welcome, don't mention it*
gern haben v ir *to like*
Geruch m (¨-e) *smell*
Gesamtschule f (-n) *comprehensive school*
gesandt von *sent by*
Geschäft n (-e) *business, shop*
Geschäftsmann/frau m/f (¨-er/-en) *businessman/woman*
geschehen v ir *happen*
Geschenk n (-e) *present (gift)*
Geschichte f (-n) *history, story*
geschieden adj *divorced*
Geschirr n *dishes, crockery*
Geschirrtuch n (¨-er) *tea towel*
geschlossen adj *closed*
Geschmack m (¨-e) *taste*
Geschwister pl *siblings*
Gesellschaft f (-en) *society*
Gesicht n (-er) *face*
Gespräch n (-e) *conversation, discussion*
gestern adv *yesterday*
gestreift adj *striped*
gesund adj/adv *healthy / healthily*
Gesundheit f *health*
Getränk n (-e) *drink*
getrennt adj/adv *separate(ly), separated*
Gewalt f (-en) *power*
gewaltig adj *huge*
gewinnen v ir *to win*
Gewitter n *thunder storm*
gewöhnen sich an v +acc *to get used to*
Gewohnheit f (-en) *habit*
gewöhnlich adj/adv *usual(ly)*
Gewürz n (-e) *spice*
Gitarre f (-n) *guitar*
Glas n (¨-er) *glass, jar*
glatt adj *smooth, straight (e.g. hair)*
Glatteis n *black ice*
glauben v *to believe/think*
gleich adv *immediately, in a moment*
gleich adj *same, similar, equal*
Gleichheit f (-en) *similarity*
Gleis n (-e) *platform, track*
global adj *global*
Glück n *happiness, luck*
glücklich adj *happy*
GmbH (= Gesellschaft mit beschränkter Haftung) *Ltd.*
Goldfisch m (-e) *goldfish*
goldig adj *sweet, cute*
Gott m (¨-er) *God*
Grad m (-e) *degree, extent*
Gramm n (-/-e) *gram*
Gras n *grass*
gratis adv *free (of charge)*
gratulieren v *to congratulate*
grau adj *grey*
Grenze f (-n) *border*
Grieche/Griechin m/f (-n/-nen) *Greek*
Griechenland n *Greece*
griechisch adj *Greek*
Grill m (-s) *grill, barbecue*
grillen v *to grill, to barbecue*
Grippe f *flu*
groß adj *big, tall*
großartig adj *magnificent*
Großbritannien n *Great Britain*
Größe f (-n) *size, height*
Großeltern pl *grandparents*
Großmutter f (¨) *grandmother*
Großstadt f (¨-e) *city*
Großvater m (¨) *grandfather*
grün adj *green*
Grund m (¨-e) *ground, reason*
Grundschule f (-n) *primary school*
Gruppe f (-n) *group*
Gruß m (¨-e) *greeting*
Grüß Gott *hello*
gültig adj *valid*
günstig adj *favourable*
Gürtel m (-) *belt*
Gummi n or m (-s) *rubber*
Gurke f (-n) *cucumber*
gut adj/adv *good / well*
gut bezahlt *well paid*
gut gelaunt *in a good mood*
gute Nacht *goodnight*
gute Reise *have a good journey*
guten Abend *good evening*
guten Appetit! *enjoy your meal!*
guten Aufenthalt *enjoy your stay*
guten Tag *hello, good day*
Gymnasium n (Gymnasien) *secondary school for more academic pupils*
Gymnastik f *exercises, gymnastics*

H

Haar n (-e) *hair*
Haarbürste f (-n) *hairbrush*
haben v ir *to have*
Hafen m (¨) *harbour, port*
Hafenstadt f (¨-e) *port*
Haferflocken f pl *porridge oats*
Hagel m *hail*
hageln v *to hail*
Hähnchen n (-) *chicken*
halb adj/adv *half*
Halbpension f *half board (at hotel)*
Hälfte f (-n) *half*
Halle f (-n) *hall*
Hallenbad n (¨-er) *indoor swimming pool*
Hallo! *Hello*
Hals m (¨-e) *throat, neck*
Halskette f (-n) *necklace*
Halsschmerzen m pl *sore throat*
halten v ir *to hold, to stop*
Haltestelle f (-n) *stop (e.g. bus)*
Hamburger m (-) *hamburger*
Hand f (¨-e) *hand*
Handball m *handball*
Händler/in m/f (-/-nen) *trader, dealer, shopkeeper*
Handschuh m (-e) *glove*
Handtasche f (-n) *handbag*
Handtuch n (¨-er) *hand towel*
Handy n (-s) *mobile phone*
Hansaplast n *'Elastoplast ®'*
hart adj *hard, harsh, severe, unkind*
Hase m (-n) *hare*
hassen v *to hate*
hässlich adj *ugly*
Hauptbahnhof m (¨-e) *main station*
Hauptgericht n (-e) *main course*
Hauptschule f (-n) *secondary school for vocational/practical training*
Hauptstadt f (¨-e) *capital city*
Hauptstraße f (-n) *major road, main street*
Haus n (¨-er) *house*
Hausarbeit f *housework, homework*
Hausaufgabe f (-n) *homework*
Hausfrau f (-en) *housewife*
Haushalt m (-e) *household*
Hausmann m (¨-er) *househusband*
Hausmeister/in m/f (-/-nen) *caretaker*
Hausnummer f (-n) *house number*
Hausschuh m (-e) *slipper*
Haustier n (-e) *pet*
Haustür f (-en) *front door*
Hauswirtschaftslehre f *home economics*
Hautfarbe f *skin colour*
Hecke f (-n) *hedge*
Heft n (-e) *exercise book*
heftig adj *violent, heavy (rain etc.)*
Heftpflaster n (-) *sticking plaster*
Heiligabend m *Christmas Eve*
Heim n (-e) *home*
Heimat f (-en) *home, homeland*
Heimfahrt f (-en) *home journey*
Heimleiter/in m/f (-/-nen) *warden of home/hostel*
Heimleitung f (-en) *person in charge of home / hostel*
Heimweg m (-e) *way home*
heiraten v *marry*
heiß adj *hot*
heißen v ir *to be called (named)*
heiter adj *bright (weather)*
Heizkörper m (-) *radiator*
Heizung f *heating*
helfen v ir *to help*
hell adj *light, pale (colour)*
Helm m (-e) *helmet*
Hemd n (-en) *shirt*
her adv *(to) here*
heraus adv *out*
Herbergseltern pl *wardens (of youth hostel)*
Herbst m (-e) *autumn*
Herd m (-e) *cooker*
herein! *come in!*
hereinkommen v sep ir *to come in*
Herr m (-en) *Mr, gentleman*
Herr Ober! *waiter!*
herrlich adj *splendid, wonderful*
herrschend adj *ruling, dominant, prevailing*
herum adv *around*
herumfahren v sep ir *to travel/drive around*
herunterladen v sep ir *to download*
hervorragend adj *outstanding, excellent*
Herz n (-en) *heart*
herzliches willkommen! *welcome!*
herzlichen Glückwunsch! *congratulations!*
heute adv *today*
heutzutage adv *nowadays*
hier adv *here*
Hilfe f *help*
hilfreich adj *helpful*
hilfsbereit adj *helpful*
Himbeere f (-n) *raspberry*
Himmel m *sky, heaven*
hin und zurück adv *return (ticket)*
hinaus adv *out*
hinein adv *in*
hinlegen sich v sep *to lie down*
hinsetzen sich v sep *to sit down*
hinten adv *behind, at the back*
hinter prep + acc/dat *behind*
historisch adj/adv *historic(al)*
Hitze f *heat*
HIV-positiv adj *HIV positive*
hoch adv *high*
hochachtungsvoll adv *yours faithfully, yours sincerely*
Hochhaus n (¨-er) *skyscraper*
hochladen v sep ir *to upload*
Hochschule f (-n) *college, university*
Hochzeit f (-en) *wedding*
Hockey n *hockey*
hoffen v *to hope*
höflich adj *polite*
holen v *to fetch*
Holland n *Holland*
Holländer/in m/f (-/-nen) *Dutch person*
holländisch adj *Dutch*
Holz n (¨-er) *wood*
Honig m (-e) *honey*
hören v *to hear*
Hörer m (-) *receiver (telephone), headphone*
Horrorfilm m (-e) *horror film*
Hose f (-n) *trousers*
Hotel n (-s) *hotel*
Hotelverzeichnis n (-se) *list of hotels*
hübsch adj *pretty*
Hubschrauber m (-) *helicopter*
Hügel m (-) *hill*
hügelig adj *hilly*
humorlos adj *humourless*
humorvoll adj *humorous*
Hund m (-e) *dog*
Hunger m *hunger*
hungrig adj *hungry*
Husten m *cough*
husten v *to cough*
Hut m (¨-e) *hat*

I

ICE-Zug m (¨-e) *intercity express train*
ideal adj/adv *ideal(ly)*
Idee f (-n) *idea*
illegal adj/adv *illegal(ly)*
Illustrierte f (-n) *magazine*
im Freien *in the open air*
Image n (-s) *image*
Imbiss m (-e) *snack*
Imbissstube f (-n) *café*
immer adv *always*
immer noch adv *still*
in prep + acc/dat *in, into*
in Ordnung *OK*
inbegriffen adj *included*
Indien n *India*
Industrie f (-n) *industry*
industriell adj *industrial*
Informatik f *ICT, computing*
Informatiker/in m/f (-/-nen) *computer scientist*
Informationsbüro n (-s) *information office*
informativ adj *informative*
Ingenieur/in m/f (-e/-nen) *engineer*
inkl. (= inklusive) adj *inclusive*
Insektizid n (-e) *insecticide*
Insel f (-n) *island*
intelligent adj *intelligent*
interessant adj *interesting*
Interesse n (-n) *interest*
interessieren sich für v *to be interested in*
Internat n (-e) *boarding school*
Internet n *internet*
Internetseite f (-n) *web page*
Interview n (-s) *interview*
inzwischen adv *in the meantime, meanwhile*

nouns — **m**: masculine **f**: feminine **n**: neuter **pl**: plural **v**: verb **v sep**: separable verb **v ir**: irregular verb **adj**: adjective **adv**: adverb

GERMAN—ENGLISH DICTIONARY

Ire/Irin m/f (-n/-nen) *Irish person*
irgend- *some-*
irgendetwas pron *something*
irgendwo adv *somewhere (or other)*
irisch adj *Irish*
Irland n *Ireland*
Italien n *Italy*
Italiener/in m/f (-/-nen) *Italian person*
italienisch adj *Italian*

J

ja *yes*
Jacke f (-n) *(casual) jacket*
Jahr n (-e) *year*
Jahreszeit f (-en) *season*
Jahrhundert n (-e) *century*
jährlich adj/adv *annual(ly)*
Januar m *January*
je prep + acc *per*
jede/r/s pron *each, every, everybody*
jedoch conj/adv *however*
jemand pron *someone, somebody*
jene/r/s pron *that*
jetzt adv *now*
jobben v *to do a job/jobs*
joggen v *to jog*
Joghurt m or n (-s) *yoghurt*
Journalist/in m/f (-en/-nen) *journalist*
Jugendherberge f (-n) *youth hostel*
Jugendklub m (-s) *youth club*
Jugendliche/r *young person*
Juli m *July*
jung adj *young*
Junge m (-n) *boy*
jünger adj *younger*
Juni m *June*
Juwelier/in m/f (-e/-nen) *jeweller*
Juweliergeschäft n (-e) *jeweller's shop*

K

Kaffee m (-s) *coffee*
Kaffeekanne f (-n) *coffee pot*
Käfig m (-e) *cage*
Kakao m (-s) *cocoa*
Kalbfleisch n *veal*
Kalender m (-) *calendar, diary*
kalt adj *cold*
Kamera f (-s) *camera*
Kamm m (-e) *comb*
kämmen v *to comb*
Kanal m (-e) *canal, channel*
Kandidat/in m/f (-en/-nen) *candidate*
Kaninchen n (-) *rabbit*
Kännchen n (-) *jug, pot*
Kantine f (-n) *canteen*
Kanufahren n *canoeing*
Kapelle f (-n) *chapel*
kaputt adj *broken*
Karneval m (-e or -s) *carnival*
Karotte f (-n) *carrot*
Karriere f (-n) *career*
Karte f (-n) *map, ticket, card*
Kartoffel f (-n) *potato*
Kartoffelbrei m *mashed potatoes*
Kartoffelchips pl *crisps*
Kartoffelpüree n *mashed potatoes*
Kartoffelsalat m *potato salad*
Karton m (-s) *cardboard box*
Käse m *cheese*
Kasse f (-n) *checkout*
Kassette f (-n) *cassette*
Kassettenrekorder m (-) *cassette recorder*
Kassierer/in m/f (-/-nen) *cashier*
Katze f (-n) *cat*
kaufen v *to buy*
Kaufhaus n (-er) *department store*
Kaugummi m *chewing gum*
kaum adv *hardly*
kegeln v *to bowl, to play skittles*
kehren v *to turn*
kein pron *no (= not any)*
Keks m (-e) *biscuit*
Keller m (-) *cellar*
Kellner/in m/f (-/-nen) *waiter/waitress*
kennen v ir *know (a person)*
kennen lernen v *to get to know*
Kenntnis f (-se) *knowledge*
Kennwort n (-er) *password*
Kfz (= Kraftfahrzeug) n *motor vehicle*
Kilometer m (-) *kilometre*
Kind n (-er) *child*

Kindheit f *childhood*
Kindergarten m (-) *nursery school*
Kinn n (-e) *chin*
Kino n (-s) *cinema*
Kiosk m (-e) *kiosk*
Kirche f (-n) *church*
Kirchturm m (-) *steeple, church tower*
Kirsche f (-n) *cherry*
Kissen n (-) *cushion*
klar adj *clear*
Klarinette f (-n) *clarinet*
Klasse f (-n) *class*
klasse adj *great*
Klassenarbeit f (-en) *test*
Klassenfahrt f (-en) *school trip*
Klassenkamerad/in m/f (-en/-nen) *classmate*
Klassenzimmer n (-) *classroom*
klassisch adj/adv *classic(al)*
Klavier n (-e) *piano*
kleben v *to stick*
Klebstoff m (-e) *glue*
Kleid n (-er) *dress*
Kleider n pl *clothes*
Kleiderschrank m (-e) *wardrobe*
Kleidung f *clothing*
Kleidungsgeschäft n (-e) *clothes shop*
klein adj *small, short*
Kleingeld n *(small) change*
Klempner/in m/f (-/-nen) *plumber*
klettern v *to climb*
klicken v *to click*
Klima n (-s) *climate*
Klingel f (-n) *bell*
klingeln v *to ring (doorbell)*
Klo n (-s) *loo*
klopfen v *to knock*
Klub m (-s) *club*
klug adj *clever*
Kneipe f (-n) *pub*
Knie n (-) *knee*
Knopf m (-e) *button*
Koch/Köchin m/f (-e/-nen) *cook*
Kochen n *cooking*
kochen v *to cook*
Koffer m (-) *suitcase, trunk*
Kohl m (-e) *cabbage*
Kohle f *coal*
Kollege/in m/f (-n/-nen) *colleague*
Köln n *Cologne*
komisch adj *funny*
kommen v ir *to come*
Kommode f (-n) *chest of drawers*
Komödie f (-n) *comedy*
kompliziert adj *complicated*
können v ir *to be able to*
Kontakt m (-e) *contact*
Konto n (Konten) *(bank) account*
Kontrolleur/in m/f (-e/-nen) *(ticket) inspector*
kontrollieren v *to check, to supervise, to control*
Konzert n (-e) *concert*
Kopf m (-e) *head*
Kopfhörer m (-) *headphones*
Kopfkissen n (-) *pillow*
Kopfsalat m (-e) *lettuce*
Kopfschmerzen m pl *headache*
kopieren v *to copy*
Korb m (-e) *basket*
Körper m (-) *body*
Korridor m (-e) *corridor*
korrigieren v *to correct, to mark*
kosten v *to cost*
kostenlos adj *free*
köstlich adj *delicious*
Kostüm n (-e) *(women's) suit, costume*
Kotelett n (-e) *cutlet, chop*
krank adj *ill*
Krankenhaus n (-er) *hospital*
Krankenpfleger m (-) *(male) nurse*
Krankenschwester f (-n) *(female) nurse*
Krankenwagen m (-) *ambulance*
Krankheit f (-en) *illness*
Krawatte f (-n) *tie*
Krebs m *cancer*
Kreditkarte f (-n) *credit card*
Kreide f (-n) *chalk*
Kreis m (-e) *circle*
Kreisverkehr m (-e) *roundabout*

Kreuzung f (-en) *crossroads*
kriegen v *to get*
Krimi m (-s) *crime story, thriller*
Kriminalität f *crime*
kritisieren v *to criticise*
Küche f (-n) *kitchen*
Kuchen m (-) *cake*
Kugelschreiber m (-) *biro, ballpoint pen*
Kuh f (-e) *cow*
kühl adj *cool*
Kühlschrank m (-e) *fridge*
Kuli m (-s) *biro*
kümmern sich um v *to take care of*
Kunde/Kundin m/f (-n/-nen) *customer*
kündigen v *to cancel, to hand in notice*
Kündigung f (-en) *cancellation, notice (to quit)*
Kunst f (-e) *art*
Kunstgalerie f (-n) *art gallery*
Künstler/in m/f (-/-nen) *artist*
Kunststoff m (-e) *plastic, synthetic material*
Kunstwerk n (-e) *work of art*
Kurs m (-e) *course*
Kurve f (-n) *bend, curve*
kurz adj *short*
kürzlich adv *recently*
Kusine f (-n) *cousin (f)*
Kuss m (-e) *kiss*
küssen v *to kiss*
Küste f (-n) *coast*

L

Labor n (-s/-e) *laboratory*
lächeln v *to smile*
lachen v *to laugh*
Lachs m (-e) *salmon*
Laden m (-) *shop*
laden v ir *to load, to charge*
Ladenbesitzer/in m/f (-/-nen) *shopkeeper*
Lagerfeuer n (-) *campfire*
Lamm m (-er) *lamb*
Lammfleisch n *lamb (meat)*
Lampe f (-n) *lamp*
Land n (-er) *country, administrative district*
landen v *to land*
Landkarte f (-n) *map*
Landschaft f (-en) *landscape*
lang adj *long*
langsam adj/adv *slow(ly)*
langweilen sich v *to get bored*
langweilig adj *boring*
Lärm m *noise*
lassen v ir *to leave*
Lastwagen m (-) *lorry, truck*
Latein n *Latin*
laufen v ir *to go, to walk, to run*
Laune f (-n) *mood*
launisch adj *moody*
laut adj/adv *loud(ly), noisy*
lautlos adj/adv *silent(ly)*
Leben n (-) *life*
leben v *to live*
lebendig adj *living, lively*
Lebenslauf m (-e) *CV*
Lebensmittel n pl *food, groceries*
Lebensmittelgeschäft n (-e) *grocer's shop*
Leber f (-n) *liver*
lebhaft adj *lively, busy*
lecker adj *delicious*
Leder n (-n) *leather*
ledig adj *single (unmarried)*
leer adj *empty*
leeren v *to empty*
legal adj/adv *legal(ly)*
legen v *to put, to lie something down*
Lehre f (-n) *apprenticeship, teaching*
lehren v *to teach*
Lehrer/in m/f (-/-nen) *teacher*
Lehrerzimmer n (-) *staff room*
Lehrling m (-e) *apprentice*
lehrreich adj *educational*
leicht adj *easy, light (weight)*
Leichtathletik f *athletics*
Leid tun v ir *to regret, be sorry (es tut mir Leid = I'm sorry)*
leiden können v *to like*
leider adv *unfortunately*

leihen v ir *to lend*
leihen sich v ir *to borrow*
leise adj/adv *quiet(ly)*
Leistung f (-en) *performance, achievement*
Leiter/in m/f (-/-nen) *manager, leader*
Leiter f (-n) *ladder*
lernen v *to learn*
Lesen n *reading*
lesen v ir *to read*
letzte/r/s adj *last*
Leute pl *people*
Licht n (-er) *light*
lieb adj/adv *kind(ly), likeable, nice(ly)*
Liebe f (-n) *love*
lieben v *to love*
lieber adv *rather*
Lieber/Liebe *Dear (in a letter)*
Liebesfilm m (-e) *romantic film*
Lieblings- *favourite*
Lied n (-er) *song*
liefern v *to deliver*
Lieferwagen m (-) *(delivery) van*
liegen v ir *to lie*
Liga f (Ligen) *league*
lila adj *purple*
Limo(nade) f (-s/-n) *lemonade*
Lineal n (-e) *ruler*
Linie f (-n) *line, route*
linke/r/s adj *left*
links adv *left*
Lippe f (-n) *lip*
Lippenstift m (-e) *lipstick*
Liste f (-n) *list*
Liter m or n (-) *litre*
Lkw (= Lastkraftwagen) m (-) *lorry*
Loch n (-er) *hole*
lockig adj *curly*
Löffel m (-) *spoon*
Lohn m (-e) *wage*
Lokal n (-e) *pub*
löschen v *to erase, to delete, to switch off (light), to extinguish*
Lotto n (-s) *national lottery*
Löwe m (-n) *lion*
lügen v *to tell a lie*
Luft f *air*
Luftverschmutzung f *air pollution*
Lunge f (-n) *lungs*
Lust (f) haben v ir *to feel like (doing something)*
lustig adj *funny*
Luxus m *luxury*

M

machen v *to make, to do*
Mädchen n (-) *girl*
Magen m (-) *stomach*
Magenschmerzen m pl *stomach ache*
mähen v *to mow*
Mahl n (-e/-er) *meal*
Mahlzeit f (-en) *meal*
Mai m *May*
Mal n (-e) *time*
malen v *to paint*
Maler/in m/f (-/-nen) *painter*
malerisch adj *picturesque*
Manager/in m/f (-/-nen) *manager*
manchmal adv *sometimes*
Mann m (-er) *man, husband*
männlich adj *male*
Mannschaft f (-en) *team*
Mantel m (-) *coat*
Margarine f (-n) *margarine*
Marke f (-n) *brand, make*
Marketing n *marketing*
Markt(platz) m (-e) *market (place)*
Marmelade f (-n) *jam, marmalade*
März m *March*
Maß n (-e) *measure, measurement*
mäßig adj/adv *moderate(ly)*
Mathe(matik) f *maths*
Mauer f (-n) *wall*
Maurer/in m/f (-/-nen) *builder*
Maus f (-e) *mouse*
Maximum n (Maxima) *maximum*
Mechaniker/in m/f (-/-nen) *mechanic*
Medienwissenschaft f *media studies*
Medikament n (-e) *medicine*
Meer n (-e) *sea*
Meerschweinchen n (-) *guinea pig*
mehr pron/adv *more*
Mehrbettzimmer n (-) *shared room*

mehrere pron *several*
Mehrfamilienhaus n (-er) *house for several families*
Mehrzweckraum m (-e) *multi-purpose room*
Meile f (-n) *mile*
mein/e/r pron *my*
meinen v *to think, to mean*
Meinung f (-en) *opinion*
meistens adv *mostly*
Meisterschaft f (-en) *championship*
Melodie f (-n) *melody*
Melone f (-n) *melon*
Menge f (-n) *quantity, load, crowd*
Mensch m (-en) *person*
merkwürdig adj/adv *strange(ly), odd(ly)*
Messe f (-n) *mass*
messen v ir *to measure*
Messer n (-) *knife*
Metall n (-e) *metal*
Meter m or n (-) *metre*
Metzger/in m/f (-/-nen) *butcher*
Metzgerei f (-en) *butcher's*
mies adj *lousy*
Miete f (-n) *rent*
mieten v *to rent*
Mikrowelle f (-n) *microwave*
Mikrowellenherd m (-e) *microwave oven*
Milch f *milk*
Million f (-en) *million*
Mindest- *minimum*
mindestens adv *at least*
Mineralwasser n *mineral water*
Minimum n (Minima) *minimum*
Minute f (-n) *minute*
mit prep + dat *with*
mit freundlichen Grüßen *yours sincerely*
mit Vergnügen! *with pleasure!*
mitgehen v sep ir *to go with*
Mitglied n (-er) *member*
mitkommen v sep ir *come (along)*
mitnehmen v sep ir *take (with you)*
Mittag m *midday*
mittags adv *at midday*
Mittagessen n (-) *lunch*
Mittagspause f (-n) *lunch break*
Mitte f (-n) *middle*
mitteilen v sep *to inform*
Mitteilung f (-en) *(text) message*
Mittel n (-) *means, method*
mittelgroß adj *medium/average height*
mittellang adj *medium/average length*
Mittelmeer n *Mediterranean Sea*
mitten adv *in the middle*
Mitternacht f *midnight*
Mittwoch m *Wednesday*
Mobbing n *workplace bullying*
Möbel n (-) *furniture*
Möbelstück n (-e) *piece of furniture*
möbliert adj *furnished*
Mode f (-n) *fashion*
Modegeschäft n (-e) *clothes shop*
modern adj *modern*
modisch adj *fashionable*
Mofa n (-s) *moped*
mögen v ir *to like*
möglich adj *possible*
Möglichkeit f (-en) *possibility*
Moment m (-e) *moment*
Monat m (-e) *month*
monatlich adj/adv *monthly*
Mond m (-e) *moon*
Montag m *Monday*
Morgen m (-) *morning*
morgen adv *tomorrow*
morgen früh *tomorrow morning*
morgens adv *in the morning(s)*
Mosel f *the Moselle (river)*
Motor m (-en) *engine*
Motorrad n (-er) *motorbike*
Motorradfahrer/in m/f (-/-nen) *motorbike rider*
müde adj *tired*
mühsam adj *laborious*
Müll m *rubbish*
Mülltonne f (-n) *dustbin*
multikulturell adj *multicultural*
München n *Munich*
Mund m (-er) *mouth*
mündlich adj/adv *oral(ly)*

prep: preposition **pron**: pronoun **conj**: conjunction **bits in brackets**: plural ending **(-)**: plural — add umlaut

GERMAN–ENGLISH DICTIONARY

Münze f (-n) *coin*
Museum n (Museen) *museum*
Musik f *music*
Musiker/in m/f (-/-nen) *musician*
musizieren v *to play a musical instrument*
müssen v ir *to have to*
Mutter f (¨) *mother*
Mutti f (-s) *mum, mummy*
Mütze f (-n) *cap, hat*
MwSt. (= Mehrwertsteuer) f *VAT*

N

nach prep + dat *after, to*
nach Hause *home*
nach oben *upwards, upstairs*
nach unten *downwards, downstairs*
Nachbar/in m/f (-n/-nen) *neighbour*
nachdem conj *after*
nachgehen v sep ir *to follow*
nachher adv *afterwards*
Nachmittag m (-e) *afternoon*
nachmittags adv *in the afternoon(s)*
Nachrichten f pl *news*
nachsehen v sep ir *to check, to look up, to watch*
Nachspeise f (-n) *dessert*
nächste/r/s adj *next*
Nacht f (¨e) *night*
Nachteil m (-e) *disadvantage*
Nachthemd n (-en) *nightshirt*
Nachtisch m (-e) *dessert*
nachts adv *at night*
Nachttisch m (-e) *bedside table*
nahe adj *near*
Nähe f *nearness, vicinity*
Nahrung f *food*
Nase f (-n) *nose*
nass adj *wet*
Natur f (-en) *nature*
natürlich adj/adv *of course, naturally*
Naturwissenschaft f (-en) *science*
Nebel m (-) *fog, mist*
nebelig adj *foggy*
neben prep + acc/dat *next to*
Nebenjob m (-s) *side job*
Neffe m (-n) *nephew*
nehmen v ir *to take*
nein *no*
nennen v ir *to name, to call*
nerven v *to get on someone's nerves*
nervös adj/adv *nervous(ly)*
nett adj *nice, kind*
Netz n (-e) *net*
neu adj *new*
neulich adv *recently*
nicht adv *not*
nicht einmal *not even*
nicht mehr *no longer*
nicht nur ... sondern auch *not only ... but also*
nicht wahr? *isn't it?*
Nichte f (-n) *niece*
nichts pron *nothing* (Das macht nichts = *It doesn't matter*)
nie adv *never*
Niederlande n pl *Netherlands*
Niederschlag m *precipitation*
niedrig adj/adv *low*
niemals adv *never*
niemand pron *no one*
nirgends adv *nowhere*
noch adv *still*
noch einmal *again*
noch nicht adv *not yet*
nochmal adv *again*
Nordamerika n *North America*
Norden m *north*
nördlich adj/adv *in/to the north*
Nordsee f *North Sea*
normal adj *normal*
normalerweise adv *normally*
Nostalgie f *nostalgia*
Not f (¨e) *need, distress, trouble*
Notausgang m (¨e) *emergency exit*
Note f (-n) *mark, grade*
notieren v *to note*
nötig adj *necessary*
Notizbuch n (¨er) *notebook*
notwendig adj *necessary*
November m *November*
Nudeln f pl *pasta, noodles*
nützlich adj *useful*
Nummer f (-n) *number*
nun adv *now*
nur adv *only*
Nuss f (¨e) *nut*
Nutzen m *use, usefulness*
nutzlos adj/adv *useless(ly)*

O

ob conj *whether*
obdachlos adj *homeless*
oben adv *at the top, above, upstairs*
Oberstufe f (-n) *6th form*
Obst n *fruit*
Obst- und Gemüseladen m (¨) *fruit and veg shop*
obwohl conj *although*
oder conj *or*
Ofen m (¨) *heater, oven*
offen adj *open*
öffentlich adj *public, municipal*
öffentliche Verkehrsmittel n pl *public transport*
öffnen v *to open*
Öffnungszeiten f pl *opening times*
oft adv *often*
ohne prep + acc *without*
ohne Zweifel *without doubt*
Ohr n (-en) *ear*
Ohrring m (-e) *earring*
Oktober m *October*
Öl n *oil*
Öltanker m (-) *oil tanker*
Oma f (-s) *granny*
Omelett n (-e/-s) *omelette*
Onkel m (-) *uncle*
Opa m (-s) *grandpa*
Oper f (-n) *opera*
Operation f (-en) *operation (medical)*
Opfer n (-) *victim, sacrifice*
optimistisch adj/adv *optimistic(ally)*
Orangenmarmelade f (n) *marmelade*
Orchester n (-) *orchestra*
ordentlich adj *tidy*
Ordnung f (-en) *order, routine*
organisch adj/adv *organic(ally)*
organisieren v *to organise*
Ort m (-e) *place*
örtlich adj/adv *local(ly)*
Osten m *east*
Ostern n *Easter*
Österreich n *Austria*
Österreicher/in m/f (-/-nen) *Austrian*
österreichisch adj *Austrian*
östlich adj/adv *in/to the east*
Ostsee f *Baltic Sea*
Ozonloch n *hole in the ozone layer*
Ozonschicht f *ozone layer*

P

Paar n (-e) *pair*
paar (ein) adj *a few/couple*
Päckchen n (-) *packet, small parcel*
Packung f (-en) *packet*
Paket n (-e) *package, packet*
Palast m (¨e) *palace*
Pampelmuse f (-n) *grapefruit*
Panne f (-n) *breakdown, flat tyre*
Papier n (-e) *paper*
Papiere n pl *papers, (official) documents*
Pappe f (-n) *cardboard*
Parfüm n (-e/-s) *perfume*
Parfümerie f (-en) *perfumery*
Park m (-s) *park*
parken v *to park*
Parkhaus n (¨er) *multistorey car park*
Parkplatz m (¨e) *parking place*
Partei f (-en) *(political) party*
Partnerstadt f (¨e) *twin town*
Pass m (¨e) *passport*
Passagier m (-e) *passenger*
passen v *to fit, to be suitable*
passieren v *to happen*
Passkontrolle f (-n) *passport control*
Patient/in m/f (-en/-nen) *patient*
Pause f (-n) *break*
Pech n *bad luck*
Pension f (-en) *guest house*
perfekt adj/adv *perfect(ly)*
Person f (-en) *person*
Personalausweis m (-e) *identity card*
Persönlichkeit f (-en) *personality*
pessimistisch adj/adv *pessimistic(ally)*
Pestizid n (-e) *pesticide*
Pfand n (¨er) *security, deposit*
Pfarrer/in m/f (-/-nen) *pastor, vicar*
Pfeffer m (-) *pepper*
Pferd n (-e) *horse*
Pfingsten n *Whitsun, Pentecost*
Pfirsich m (-e) *peach*
Pflanze f (-n) *plant*
Pflaume f (-n) *plum*
Pflichtfach n (¨er) *(compulsory) subject*
Pfund n (-e) *pound*
Pfund Sterling n *pound sterling*
Physik f *physics*
physisch adj/adv *physical(ly)*
Picknick n (-e/-s) *picnic*
picknicken v *to (have a) picnic*
Pilz m (-e) *mushroom, toadstool*
Plakat n (-e) *poster*
Plan m (¨e) *plan*
planen v *to plan*
Plastik n *plastic*
Platz m (¨e) *place, room, seat, square, court*
plaudern v *to chat*
plötzlich adv *suddenly*
PLZ (= Postleitzahl) f *post code*
Polen n *Poland*
Polizei f *police*
Polizeiwache f (-n) *police station*
Polizist/in m/f (-en/-nen) *policeman/woman*
Pommes frites n pl *chips*
Popmusik f *pop music*
Portemonnaie n (-s) *wallet, purse*
Portion f (-en) *portion, helping*
Post f *post, post office*
Postamt n (¨er) *post office*
Postbote/botin m/f (-n/-nen) *postman/woman*
Poster n (-/-s) *poster*
Postkarte f (-n) *postcard*
Postleitzahl f (-en) *post code*
praktisch adj/adv *practical(ly)*
Pralinen f pl *chocolates*
Preis m (-e) *price*
Preisliste f (-n) *price list*
preiswert adj *cheap, good value*
Priester m (-) *priest*
prima adj *great*
privat adj *private, personal*
Privatschule f (-n) *private school*
pro prep *per*
pro Stunde *per hour*
probieren v *to try out*
Problem n (-e) *problem*
produzieren v *to produce*
Programm n (-e) *program(me)*
Programmierer/in m/f (-/-nen) *computer programmer*
Projekt n (-e) *plan, project*
Projektor m (-en) *projector*
Prospekt m (-e) *leaflet*
prost! *cheers!*
Prozent n (-e) *per cent*
prüfen v *to test, to examine, to check*
Prüfung f (-en) *exam*
Pullover, Pulli m (-, -s) *pullover*
Punkt m (-e) *point, full stop*
pünktlich adj/adv *punctual, on time*
putzen v *to clean*

Q

Quadrat n (-e) *square*
Qualifikation f (-en) *qualification*
Qualität f (-en) *quality*
Quantität f (-en) *quantity*
Quatsch m *rubbish (nonsense)*
Querflöte f (-n) *flute*
Quittung f (-en) *receipt*
Quizsendung f (-en) *quiz show*

R

Rabatt m (-e) *discount*
Rad n (¨er) *bicycle, wheel*
Radfahren n *cycling*
Radfahrer/in m/f (-/-nen) *cyclist*
Radiergummi m (-s) *rubber, eraser*
Rand m (¨er) *edge*
Rapmusik f *rap*
Rasen m *lawn*
Rasse f (-n) *race (people)*
Rassenproblem n (-e) *race problem*
Rassismus m *racism*
rassistisch adj *racist*
Raststätte f (-n) *motorway services*
raten v ir *to advise*
Rathaus n (¨er) *town hall*
Rauch m *smoke*
rauchen v *to smoke*
Raucher(in) m/f (-/-nen) *smoker*
Realschule f (-n) *secondary school*
rechnen v *to count, to calculate*
Rechnung f (-en) *bill*
recht haben v ir *to be right*
Rechteck n (-e) *rectangle*
rechts adv *right*
Rechtsanwalt/anwältin m/f (¨e/-nen) *lawyer*
rechtzeitig adj/adv *punctual / on time*
recyceln v *to recycle*
Rede f (-n) *speech*
reden v *to talk*
reduziert adj *reduced*
Regal n (-e) *shelves*
Regel f (-n) *rule*
regelmäßig adj/adv *regular(ly)*
Regen m *rain*
Regenmantel m (¨) *raincoat*
Regenschirm m (-e) *umbrella*
regnen v *to rain*
regnerisch adj *rainy*
reich adj *rich*
reichen v *to be enough, to react*
reif adj *mature, ripe*
Reifen m (-) *tyre*
Reifenpanne f (-n) *puncture*
Reihe f (-n) *row (of seats etc.)*
Reihenhaus n (¨er) *terraced house*
reinigen v *to clean*
Reinigung f *cleaning, dry cleaning*
Reis m *rice*
Reise f (-n) *journey*
Reisebüro n (-s) *travel agency*
Reisebus m (-se) *coach*
reisen v *to travel*
Reisende(r) m/f *traveller*
Reisepass m (¨e) *passport*
Reisescheck m (-s) *traveller's cheque*
Reisetasche f (-n) *holdall, travel bag*
Reiseziel n (-e) *destination*
reiten v ir *to ride*
Reiten n *horse riding*
Reklame f (-n) *advert*
Religion f (-en) *religion, R.E.*
rennen v ir *to run*
Rennen n (-) *running, racing, race*
Rentner/in m/f (-/-nen) *pensioner*
Reparatur f (-en) *repair*
reparieren v *to repair*
reservieren v *to reserve*
Reservierung f (-en) *reservation*
Rest m (-e) *rest, remainder*
Resultat n (-e) *result*
retten v *to save*
Rezept n (-e) *prescription, recipe*
Rezeption f (-en) *reception*
Rhein m *the Rhine*
richtig adj *right, true*
Richtung f (-en) *direction*
riechen v ir *to smell*
Riegel m (-) *bar (of chocolate etc.)*
Rindfleisch n *beef*
Ring m (-e) *ring*
Risiko n (-s/Risiken) *risk*
Rock m (¨e) *skirt*
Rockmusik f *rock music*
roh adj/adv *raw, rough(ly)*
Rollbrett n (-er) *skateboard*
Roller m (-) *scooter*
Rollschuh laufen v ir *to go roller-skating*
Rolltreppe f (-n) *escalator*
Roman m (-e) *novel*
romantisch adj *romantic(ally)*
rosa adj *pink*
Rosenkohl m (-e) *Brussels sprout*
rot adj *red*
Rücken m (-) *back*
Rückfahrkarte f (-n) *return ticket*
Rückfahrt f (-en) *return journey*
Rucksack m (¨e) *rucksack*
rückwärts adv *backwards*
rudern v *to row*
Ruderboot n (-e) *rowing boat*
rufen v ir *to call, to shout*
Rugby n *rugby*
Ruhe f *peace, calm*
ruhig adj *peaceful, calm*
rund adj *round (shape)*
Rundfahrt f (-en) *tour (on transport)*
Rundgang m (¨e) *tour (walking)*
Russe/Russin m/f (-n/-nen) *Russian*
russisch adj *Russian*
Russland n *Russia*

S

Saal m (Säle) *hall, ballroom*
Sache f (-n) *thing*
Sackgasse f (-n) *cul-de-sac*
Saft m (¨e) *juice*
sagen v *to say, to tell*
Sahne f *cream*
Salat m (-e) *salad, lettuce*
Salz n *salt*
Salzkartoffeln f pl *boiled potatoes*
sammeln v *to collect*
Sammlung f (-en) *collection*
Samstag m *Saturday*
Sand m (-e) *sand*
Sandburg f (-en) *sand castle*
Sandale f (-n) *sandal*
sanft adj/adv *soft(ly), gentle/gently*
Sänger/in m/f (-/-nen) *singer*
Satellitenfernsehen n *satellite TV*
satt adj *full (having eaten)*
satt haben v ir *to be fed up with something*
sauber adj *clean*
sauer adj *sour, angry*
Sauerkraut n *pickled cabbage*
Sauerstoff m *oxygen*
saurer Regen m (-) *acid rain*
S-Bahn f *suburban railway*
Schach n *chess*
Schachtel f (-n) *small box (e.g. of chocolates)*
schade adj *(what a) shame*
schaden v *to damage, to harm*
Schaden m (¨) *damage*
schädlich adj *harmful*
Schaf n (-e) *sheep*
schaffen v ir *to create, to make*
Schal m (-s/-e) *scarf, shawl*
Schale f (-n) *skin, peel, shell*
Schalter m (-) *ticket office, switch*
schämen sich v *to be ashamed*
scharf adj *sharp, hot (spicy)*
Schaschlick n (-s) *kebab*
Schatten m (-) *shadow*
schattig adj *shady*
schauen v *to look*
Schauer m (-) *(rain) shower*
Schaufenster n (-) *display window*
Schauspieler/in m/f (-/-nen) *actor/actress*
Scheck m (-s) *cheque*
Scheckheft n (-e) *cheque book*
Scheibe f (-n) *slice*
scheiden (sich scheiden lassen) v ir *to get divorced*
Schein m (-e) *banknote*
scheinen v ir *to seem, to appear, to shine*
Scheinwerfer m (-) *headlight*
schenken v *to give (a present)*
Schere f (-n) *pair of scissors*
Schichtarbeit f *shift work*
schick adj/adv *stylish(ly)*
schicken v *to send*
schießen v ir *to shoot, to score*
Schiff n (-e) *ship*
Schild n (-er) *signpost*
Schildkröte f (-n) *tortoise*
Schinken m *ham*
Schlafanzug m (¨e) *pyjamas*
schlafen v ir *to sleep*
Schlafraum m (¨e) *dormitory, bedroom*
Schlafsack m (¨e) *sleeping bag*
Schlafwagen m (-) *sleeping car*
Schlafzimmer n (-) *bedroom*
schlagen v ir *to hit, to knock*
Schläger m (-) *racquet, stick, bat*
Schlagsahne f *whipped cream*
Schlagzeug n (-e) *drums*
Schlange f (-n) *snake*
Schlange stehen v ir *to queue*
schlank adj *slim*

nouns — **m**: *masculine* **f**: *feminine* **n**: *neuter* **pl**: *plural* **v**: *verb* **v sep**: *separable verb* **v ir**: *irregular verb* **adj**: *adjective* **adv**: *adverb*

GERMAN—ENGLISH DICTIONARY

schlecht adj bad
schließen v ir to close
Schließfach n (-̈er) locker
schließlich adv eventually, after all, finally
schlimm adj bad
Schlips m (-e) tie
Schlittschuhlaufen n ice skating
Schloss n (-̈er) castle, lock
Schlüssel m (-) key
Schlüsselbund m or n (-e) keyring, bunch of keys
Schlussverkauf m (-̈e) (end-of-season) sale
schmal adj narrow
schmecken v to taste, to taste good
Schmerz m (-en) pain
schmerzhaft adj painful
Schmuck m jewellery
schmutzig adj dirty
Schnaps m (-̈e) schnapps, spirits
Schnee m snow
schneiden v ir to cut
schneien v to snow
schnell adj/adv quick(ly)
Schnellimbiss m (-e) snack bar
Schnitzel n (-) (veal/pork) escalope
Schnupfen m (-) a cold
Schnurrbart m (-̈e) moustache
Schokolade f (-n) chocolate
schon adv already
schön adj beautiful, fine (weather)
Schornstein m (-e) chimney
Schotte/Schottin m/f (-n/-nen) Scot
schottisch adj Scottish
Schottland n Scotland
Schrägstrich m (-e) forward slash
Schrank m (-̈e) cupboard
schrecklich adj/adv terrible/terribly
Schreibblock m (-s or -̈e) writing pad
schreiben v ir to write
Schreibpapier n writing paper
Schreibtisch m (-e) desk
Schreibwarengeschäft n (-e) stationer's
schreien v ir to scream/shout
schriftlich adj written
Schublade f (-n) drawer
schüchtern adj/adv shy(ly)
Schuh m (-e) shoe
Schulabschluss m (-̈e) school leaving certificate
Schulbildung f education
Schulbuch n (-̈er) school book
Schulbus m (-se) school bus
Schuldirektor/in m/f (-en/-nen) head teacher
Schule f (-n) school
Schüler/in m/f (-/-nen) school pupil
Schüleraustausch m (-e) school exchange
Schülerzeitung f (-en) school magazine
Schulhof m (-̈e) school playground
Schulleiter/in m/f (-/-nen) headmaster/mistress
Schulstunde f (-n) lesson
Schultag m (-e) school day
Schultasche f (-n) school bag
Schulter f (-n) shoulder
Schüssel f (-n) bowl
schützen v to protect
schwach adj weak, poor (e.g. schoolwork)
Schwager/Schwägerin m/f (-̈e/-nen) brother/sister-in-law
schwänzen v to skip, to play truant
schwarz adj black
schwarze Johannisbeere f (-n) blackcurrant
Schwarzwald m the Black Forest
schwatzen v to chat
schweigen v ir to be silent, to say nothing
Schweinefleisch n pork
Schweiz f Switzerland
Schweizer/in m/f (-/-nen) Swiss person
schweizerisch adj Swiss
schwer adj/adv heavy / heavily, difficult / with difficulty, serious(ly)
Schwester f (-n) sister
schwierig adj difficult
Schwimmbad n (-̈er) swimming pool
Schwimmen n swimming
schwimmen v ir to swim
See f/m (-n) sea (f); lake (m)
seekrank adj seasick
Segelboot n (-e) sailing boat
segeln v to sail
sehen v ir to see
sehenswert adj worth seeing
Sehenswürdigkeit f (-en) sight (something worth seeing)
sehr adv very
Seide f silk
Seife f (-n) soap
Seifenoper f (-n) soap opera
sein v ir to be
seit prep + dat since
seitdem conj since
Seite f (-n) side, page
Sekretär/in m/f (-e/-nen) secretary
Sekretariat n (-e) office
Sekt m (-e) (German) champagne
Sekunde f (-n) second
selbst pron/adv self/even
selbständig adj/adv independent(ly)
Selbstbedienung f self-service
selten adj/adv rare(ly), infrequent(ly), seldom
Semester n (-) term, semester
senden v to send
Sendung f (-en) (TV) programme
Senf m mustard
sensibel adj/adv sensitive(ly)
September m September
Serie f (-n) series (e.g. on TV)
servieren v to serve
Serviette f (-n) serviette, napkin
Sessel m (-) armchair
setzen sich v to sit down
sicher adj/adv certain(ly), sure(ly)
Sicherheitsgurt m (-e) seat belt
Silber n silver
Silvester n New Year's Eve
simsen v to text
singen v ir to sing
Sitz m (-e) seat
sitzen v ir to sit
sitzen bleiben v ir to repeat a (school) year
Ski fahren v ir to ski
Skifahren n skiing
Skilehrer/in m/f (-/-nen) ski instructor
Slip m (-s) briefs
SMS f text message
SMV (= Schülermitverwaltung) f school / student council
sniffen v to sniff/snort (drugs)
so ... wie as ... as
so dass so that
so viel wie as much as
sobald conj as soon as
Socke f (-n) sock
Sofa n (-s) sofa
sofort adv immediately
sogar adv even
Sohn m (-̈e) son
Soldat/in m/f (-en/-nen) soldier
sollen v ir to be supposed to
Sommer m (-) summer
Sonderangebot n (-e) special offer
Sonnabend m Saturday
Sonne f (-n) sun
sonnen sich v to sun oneself
Sonnenbrand m sunburn
Sonnenbrille f (-n) sunglasses
Sonnencreme f (-s) suncream
Sonnenschirm m (-e) sunshade
sonnig adj sunny
Sonntag m Sunday
sonst adv otherwise
sonst nichts nothing else
Sorge f (-n) worry
sorgen für v to take care of
Soße f (-n) sauce, gravy
Souvenir n (-s) souvenir
sowohl ... als (auch) both ... and
Spanien n Spain
Spanier/in m/f (-/-nen) Spaniard
Spanisch n Spanish (language)
spanisch adj Spanish
spannend adj exciting, tense
sparen v to save (up)
Sparkasse f (-n) savings bank
sparsam adj/adv thrifty, economic(al), sparing(ly)
Spaß m fun
spät adj late
später adj/adv later
spazieren v to walk
spazieren gehen v ir to go for a walk
Spaziergang m (-̈e) walk
Speck m bacon
speichern v to store
Speisekarte f (-n) menu
Speisesaal m (-säle) dining room
Speisewagen m (-) restaurant car
spenden v to donate, to give
Spezialität f (-en) speciality
Spiegel m (-) mirror
Spiegelei n (-er) fried egg
Spiel n (-e) game, match
spielen v to play
Spieler/in m/f (-/-nen) player
Spielfilm m (-e) feature film
Spielplatz m (-̈e) play area
Spielzeug n (-e) toy
Spielzimmer n (-) playroom
Spinat m (-e) spinach
Spitze! brilliant!
Spitzname m (-n) nickname
Sport m sport, PE
Sport treiben v ir to do sport
Sportausrüstung f sports equipment
Sporthalle f (-n) sports hall
sportlich adj sporty
Sportplatz m (-̈e) sports field
Sportzentrum n (-zentren) sports centre
Sprache f (-n) language
Sprachlabor n (-s or -e) language lab
Spraydose f (-n) aerosol (can)
sprechen v ir to speak
Sprechstunde f (-n) surgery / consulting hours
springen v ir to jump
Spritze f (-n) syringe, injection
spritzen v to spray, to inject
Sprudel m (-) sparkling mineral water, fizzy drink
Spülbecken n (-) sink
Spüle f (-n) sink
spülen v to wash up
Spülmaschine f (-n) dishwasher
staatlich adj state
Stadion n (Stadien) stadium
Stadt f (-̈e) town
Stadtbummel m (-) stroll around town
Stadtführer m (-) town/city guidebook
Stadtführung f (-en) guided tour of town/city
Stadtmitte f (-n) town centre
Stadtplan m (-̈e) street map
Stadtrand m (-̈er) edge of the town
Stadtrundfahrt f (-en) guided tour of the town
Stadtteil m (-e) district
Stadtviertel n (-) district
Stadtzentrum n (-zentren) town centre
Stahl m steel
Star m (-s) celebrity
stark adj strong
starten v to start, to take off (plane)
statt prep + gen instead of
Stau m (-e or -s) traffic jam
Staub saugen v to hoover/vacuum
stecken v to place, to insert, to stick
Stehcafé n (-s) stand-up cafe
stehen v ir to stand, to suit someone (e.g. clothing)
stehlen v ir to steal
steigen v ir to climb, to rise, to get on
steil adj/adv steep(ly)
Stein m (-e) stone
Stelle f (-n) job (position)
stellen v to put/place
Stellenangebote n pl situations vacant
Steppdecke f (-n) duvet, quilt
sterben v ir to die
Stereoanlage f (-n) stereo
Steward/ess m/f (-s/-en) air steward/stewardess
Stiefel m (-) boot
Stift m (-e) pen
still adj quiet, peaceful
stimmt! right!
Stock m (-) storey
Stockwerk n storey
Stoff m (-e) material
stolz adj proud
stoppen v to stop
Strand m (-̈e) beach
Straße f (-n) street
Straßenbahn f (-en) tram
Straßenkarte f (-n) street map
Straßenschild n (-er) roadsign
Streik m (-s) strike
Streit m (-e) argument, quarrel
streiten v ir to quarrel
streiten sich v ir to argue, to quarrel
streng adj strict
stressig adj stressful
Strom m electricity
Strumpf m (-̈e) sock, stocking
Strumpfhose f (-n) tights
Student/in m/f (-en/-nen) student
studieren v to study
Stück n (-e) piece, coin
Stückchen n (-) (little) piece, bit
Studium n (Studien) (course of) study
Stufe f (-n) stair, level
Stuhl m (-̈e) chair
Stunde f (-n) hour, lesson
Stundenplan m (-̈e) timetable
Sturm m (-̈e) storm
stürmisch adj stormy
suchen v to seek, to look for
Sucht f (-̈e) addiction
süchtig adj addicted
Südamerika n South America
Süden m the South
südlich adj/adv in/to the south
Supermarkt m (-̈e) supermarket
Suppe f (-n) soup
Surfbrett n (-er) surfboard
surfen v to surf (im Internet surfen = to surf the internet)
süß adj sweet
Süßigkeiten f pl sweets
sympathisch adj nice (person)

T

Tabak m tobacco
Tabakwarengeschäft n (-e) tobacconist's
Tablett n (-s or -e) tray
Tablette f (-n) tablet, pill
Tafel f (-n) (black)board, bar (e.g. of chocolate)
Tag m (-e) day
Tagebuch n (-̈er) diary
Tagesgericht n (-e) dish of the day
Tageskarte f (-n) menu/dish (of the day)
Tagesmenü n (-s) menu of the day
täglich adv daily
Tal n (-̈er) valley
tanken v to fill up (e.g. petrol tank)
Tankstelle f (-n) petrol station
Tannenbaum m (-̈e) fir tree, Christmas tree
Tante f (-n) aunt
Tanz m (-̈e) dance
tanzen v to dance
Tanzen n dancing
Tapete f (-n) wallpaper
Tasche f (-n) bag, pocket
Taschenbuch n (-̈er) paperback
Taschengeld n pocket money
Taschenlampe f (-n) torch
Taschenmesser n (-) pocket knife, pen-knife
Taschenrechner m (-) calculator
Taschentuch n (-̈er) handkerchief
Tasse f (-n) cup
Tastatur f (-en) keyboard
Taste f (-n) key (of keyboard)
Tätowierung f (-en) tattoo
Taufe f (-n) baptism, christening
Taxi n (-s) taxi
Taxifahrer/in m/f (-/-nen) taxi driver
Techniker/in m/f (-/-nen) technician
Technologie f (-n) technology
Tee m (-s) tea
Teekanne f (-n) teapot
Teelöffel m (-) teaspoon
Teil m or n (-e) part
teilen v share, split
Teilnahme f participation
Teilzeit f part-time
Telefon n (-e) telephone
Telefonanruf m (-e) telephone call
Telefonbuch n (-̈er) phone book
telefonieren v to telephone
Telefonnummer f (-n) phone numbe
Telefonzelle f (-n) phone box
Teller m (-) plate
Tellerwäscher/in m/f (-/-nen) dishwasher
Temperatur f (-en) temperature
Tennis n tennis
Teppich m (-e) carpet
Termin m (-e) date, appointment, deadline
Terminkalender m (-) diary (for appointments)
Terrasse f (-n) terrace, patio
teuer adj expensive
Theater n (-) theatre
Theatergruppe f (-n) theatre group
Theaterstück n (-e) play
Theke f (-n) counter
Therapie f (-n) therapy
Thunfisch m (-e) tuna
tief adj deep
Tiefkühlschrank m (-̈e) freezer
Tiefkühltruhe f (-n) chest freezer
Tier n (-e) animal
Tierarzt/ärztin m/f (-̈e/-nen) vet
Tierheim n (-e) animal home
tippen v to type
Tisch m (-e) table
Tischdecke f (-n) tablecloth
Tischler/in m/f (-/-nen) joiner, carpenter
Tischtennis n table tennis
Tischtuch n (-̈er) tablecloth
Toastbrot n bread for toasting
Tochter f (-̈) daughter
Tod m (-e) death
Toilette f (-n) toilet
Toilettenpapier n toilet paper
toll adj great
Tomate f (-n) tomato
Ton m (-̈e) tone, sound
Topf m (-̈e) pot, pan
Tor n (-e) gate, goal
Torte f (-n) gateau, cake
tot adj dead
total adj/adv total(ly)
Tour f (-en) tour
Tourismus m tourism
Tourist/in m/f (-en/-nen) tourist
Touristeninformation f (-en) tourist information (office)
tragen v to carry, to wear
Tragödie f (-n) tragedy
trainieren v to train, to coach
Trainingsanzug m (-̈e) track suit
Trainingsschuhe m pl trainers
Traube f (-n) grape
Traum m (-̈e) dream
traurig adj sad
Trauring m (-e) wedding ring
treffen v to meet
Treffpunkt m (-e) meeting place
Treibhauseffekt m greenhouse effect
Treibhausgas n (-e) greenhouse gas
trennen sich v to split up
Treppe f (-n) staircase
Treppenhaus n (-̈er) stairwell
treten v ir to step, to kick
Trimester n (-) term
trinken v ir drink
Trinkgeld n (-er) tip
Trinkwasser n drinking water
trocken adj dry
trocknen v to dry
Trompete f (-n) trumpet
trotz prep + gen despite
trotzdem adv nevertheless
Truthahn m (-̈e) turkey
tschüss bye
Tube f (-n) tube
Tuch n (-̈er) cloth
tun v ir to do
Tunnel m the Channel Tunnel
Tür f (-en) door
Türkei f Turkey
Turm m (-̈e) tower
turnen v to do gymnastics

prep: preposition **pron: pronoun** **conj**: conjunction **bits in brackets**: plural ending **(-̈)**: plural — add umlaut

German—English Dictionary

rnen n *gymnastics, PE*
rnhalle f (-n) *gym*
rnschuhe m pl *trainers*
te f (-n) *small bag*
p m (-en) *type, bloke*
pisch adj/adv *typical(ly)*

Bahn f *underground (railway)*
Bahnstation f (-en) *underground station*
el adj *nasty, ill*
en v *to practise*
er prep + acc/dat *over, above*
erall adv *everywhere*
erbevölkert adj *overpopulated*
erfahrt f (-en) *(sea) crossing*
erhaupt nicht *not at all*
ermorgen adv *the day after tomorrow*
ernachten v *to stay the night*
ernachtung f (-en) *overnight stay*
erqueren v *to cross*
errascht adj *surprised*
erwachen v *to supervise*
rigens adv *moreover, by the way*
ung f (-en) *practice*
er n *(river) bank*
r f (-en) *watch, clock, o'clock*
raviolette Strahlen m pl *UV rays*
n prep + acc *around*
n… zu conj *in order to*
nfrage f (-n) *opinion poll, survey*
ngeben von *surrounded by*
nkleidekabine f (-n) *changing cubicle*
nkleideraum m (¨-e) *changing room*
nleitung f (-en) *diversion, detour*
nschlag m (¨-e) *envelope*
nsteigen v sep ir *change (trains)*
nwelt f *environment*
nweltfeindlich adj *environmentally damaging*
nweltfreundlich adj *environmentally friendly*
nweltproblem n (-e) *environmental problem*
nziehen v sep ir *to move (house)*
nziehen sich v sep ir *to get changed*
nd conj *and*
nfall m (¨-e) *accident*
nfit adj *unfit*
nfreundlich adj *unfriendly*
ngeduldig adj *impatient*
ngefähr adv *about, approximately*
ngerecht adj *unjust, unfair*
ngesund adj *unhealthy*
nglaublich adj *unbelievable*
nhöflich adj *impolite*
niform f (-en) *uniform*
niversität f (-en) (Uni) *university*
nmöglich adj *impossible*
nordentlich adj *untidy*
nrecht haben v ir *to be wrong*
nsicher adj *uncertain, insecure*
nsympathisch adj *unpleasant*
nten adv *at the bottom, below, downstairs*
nter prep + acc/dat *under*
ntergeschoss n *basement*
nterhalten sich v ir *to converse*
nterhaltung f *entertainment*
nterhaltungsmöglichkeiten f pl *entertainment, things to do*
nterhose f (-n) *underpants*
nterkunft f (¨-e) *accommodation*
nternehmungslustig adj *enterprising, adventurous*
nterricht m *lessons, classes*
nterrichten v *to teach, to inform*
nterschied m (-e) *difference*
nterschiedlich adj *different, variable*
nterschreiben v ir *to sign*
nterschrift f (-en) *signature*
nterstützen v *to support*
ntertasse f (-n) *saucer*
nterwäsche f *underwear*
nterwegs adv *on the way*
nvorstellbar adj *unimaginable*
nzufrieden adj *discontented*
Urlaub m (-e) *holiday*
usw. (= und so weiter) *etc.*

V

Vandalismus m *vandalism*
Vanille f *vanilla*
Vater m (¨) *father*
Vati m (-s) *dad*
Vegetarier/in m/f (-/-nen) *vegetarian*
verantwortlich adj *responsible*
Verantwortung f (-en) *responsibility*
verbal adj *verbal*
verbessern v *to improve*
Verbesserung f (-en) *improvement, correction*
verbieten v ir *to forbid*
verbinden v ir *to connect*
Verbindung f (-en) *connection*
verboten adj *prohibited, forbidden*
Verbrauch m *use, consumption*
Verbrechen n (-) *crime*
verbringen v ir *spend (time)*
verdienen v *to earn, to deserve*
Verein m (-e) *club, organisation*
Vereinigte Staaten m pl *USA*
Verfallsdatum n *use-by date*
Vergangenheit f *past, past tense*
vergeben v ir *to forgive, to give away*
vergessen v ir *to forget*
Vergleich m (-e) *comparison*
Verhältnis n (-se) *relationship, ratio*
verheiratet adj *married*
verhindern v *to prevent*
verkaufen v *to sell*
Verkäufer/in m/f (-/-nen) *salesperson*
Verkehr m *traffic*
Verkehrsamt n (¨er) *tourist information office*
Verkehrsmittel n (-) *mode of transport*
Verkehrsunfall m (¨-e) *road accident*
verlassen v ir *to leave, to abandon*
verletzen v *to injure*
Verletzung f (-en) *injury*
verlieren v ir *to lose*
verloben sich v *to get engaged*
verlobt adj *engaged*
Verlobungsring m (-e) *engagement ring*
vermeiden v ir *to avoid, to prevent, to warn*
vermieten v *to rent out*
verpacken v *to pack, to wrap up*
Verpackung f (-en) *packing*
verpassen v *to miss (bus / train etc.)*
Versammlung f (-en) *meeting, assembly*
verschieden adj/adv *different(ly), various(ly)*
verschmutzen v *to dirty, to pollute*
Verschmutzung f *pollution*
verschwinden v ir *to disappear*
verspäten sich v *to be late*
Verspätung f (-en) *delay, lateness*
versprechen v ir *to promise*
verstehen v ir *to understand*
verstehen sich v ir *to get on well*
Versuch m (-e) *experiment, attempt*
versuchen v *to try*
Vertreter/in m/f (-/-nen) *representative*
Verwandte(r) *relative*
verzeihen v ir *to forgive*
Verzeihung! *Sorry!*
Vetter m (-n) *cousin*
viel/e pron/adj *lots, many*
Viel Glück! *good luck*
vielleicht adv *perhaps, maybe*
viereckig adj *rectangular*
Viertel n (-) *quarter*
Virus n/m (Viren) *virus*
Vitamine n pl *vitamins*
Vogel m (¨) *bird*
Volksmusik f *folk music*
voll adj *full*
völlig adv *completely*
Vollpension f *full board (at hotel)*
von prep + dat *from, of*
vor prep + acc/dat *before, in front of, outside*
vor kurzem *recently*
voraus adv *in front, ahead*
(im Voraus = *in advance*)
vorausgesetzt, dass *provided that*
vorbei adv *past, by*
vorbeifahren v sep ir *to go past*
vorbeigehen v sep ir *to pass by, to go by*
vorbereiten v sep *to prepare*
Vorfahrt f *right of way*
vorgehen v sep ir *to go forward, to go on ahead*
vorgestern adv *the day before yesterday*
vorhaben v sep ir *to intend, to have planned*
Vorhang m (¨e) *curtain*
vorher adv *beforehand, previously*
Vorliebe f (-n) *preference*
Vormittag m (-e) *morning*
vormittags adv *in the morning(s)*
vorn/e adv *at the front, in front*
Vorname m (-n) *first name*
Vorort m (-e) *suburb*
vorschlagen v sep ir *to suggest, to propose*
Vorspeise f (-n) *starter*
vorstellen v sep *to introduce*
vorstellen sich v sep *to introduce oneself, to imagine*
Vorstellung f (-en) *showing, performance, idea*
Vorteil m (-e) *advantage*
Vorwahl f (-en) *area code*
vorwärts adv *forwards*
vorziehen v sep ir *prefer*

W

Wagen m (-) *car*
Wahl f (-en) *choice*
Wahlfach n (¨er) *option subject*
wählen v *to choose, to dial*
wahr adj *true* (nicht wahr? = *isn't it?*)
während conj *during, while*
Wahrheit f (-en) *truth*
wahrscheinlich adv *probably*
Wald m (¨er) *forest*
Wales n *Wales*
Waliser/in m/f (-/-nen) *Welsh person*
walisisch adj *Welsh*
Wand f (¨e) *wall*
wandern v *to walk, hike*
Wanderung f (-en) *walk, hike*
wann adv *when*
Warenhaus n (¨er) *(department) store*
warm adj *warm*
warnen v *to warn*
warten v *to wait*
warten auf v *to wait for*
Warteraum m (¨e) *waiting room*
Wartesaal m (-säle) *waiting room*
Wartezeit f *waiting period, wait*
Wartezimmer n (-) *waiting room*
warum adv *why*
was pron *what*
was für… *what kind of…*
Waschbecken n (-) *washbasin*
Wäsche f *washing, underwear*
waschen (sich) v ir *to wash (oneself)*
Wäscherei f (-en) *laundry*
Waschküche f (-n) *laundry room*
Waschmaschine f (-n) *washing machine*
Waschpulver n (-) *washing powder*
Waschsalon m (-s) *launderette*
Wasser n *water*
Wasserhahn m (¨e) *tap*
Wasserski n *waterskiing*
Wasserskilaufen n *waterskiing*
Wasserverschmutzung f *water pollution*
Webseite f (-n) *web page*
Website f (-s) *website*
Wechselgeld n *change*
Wechselkurs m (-e) *exchange rate*
wechseln v *to change*
Wechselstube f (-n) *bureau de change*
wecken v *to wake someone*
Wecker m (-) *alarm clock*
weder ... noch conj. *neither ... nor*
Weg m (-e) *way, path*
wegen prep + gen *because of*
weggehen v sep ir *to go away*
wegwerfen v sep ir *to throw away*
wehtun v ir sep *to hurt*
weiblich adj *female*
weich adj/adv *soft(ly)*
Weihnachten n (-) *Christmas*
Weihnachtsbaum m (¨e) *Christmas tree*
Weihnachtsmarkt m (¨e) *Christmas market*
weil conj *because*
Wein m (-e) *wine*
weinen v *to cry*
Weintraube f (-n) *grape*
Weise f (-n) *way*
weiß adj *white*
Weißbrot n *white bread*
weit adj *far*
weiterfahren v sep ir *to continue*
weitermachen v sep *to continue (e.g. studies), to carry on*
Welle f (-n) *wave*
Wellensittich m (-e) *budgerigar*
Welt f (-en) *world*
weltweit adj/adv *worldwide*
wem pron *who, to whom*
wen pron *who, whom*
wenig pron/adj *little, few*
weniger adv *less*
wenigstens adv *at least*
wenn conj *if, when*
wer pron *who*
werden v ir *to become, to get*
werfen v ir *to throw*
Werken n *handicrafts*
Werkstatt f (¨en) *workshop, garage*
Werkzeuge n pl *tools*
wertvoll adj *valuable*
Wespe f (-n) *wasp*
wessen pron *whose*
Westen m *the west*
westlich adj/adv *in/to the west*
Wetter n *weather*
Wetterbericht m (-e) *weather report*
Wettervorhersage f (-n) *weather forecast*
wichtig adj *important*
wie adv *how, as, like*
wie bitte? *pardon?*
wie geht's? *how are you?*
wie viel(e) adv *how much / many*
wieder adv *again*
wiederholen v *to repeat*
wiegen v ir *to weigh*
Wien n *Vienna*
Wiese f (-n) *meadow*
wieso adv *why*
willkommen adj *welcome*
Wind m (-e) *wind*
windig adj *windy*
windsurfen v *to windsurf*
Winter m (-) *winter*
wirklich adv *really*
wissen v ir *to know (facts)*
witzig adj *funny*
wo adv *where*
Woche f (-n) *week*
Wochenende n (-n) *weekend*
wöchentlich adj/adv *weekly*
woher adv *where from*
wohin adv *where to*
Wohltätigkeit f *charity*
Wohnblock m (¨e or -s) *block of flats*
wohnen v *to live*
Wohnort m (-e) *place where you live*
Wohnung f (-en) *flat*
Wohnwagen m (-) *caravan*
Wohnzimmer n (-) *living room*
Wolke f (-n) *cloud*
wolkenlos adj *cloudless*
wolkig adj *cloudy*
Wolle f *wool*
wollen v ir *to want*
Wort n (-e or ¨er) *word*
Wörterbuch n (¨er) *dictionary*
Wunde f (-n) *wound*
wunderbar adj *wonderful*
wunderschön adj *really beautiful*
Wunsch m (¨e) *wish*
wünschen v *to wish, to want*
wünschen sich v *to desire, to wish for*
Wurst f (¨e) *sausage*
Wurstbude f (-n) *sausage stand*

Z

z.B. (= zum Beispiel) *for example (e.g.)*
Zahl f (-en) *figure*
zahlen v *to pay*
zählen v *to count*
zahlreich adj *numerous*
Zahn m (¨e) *tooth*
Zahnarzt/ärztin m/f (¨e/-nen) *dentist*
Zahnbürste f (-n) *toothbrush*
Zahnpasta f (-pasten) *toothpaste*
Zahnschmerzen m pl *toothache*
ZDF *German television company*
Zebrastreifen m *zebra crossing*
Zeichentrickfilm m (-e) *cartoon*
Zeichnen n *drawing (subject)*
zeichnen v *to draw*
zeigen v *to show*
Zeit f (-en) *time*
Zeitpunkt m (-e) *moment*
Zeitschrift f (-en) *magazine*
Zeitung f (-en) *newspaper*
Zeitungskiosk m (-e) *newspaper stall*
Zelt n (-e) *tent*
zelten v *to camp*
Zelten n *camping*
Zentimeter n/m (-) *centimetre*
Zentralheizung f *central heating*
Zentrum n (Zentren) *centre*
zerbrechlich adj *fragile*
zerstören v *to destroy*
Zettel m (-) *piece of paper, note*
Zeugnis n (-se) *school report*
ziehen v ir *to pull*
Ziel n (-e) *aim, goal*
ziemlich adv *quite*
Zigarette f (-n) *cigarette*
Zimmer n (-) *room*
Zimmermädchen n (-) *maid*
Zitrone f (-n) *lemon*
Zoll m (¨e) *customs, toll*
Zoo m (-s) *zoo*
zornig adj *angry*
zu adj/adv/prep + dat *to, too (e.g. too old), closed*
zu Ende *over, finished*
zu Fuß *on foot*
zu Händen von *for the attention of*
zu Hause *at home*
Zucker m *sugar*
zuerst adv *at first, first of all*
zufällig adj *accidental, random*
zufrieden adj *satisfied*
Zug m (¨e) *train*
Zugführer/in m/f (-/-nen) *guard (on train)*
Zuhause n *home*
zuhören v sep *to listen to*
Zukunft f *future*
zuletzt adv *at last, in the end*
zum Beispiel *for example*
zum Mitnehmen adj *take away (meals)*
zum Wohl! *cheers!*
zumachen v sep *to close, to shut*
zunehmen v sep ir *to increase, to put on weight*
zurück adv *back*
zurückfahren v sep ir *to go back, to drive back*
zurückgehen v sep ir *to return*
zurückkommen v sep ir *to come back*
zurücklassen v sep ir *to leave*
zurückrufen v sep ir *to call back*
zurückstellen v sep *to put back*
zusammen adv *together*
Zuschauer/in m/f (-/-nen) *spectator, audience*
Zuschlag m (¨e) *supplement*
zusehen v sep ir *to look on, to watch*
zustimmen v sep *to agree*
Zweibettzimmer n (-) *twin-bed room*
zweitens adv *secondly*
zweiter Klasse *second class*
Zwiebel f (-n) *onion*
Zwilling m (-e) *twin*
zwischen prep + acc/dat *between*
zwo = zwei (telephone)

nouns — ***m****: masculine* ***f****: feminine* ***n****: neuter* ***pl****: plural* ***v****: verb* ***v sep****: separable verb* ***v ir****: irregular verb* ***adj****: adjective* ***adv****: adverb*

Index

A

accusative case 84
adjectives 91, 92
adverbs 93
alcohol 25
amounts 1
apologising 6
appearances 17
articles 90
asking for things 14, 15, 37
asking questions 4

B

because 9, 89
blogs 34
bodies 22
booking a room 48
buildings 58
businesses 82

C

CVs 79
camping 47, 48
cases 84, 85
catching the train 44
celebrations 64
celebrities 32
cinemas 41
classroom language 71
clothes 38
colours 38
comparatives 94
complaints 52
computers 33
conjunctions 89
countries 43, 60

D

daily routine 16
dates 3
dative case 85
days of the week 2
definite articles 90
describing people 17–19
diet 24
directions 59
drugs 25

E

e-mail 34
environment 65, 66
equal opportunities 21
exchange trips 55
excursions 46
exercise 24
extracurricular activities 72

F

families 18
famous people 32
films 30, 41
food 13
foreign places 43
formal letters 11
free time 28
furniture 63
future plans 20, 75
future tense 103

G

gardens 63
gender of nouns 86
genitive case 85
German schools 72
Godzilla 29
going out 39–41
grades 72

H

health 24, 25
helping at home 16
hobbies 27, 28
holidays 53–55
hostels 47–50
hotels 47–50
houses 62, 63
how long...? 71

I

I would like... 36, 111
illness 22, 23
imperatives 106
imperfect tense 105
impersonal verbs 112
in order to... 112
infinitives 100
informal letters 10
internet 33
interviews 80
inviting people out 39
irregular verbs 102

J

job vacancies 79
jobs 76–80

L

letters 10, 11
listening to music 31

M

materials 38
mealtimes 14, 15
modal verbs 110, 111
money 36
months 3
music 31

N

nationalities 43, 60
negatives 109
nominative case 84
noun endings 85
nouns 85–87
numbers 1

O

opinions 7–9
ordering food 51

P

parts of the body 22
pen friends 55
perfect tense 104
personality 19
pets 18
plots 30
pluperfect tense 106
plurals 87
politeness 5, 6
prepositions 95, 96
present tense 101, 102
problems at school 73
problems with accommodation 50
pronouns 97–99

Q

quantities 37
questions 4

R

reflexive verbs 107
relationships 20
relative pronouns 99
requests 14, 15, 37
restaurants 51, 52

S

school routine 69
school rules 70
school subjects 68
schoolbag 70
separable verbs 108
shopping 35–38
shops 35
smoking 25
social issues 21
spelling 17
sports 27, 28
stress 73
superlatives 94
swimming pools 40

T

technology 33
telephones 81
television 29
tenses 100
   future 103
   imperfect 105
   perfect 104
   pluperfect 106
   present 101, 102
text messages 34
times 2
timetables 69
tourist information 46
towns 61, 62
transport 45
travelling by train 44
TV 29

U

unemployment 21

V

verbs 100

W

weather 56
when is...? 35, 49
where is...? 35, 49
word order 88
work experience 74
working abroad 78

Y

yourself 17